• • • •

The Stages of Acting

A Practical Approach for Beginning Actors

Mack Owen

San Diego State University

📖 HarperCollinsCollegePublishers

Acquisitions Editor: Daniel F. Pipp
Project Editor: Claire M. Caterer
Design Supervisor/Text Design: Mary Archondes
Cover Photo: Ken Howard
Production Manager/Assistant: Willie Lane/Sunaina Sehwani
Compositor: American-Stratford Graphics Services, Inc.
Printer and Binder: R. R. Donnelley & Sons Company
Cover Printer: The Lehigh Press, Inc.

The Stages of Acting: A Practical Approach for Beginning Actors
Copyright © 1993 by HarperCollins College Publishers

Library of Congress Cataloging-in-Publication Data

Owen, Mack.
    The stages of acting : a practical approach for beginning actors /
  by Mack Owen.
        p.   cm.
    ISBN 0-06-500632-1
    1. Acting.   I. Title.
  PN2061.O87   1992
  792'.028—dc20   92-20698
                                                          CIP

92 93 94 95   9 8 7 6 5 4 3 2 1

This book is for my all-time favorite
beginning acting student:
Megan Owen

• • • •
CONTENTS

• • • •

LIST OF EXERCISES

· · · ·

PREFACE

Learning to act in the classroom is like learning to fly in a flight simulator. No matter how clever and lifelike the computerized emergencies flashing on the video screen, the new pilot must feel a certain shock when faced with the actuality of flight. So, too, all new actors face that frightening and jarring moment when the theories and exercises of the beginning acting class are put to the practical, rigorous test of rehearsing for and performing in a real play in a real theater. There's no way of completely avoiding this awkward transition, but this book is organized to minimize the shock.

This is a nuts-and-bolts book. In it, I have used the same approach that I have used in my acting classes for the last twenty years: The process of learning to act is organized in exactly the same way and in the same order as are the series of rehearsals that eventually lead to performance. This method not only prepares students for the most common approach to rehearsals in the theater today,

but helps them anticipate the practical, everyday questions and answers that working actors face in preparing a role.

The learning process as presented here is concise, straightforward, presumes no previous knowledge, and, above all, is *practical,* with many on-the-feet and on-the-floor exercises to directly illustrate the ideas. Characterization and what makes it tick are taken apart, bared to the skeleton, and then put back together again so that it will, one hopes, run properly. These practical nuts and bolts are used in the construction and exercising of internal as well as external technique. Actors must be possessed by the mental and emotional urgency of their characterizations, so there is ample discussion of ways to explore, determine, and express the inner life of performance.

ORGANIZATION OF THE TEXT

Chapter 1 defines the *internals and externals:* the ways in which an actor's body becomes the external reflection of the internal thought structure of the character. The actor's task of making the character's thoughts visible and audible through action is not only the major premise of this book; it is also, I believe, the vital core of all acting.

Chapter 2 concentrates on externals—showing students how to prepare their voices and bodies for the work of rehearsals and performances. The exercises in this chapter help students relax and effectively use their bodies; coordinate mental and physical focus and readiness (often called *centering*); and prepare their vocal equipment for effective voice production and speech.

Chapter 3 deals with the internals: finding and understanding the thoughts and emotions of the character. The text discusses the techniques used to analyze and understand the text of a play so as to bring about a full and complete understanding of the play's language and subject matter as well as the various ways actors discover the thoughts and emotions underneath the text that produce the character's speech and action. These motivating forces are usually referred to as the *subtext*, which is further analyzed later in the book.

Chapters 4, 5, and 6 take the student directly into the rehearsal process: the *readthrough,* in which the play is read and intellectually understood; the *blocking rehearsals,* where the director familiarizes the actors with the physical environment of the set and works with them to decide on movement patterns and orientation within the set in combination with other actors; and the *working rehearsals,* in which each actor examines the internal process in great detail, making choices about the meaning of the text and subtext, as well as the external process which they motivate.

Chapters 7 and 8 put the internal and external information together into a coherent and dynamic whole. *Running rehearsals,* in which problems of rhythm (pace, rate, build) and the creation of an ensemble are added to the continuing work on characterization, are discussed in Chapter 7. Chapter 8 considers the performance itself, the ongoing task of maintaining and repeating the play in front of an audience, including such matters as concentration, focus, warm-up, coping with the unexpected, and keeping the performance fresh.

Finally, Chapters 9 and 10 deal with practical matters, some of which are beyond the scope of a beginning class but are discussed here simply to provide students with an introduction to their future as actors and to provide them with a basis on which to begin to make some decisions about it. These matters are too often left for beginning actors to discover for themselves, so, to avoid such haphazard learning, Chapter 9 outlines some of the most common questions of conduct and procedure that occur in *technical* and *dress rehearsals* as well as the performances themselves. Chapter 10 offers a broad overview of the various kinds of theater found in the United States in these last years of the twentieth century, allowing students to think about where they most likely will fit in and helping them make sure their next steps in the learning process are appropriate ones. Also found in this chapter are some very general notes on auditioning: suggestions about how to approach the audition, which kinds of material to choose, and a hint or two about the psychological pressures of this nerve-wracking situation.

To help make these ideas immediate and workable, Appendix A consists of five short, gender-neutral exercise plays that contain situations and problems derived from the material discussed in the body of the book. These brief plays were written especially for this book and are designed to provide a laboratory wherein the specific problems discussed in the classroom may be worked on at an immediate and practical level. Further exercise scenes of this type are found in my text *The Actor's Scenebook: Scenes for Beginning Actors to Create* (HarperCollins: 1993), and they make ideal companions to this book. Appendix B takes students step by step through the important process of character analysis.

I have used the word *actor* throughout the text to refer to acting students of both sexes in the same way that both male and female physicians are spoken of as *doctors*. The term *actress* is, to me, as demeaning and ridiculous as *doctoress* would be. I hope no one sees it as foisting a male gender word on women, as that is most certainly not my intent. So, too, since there is no neuter personal pronoun in English, I have adopted the simple but somewhat arbitrary method of alternating gender pronouns. I could not bring myself to use male pronouns exclusively, excusing such usage on the grounds that everyone knows I really mean both men and women.

Finally, then, learning these basic ideas about acting in the practical order in which most rehearsals occur will, I hope, make the process more familiar and less intimidating when young actors first encounter the real world of the theater. They can use this text as an ongoing reference as they move from the flight simulator phase of classroom scene study to the practical—and very exhilarating—task of acting a role in a real play.

ACKNOWLEDGMENTS

I am very grateful to the people who gave me so much valuable help as this book was being written: Christina Courtenay, Martin Katz, and Peter Larlham, who read it all and whose comments were most helpful; Steven Gallion, who was the first person other than myself to teach the material on which the book is based; Kandis Chappell and Nick Reid, good friends who gave good advice and much needed support; and Diana Owen, whose careful reading of the manuscript was so helpful in catching mistakes. In addition, I would like to thank my reviewers, including Sally Askins, Texas Tech University; Dorothy Corvinus, University of North Carolina at Chapel Hill; Coleen Kelly, University of Virginia; Michael King, Northern Kentucky University; Norman Myers, Bowling Green State University; and Ronald Woodland, Edinboro University of Pennsylvania. Thanks finally to the people at HarperCollins: Melissa Rosati, who first liked the idea of the book and was constantly encouraging; Judith Anderson and Claire Caterer, who patiently answered so many questions; and Dan Pipp, who saw it all through.

Mack Owen

CHAPTER 1

• • • •

INTERNALS AND EXTERNALS

Acting is the external manifestation of an internal process. This is an obvious over-simplification, but I think it states the basic problem of acting pretty well. What exactly does this statement mean? Let's look at it more closely.

The "internal process" involves assimilating the myriad details of the mental and emotional life of a character so that it coexists with the mental and emotional life of the actor and motivates—produces—the "external manifestation."

The "external manifestation" consists of the voice and body of the actor speaking and moving as the textual character would speak and move: *embodying* the internal thought process. We might say that the character inhabits the physical body of the actor to produce the person in the play the audience sees.

Both internal process and external manifestation are equally important and work together; both must be developed, practiced, and refined. This mutually dependent relationship between the internal and external will be the basis of every characterization you ever develop.

As I mentioned in the preface, the first work you do in acting will probably be to produce a character we have defined as realistic, a recognizable and contemporary human being complete and solid enough to exist effectively in the artificial environment of the performance area. In such a characterization, both the mental and emotional framework you create and the physical response of your body should be immediately recognizable as belonging to the everyday world.

As you go forward in your training, however, you will work on roles requiring you to create a characterization that is beyond simple recognition as "real." In some roles you will need to develop mental, physical, and linguistic skills that will take a performance into the complicated and multifaceted world of *style*. A character may need to be larger than life, might perform ritualistically, or speak and move in many and varied unusual ways. What sometimes happens, as characterization moves further away from reality, is that the internal/external interdependence gets thrown off balance. Try to remember that no matter how heightened, abstracted, or strange the material, the mental and physical combination which produces the characterization must stay in proportions of equal importance. No matter what unusual elements are involved, the performance always derives from the partnership of the internal thought process and the external physical manifestation.

Some actors may be performing a serious drama in a small open space completely surrounded by an intimately seated audience; another group of actors may be singing and dancing in a large-scale musical on a technologically complex stage behind a picture-frame opening in a theater seating thousands of people; still other actors may be speaking in near-ordinary tones and moving in restrained and natural ways in fragmented but instantly recognizable rooms in front of television or film cameras. No matter in which of these situations theater is practiced, no matter what style is employed by the actors, the performance must come from the direct and honest communication of genuine, immediate thought and emotion. Sometimes, though, actors fall into the trap of emphasizing one side or the other of this equation—either internal or external—to the detriment of the performance. This seems particularly apt to happen when actors are dealing with a play or characterization that is thought of as non-realistic or stylized.

Perhaps nowhere is this problem more readily identifiable than in today's large-scale musicals. Here the level of energy on the stage is often so heightened and the visual and audio components so magnified that the performers seem tempted to rely solely on these external factors to define characterization. After all, they seem to think, singing is not the way ordinary people communicate, dancing is not the way people usually move, so why should we try to be real? Well, the question is not one of being real in the sense of being ordinary or low in energy; it is instead a question of being truthful and immediate: to trust the internal process to produce accurately even their heightened, highly energized characterizations. The equation is simple: if the external manifestation (voice, movement) must be extraordinary or highly magnified, then the internal process (thoughts, emotions) that produces it must also be extraordinary or of a higher magnitude. The internal process must never simply be bypassed; if it is, the performance will be artificial and empty, no matter how energetic or how skilled the singing and dancing.

When the actor seeks to entertain the audience with external energy alone, the audience may perhaps be momentarily distracted or amused; but if they see an actor really thinking the character's thoughts and allowing these thoughts to motivate all the dazzling singing and dancing the role requires, the audience will still be entertained, but they will also see the human being underneath. Of course, for this process to work effectively, the actor must have worked long hours to train the body in the external skills of singing and dancing. No matter how hard the actor in a musical may *think*, the internal thought process alone cannot produce beautiful musical sounds or complicated dance movements.

The reverse, obviously, can also be true. Some actors may rely too heavily on the internal process to produce effective communication of characterization. Often they immerse themselves—sometimes to an alarming degree—in what they see as the necessity of completely eliminating their own awareness and totally becoming the character, trusting the depth of their emotions to produce an appropriate physical response automatically. Well, sometimes it does and sometimes it doesn't. What these actors ignore is that the external manifestation of *all* acting, not just those perfomances involving singing and dancing, must be trained and refined as thoroughly as the internal process; actors' bodies must know precisely what to do in order to serve most effectively as the external expression of the emotional truth the actors have rightly worked so hard to obtain. All well-trained actors need bodies in excellent physical condition that can fence and fight and sing and dance when called upon to do so. Moreover, none of these physical actions, no matter how extreme or unusual, will be perceived as artificial if they are fully motivated by thought. Both the internal process and the external manifestation are created by the actor and must work in cooperation with each other.

There is another reason why becoming the character is both impossible and undesirable. Some part of you—the actor—must always be present in all of your characterizations to control the performance. The much abused and much mis-understood theory often called method acting has led some young actors to believe that such control will inevitably produce a shallow or superficial perfor-mance. This is not true. Certainly, the join between actor and character must be finely made and as unobtrusive as possible, but some conscious control by the actor is necessary. Each performance of a scene or play is going to be different no matter how much attention is rightly paid to consistency: energy levels vary, other performers react in different ways from night to night, physical conditions vary, and, above all, each and every audience is an individual entity, each reacting in its own way to the same material. Spontaneity itself demands that the actor respond to these varying conditions as they occur and not according to some preordained and unbending in character unconsciousness. The actor must be aware and in control to some minimal degree—the exact proportion will vary from actor to actor—in order to adjust to such variables. I should point out here, although there's a longer discussion later in the section on performance, that this control must never involve actor evaluation of the performance as it is going on. This tendency is very bad for concentration and immediacy.

The point is that the art of acting comes from the interdependency of the internal (thought and emotion) and external (voice and movement) processes that must work together in such a way that the performance appears seamless:

there must never appear to be a visible line between thought and action, between actor and character. Whether the characterization the audience sees is realistic (recognizable as an everyday human being who could walk down a major city street and cause no comment), or stylized (heightened or extended in a number of ways for a variety of theatrical purposes)—either way, the actor's process is to make sure that the character is motivated by real and immediate thought, operates consistently within its own carefully constructed mode of behavior, and is controlled and conveyed to the audience by highly trained and carefully chosen physical and vocal techniques so as to appear spontaneous and immediate. (See Fig. 1.1.)

I'm sure you are beginning to see that establishing your own balance between these two processes can be tricky. Over the years, though, you will find the proportion between the two that is right for you.

Having commented about balance and spontaneity, let me end with a very dangerous analogy that I hope will shed some further light on all this. In order to program a computer, meticulous care must be maintained in following the first, often very tedious process. Step by step, the programmer stores a bewildering and apparently unrelated array of instructions in the computer's mem-

Figure 1.1   The members of an acting class should look on the time they spend there as "laboratory" time, helping and critiquing each other's work and, above all, not being afraid to take risks.

ory. These instructions can consist of the order in which numbers appear on the screen, the precedence one command takes over another, or bits of factual information needed to answer difficult questions. All of these various instructions are interrelated but have no real life of their own until the entire program is completed. Once this is done—the factual information necessary to do the job is installed in the memory bank—then all the operator has to do to run the program is push the Enter button. When that button is pushed, all the many details that have been so laboriously gathered and stored in the program begin to function as a whole, and, most importantly, begin to evoke reactions from each other to create something completely different—a solution to a problem or maybe a new game: a picture or graph or chart on the display screen, often accompanied by sound, and moving smoothly from one function to another. All the person running the program had to do was push one button and this elaborate sequence of events was set into motion. But remember: the program only works if all the tiny bits of information have been correctly assimilated into the computer's memory! If any piece is missing from the program, or if any bit has not been properly installed in deep memory, then the entire structure breaks down: the program will not run no matter how many times the operator hits the Enter button.

Relate this to the process of acting. As you begin to study your character and the play in which it appears, you will be assembling a wide variety of information all ready to go into action when the program is complete. What are these bits of information to the actor? The first is probably a clear intellectual understanding of the play and of your character (your character's biography, for instance); memorizing the words of the play is probably the second set of instructions to go into the memory bank (learning the lines); next you may memorize your physical location on the set (the director's blocking); then would come the delineation and assimilation of the many and varied thoughts, emotions, and sensory impressions of the character (the subtext); and finally you would decide on the physical and vocal choices that will convey all of this to the audience. Each of these pieces of information must be firmly established in the memory of the computer, in this case the brain of the actor, in order for the program—the performance—to function smoothly and effectively; in fact, the memory level to which all this must be consigned should almost be that of the autonomic processes: those which are beyond conscious will. Certainly, these elements must be memorized to the extent that they can be recalled without conscious thought.

If we consider all the preparation time of reading the play, blocking it, and working through each section as the time in which information is assembled (when the computer is programmed), then later rehearsals are those times in which the program is run. In this crucial last stage of rehearsals, the actor and the director must put all the pieces together: they must work on rhythm and begin to feel the natural emotion level of the scene establish itself in terms of build and pace and rate. If all the separate parts of the scene have been properly constructed, then the actor can release almost all conscious control and allow the program to run on something close to an instinctive level, allowing the performance to develop spontaneously as the immediate situation warrants. When this happens as it should, all the parts come together and produce the whole.

The Enter button that initiates this smoothly running program may be considered the stimulus of the performance situation itself. Actors must prepare themselves to begin the scene, then set off a trigger mechanism that involves concentration as well as physical and mental readiness. This trigger mechanism might be the ability to place yourself in the physical environment of the scene or the emotional state of the character at the beginning of the scene. It will vary from actor to actor, from scene to scene, from play to play, but the important thing to remember is that the mind and body of the actor must be relaxed, alert, and centered in order to be ready to press Enter. And once that button is pressed, once the program is running, conscious control can be, indeed should be, much less. Just remember, the more detailed, complete, and solid the information gathered and put into the program, the less control will be needed when the program—performance—is running.

Now here comes an even more dangerous part of this analogy. Let me suggest that all we have to do now is visualize the computer as a robot—a moving computer with arms and legs and facial muscles and a voice—to understand that the internal process composed of hundreds or thousands of pieces of information must be actually gone through before the robot will move its arms and legs or smile or speak. The thought, in other words, must be *actually thought* in order to motivate any physical action. To the robot, movement and speech are the result of the preprogrammed bits of information. To the actor, the external manifestation is the result of the internal process. (See Fig. 1.2.)

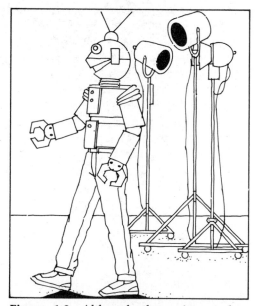

Figure 1.2 Although the acting student must be very aware of external technique, the internal thought process must always motivate action or the result will be stiff and mechanical.

Why is all this so dangerous? *Because I very much do not wish you to believe— having written the dread words* computer *and* robot—*that a performance can ever be in any way mechanical!* Quite the contrary is true. The body of the character must move and speak as naturally as you do in your everyday life and always as a result of apparently spontaneous thought. All that the actor has done at the end of the programming task is supply the brain with facts. In beginning to run the performance, those facts fit together in new ways, producing completely new actions and reactions. The key here is to release enough control of the performance to allow the carefully assembled program to run with as much spontaneity as possible. And a great deal of spontaneity *is* possible. Allowing all this meticulously gathered network of factual information to run on the autonomic level allows the actor the freedom to listen to the words and actions of the other characters as if he or she were seeing and hearing them for the first time. It lets the actor concentrate on all the reactions and interrelationships of the play as if they were occurring freshly in the immediate present and originating from deep, immediate, personal wellsprings of emotion. This comes close to being a definition of the spontaneity that we have spoken of at such length, and it is certainly the lifeblood of performance: to create within the artificial environment of the theater a human being who is real and immediate to the observer and who seems to be participating in the events of the play for the first time just as the observer is, but which is the result of weeks of careful planning and rehearsal.

Of course, we all understand that a character in a play is absolutely not a computer or a robot. Programming a real computer with bits of information— though certainly complex enough—is not nearly as complicated as absorbing and exhibiting the thoughts and emotions of a human being. What exactly, then, are these bits of information and the tools of their expression—these externals and internals—which make up acting?

The physical externals are, perhaps, easier to list, simply because they are more visible and more easily measurable. This, of course, does not make them less important or any easier to develop. Chapter 2 discusses these skill areas, all of which have to do, in one way or another, with the body. Along with the discussions are exercises to help you develop competence in each area. All of these skills depend on a relaxed body. Relaxation of the body is discussed in a separate section at the beginning of Chapter 2, and a number of exercises that will help you with relaxation are listed. Remember always to start slowly and gently when you do these exercises. Work on them every day, but never try to force the body to do anything. Take it easy!

The Body as Occupier of Space
1. Stance: the way the body stands or sits or lies at rest.
2. Movement: the way the whole body moves in space.
3. Hand/arm gesture: the movement of the hands and arms apart from the body.
4. Body gesture: the movement of the hands and arms as they relate to the body.
5. Facial gesture: movement of the muscles in the face.

The Body as Producer of Sound

1. Diaphragmatic breathing: natural deep breathing controlled by the diaphragm muscle.
2. Articulation: the shaping of sound by the lips, tongue, palate, and lower jaw.
3. Diction: the correct or accepted pronunciation of words.
4. Vocal placement: the placement of the voice in any of several resonating areas for the production of a variety of centered and resonant sounds.
5. Projection: the specific directing of sound so as to be heard by the audience clearly and easily.

The internal process involves the intellect and the emotions, and is therefore less easy to define, but a start may be made by grouping the ideas into three basic sections.

Concentration

1. First circle of concentration: being alone onstage.
2. Second circle of concentration: focusing within the ensemble.
3. Third circle of concentration: focusing on memory and infinity.

Understanding the Text

1. Who am I?
2. Where am I?
3. What am I doing?

Understanding the Subtext

1. Motivational unit: smallest unit of intent.
2. Spine: through-line of character's intent.
3. Superobjective: overall intent of the play.

I hope this chapter has given you a clear idea about the internals and externals of acting and how your use of them must be balanced. It's quite a simple concept, but it needs to be treated with a good deal of seriousness, attention to detail, and lots of hard work. Let's begin that work in the next chapter by learning some ways to relax your body and prepare the most important of your external skills.

Chapter 2
• • • •
PREPARING
THE
EXTERNALS

RELAXATION

The actor's body—yours—is the body the character must inhabit. In order for this mutually shared body to move as the character would move, the actor's body—yours—must be relaxed; the character's stance and gesture pattern, for instance, must not be applied on top of the actor's own tension: there must be a clean slate on which to apply character movement. If you are tense, conflicting muscle strains are produced that often prevent effective movement, frequently making it look halting and awkward. As an acting student, you must find an effective method of relaxation that you practice in the classroom on a daily basis, just as dancers do their barre work. These exercises should also be a part of your warm-up sequence done before rehearsing or performing a role.

There are many relaxation exercises acting students may use, some of which you may have already mastered as part of a meditative or martial arts discipline. Actors do have some specific needs, however.

First of all, physical relaxation for the actor must leave the body alert: this is not the kind of relaxation that leads to sleep—loose muscles must not lead to slack mental activity. Ideally, the relaxed actor is physically free of tension and mentally concentrated, ready to operate in the immediate present, with a body open to the development of character movement.

Second, physical relaxation must leave the body centered. This idea of centering may be a bit difficult to understand at first, but after a while it will seem natural to you; certainly once you're used to moving from your natural center, you'll wonder how you could ever have worked without it. Don't think of centering as anything mystical or trendy. It's a natural process that is both psychological and physical and simply provides you with a point of focus and balance. Begin by trying to visualize and locate your body's natural center point. It is usually an inch or so below the navel and is sometimes called the solar plexus. This point is quite close to the place where breath—and therefore sound—is produced, so it's a good focal point for breathing, but it also works well in balancing stance and focusing concentration. Any relaxation exercise for an actor should begin by finding and focusing on that center point. After a while you'll begin to move (and speak and think) from your center point without thinking about it.

Third, these exercises must also leave you with a balanced stance firmly related to the floor. The relaxation process should leave the muscles of the legs, particularly, lose and pliant so that they will easily and naturally support the body on whatever surface is under the feet. This is often called *grounding*, for the simple reason that it is so important for the actor to be easily but firmly related to the ground (or floor) so that the rest of the body can relax and move freely and creatively. A grounded, natural, centered stance is the basis of all movement.

Physical relaxation for the actor is also necessary for good voice production. Particularly important in this regard are the muscles of the shoulders, the neck, the jaw, the throat—all areas that must be relaxed in order to produce good speech.

Specific relaxation and warm-up exercises depend to a great extent on the individual requirements of the body being relaxed and on the kind of role for which it is being prepared. Let's begin, however, with a general exercise that both relaxes the whole body and provides a focal point for concentration. As you do this exercise, your breathing should settle to its autonomic level where diaphragmatic breathing will begin, the rib cage expanding as you breathe in the relaxing as you breathe out. This kind of natural breathing is the basis of good vocal production. Take note of it at this point, but don't worry about trying to develop it right now. We'll talk about it in more detail later in this chapter.

As we begin this first exercise, by the way, I think it is important to note that the visualizations found in all the exercises in this book are important psychological aids that support—and sometimes produce—the physical processes, so get used to doing them completely, thoroughly, and without embarrassment.*

● ● ●

EXERCISE 1

RELAXATION EXERCISE FOR THE WHOLE BODY

Lie flat on the floor in a comfortable position with your arms on either side of your body. You might want to put a pad under your head for comfort, and a thin one under your lower back. Your feet should flop to the sides, not point up. Be sure

---

* All exercises should be done carefully. Consult your physician before attempting any exercises that might be harmful to your personal physical condition.

there's no strain on the muscles of your lower back. Close your eyes and let the thought processes of everyday activity slow down a bit: try visualizing a warm gray fog, for instance. Don't say to yourself, "I must empty my mind!" as that will set up its own resonances, creating rather than lessening tension. Instead of trying to force your mind to empty, focus on the positive image of the fog, allowing it to surround and support your body, to inhibit and lull your mind. Once your body is floating, relaxed, in this fog, visualize a portion of this fog as a blob of softly glowing light hovering just over your face. Once this ball of light is as real as possible to you, allow it to suffuse your entire head with a warm, soft glow. Once this is established, begin a slow mental count from 1 to 20. As you begin the count, let your focused ball of light (gently! don't force it!) drift down your body, relaxing each body section as you come to it: your head, including eyes, mouth, and jaw; neck; shoulders; arms, including wrists and fingers; upper chest; stomach (top of the rib cage); abdomen (bottom of the rib cage); pelvis; knees; calves; ankles; feet (particularly the soles); toes. Then begin with the toes and go back up your body, allowing the ball of light to envelope each part of the body again. Do this a few times going very slowly up and down your body. After a few minutes, increase the speed of the count a bit, but never get very fast. At its peak, the light should be traveling up and down your body in a slow, steady stream. Gradually the light should seem to expand and enclose your whole body in a pulsing wave. As this wave of light moves up and down the body, begin to visualize your body melting into the floor, becoming limp and flexible; it might help if the light feels a little warmer at this point. Continue this exercise until the process is automatic and the light moves freely, relaxing your body as it goes.

● ● ●

If, after doing an exercise like this one, your entire body is functioning easily and naturally, we need to see if this relaxed state can be maintained as the body becomes more alert. To do this, move easily and loosely to an erect posture. Exercise 2 continues the relaxation process, but allows the lower body to maintain an easy and alert balance while the upper body is loose and relaxed; it also helps you with centering.

● ● ●

EXERCISE 2
STACKING VERTEBRAE

Stand comfortably with your feet about as wide apart as your shoulders are wide: too narrow a stance makes for instability, too wide and the muscles on the insides of the thighs will be improperly stretched. Arms and hands should hang loosely from the shoulders. Keeping the knees slightly flexed (*not locked!*) let the upper part of your body—from the pelvis up—flow *gently* forward to hang as loosely as possible from the pelvis. Letting the upper part of your body sag from the pelvis, begin to pulse (gently!) up and down, allowing the torso muscles gradually to loosen. Don't worry if your hands don't touch the floor like those of the dance student next to you! Don't force it! Take it easy! As you loosen up over the next weeks or months you do this exercise, they may do so, or at least get a bit closer to the floor, but this isn't necessary; you are just trying to relax your muscles, not become an acrobat or dancer. Keep well within your own limits. Let progress come easily and slowly without trying too hard. After a few bounces, return to an erect posture slowly, counting to ten, rolling your back up and visualizing the vertebrae stacking themselves up, one by one as you do so. Let your arms hang loose and watch that your shoulders don't get tense and thrust themselves forward. At ten, gently rotate shoulders into place, allowing your neck to place your head on the top of the stack with no shoulder tension, the arms hanging very loosely. You will find it helps concentration if you focus on the same spot—real if you have your eyes open, imagined if you have your eyes shut—each time you return to an erect posture.

● ● ●

Stacking vertebrae, as well as these other basic exercises, are the beginnings of physical relaxation and must be executed within the specific limitations of your own body and its readiness for these exercises. *Don't overdo! Don't force it! Take it easy!* I will say this so many times you will probably get tired of hearing it, but it is important enough to risk that. I don't want you to hurt yourself, and if you try to push and force your body, that is exactly what will happen. Resist the temptation to push ahead too fast. Preparing your body is a time-consuming process that must be approached slowly over a long period. Like any other physical discipline, it works best when practiced daily and in moderation. After each exercise it is wise to shake out the entire body: imagine yourself a dog emerging from the water and shake your body easily but thoroughly to remove all the imaginary water drops. Jog lightly or hop gently around your part of the room as you do this.

Now let's pay some special attention to one of the most important areas for the actor: the neck and the jaw, which must absolutely be relaxed in order to develop vocal skills. The neck and jaw are also muscles that frequently tense as a result of the daily stress of living. Let's relax them.

● ● ●

EXERCISE 3

NECK ROLLS

At the end of one of the stacking vertebrae sequences, remain in the erect posture with your head sitting on your shoulders easily and naturally. With your eyes closed, visualize a 10-foot pole growing from the top of your head. Again, don't skimp on these visualizations! They may seem a bit silly at first, but you'll soon discover that they're important parts of the process, not just a fanciful game. When you have established this pole as a real object within your imagination, place a small iron ball—a little bigger than a tennis ball—attached and balanced at the top of the pole. Imagine that this pole and the iron ball balance on your head, firmly attached but *exerting no pressure on the head and neck.* Do not let this stress create pressure or tension. Keeping the shoulders still and relaxed, imagine the ball, taking the pole with it, tipping *slowly* forward until your head, on your completely relaxed neck, is *gently* and *easily* lolling on your chest. *Don't let the neck snap as it comes forward!*

Let it pulse a little (gently) as the chin rests on the chest. Keeping the neck loose and relaxed, slowly swing the *pole* to the right, then to the left: shoulder to shoulder; the *loose neck* allows the head to follow. *Gently now! Don't force it! Take it easy!* Swing the pole from shoulder to shoulder, easily and with a loose, relaxed neck. Let your head *loll* as it swings from side to side. Never force the neck or let it snap into any position! Let the jaw relax, let the mouth hang open as the head reaches each shoulder. Keep everything loose! Repeat this process, always remembering to focus on the iron ball at the tip of the pole: direct *it* to move, not your head; this will take focus away from the neck muscles and help to keep your neck relaxed. You might want to visualize your neck as being limp like wet spaghetti. Again, take your time with this exercise, never forcing, never allowing your neck to move sharply or to jerk or snap into position.

● ● ●

Practicing these fundamental exercises in relaxation on a daily basis will bring you to a point where you may begin to recognize how much further you need to go in loosening your body. These are only three very basic exercises, and you may need to find others—there are a great number of them in many excellent books—that focus on other specific parts of the body. In fact, as you continue to study acting, you will want to find other courses and new disciplines to help you. Or you may find that you need to spend a longer time working on the fundamental exercises found here before proceeding further. Ask yourself if you can satisfactorily relax the whole body or any of its individual parts in isolation and still remain alert and balanced; if the answer is yes, take the next step.

THE BODY AS OCCUPIER OF SPACE

Stance

At the completion of one of the stacking vertebrae exercises, your body should be in a natural, well-aligned, centered stance: the feet should be easily but firmly connected to the floor, the legs should be relaxed (never lock the knees!), using only the muscles necessary to maintain a relaxed erect posture, the torso sitting easily and comfortably on the pelvis (the shoulders hanging easily; no military bracing), the neck and head (very important) sitting comfortably on the top of the torso (no jaw tension), arms hanging loosely at your sides, hands lightly and naturally cupped. You should feel comfortable but balanced and alert, able to return to this basic stance after the completion of any exercise. If you feel this is accomplished, let's work on variations of stance.

● ● ●

EXERCISE 4

STANCE EXERCISES

Maintaining the natural, connected stance just described, transfer most of the control of the stance to your toes: raise your body up and down easily, using only the toes and assigning the job of keeping the body erect and balanced to your legs. Maintaining the stance, bounce gently on your toes several times. Now imagine a wire coming out of the top of your head that is gently pulling your body upward, extending and stretching it to maximum height. Your visualization of the wire is to motivate upper body relaxation: your toes are providing the lift. Use as few muscles as possible. Keep your body from the toes upward as relaxed as you can. Transfer as much of the active muscle use as possible to your feet and toes. You can control shaking of your legs by keeping your eyes fixed on a point of concentration directly ahead of you at easy eye level, thus taking concentration (and insecurity!) away from the leg muscles. Hold this extension for a moment, then lower back to a flatfooted, connected stance. Rest for a moment, shake out if you need to, then try this exercise using only one foot, alternating left and right. Keep concentration by maintaining your point of focus. Now repeat this exercise, this time also raising your arms as your body rises on the toes. Imagine invisible wires attached to the tops of your hands, and let them pull the arms to full extension over your head. Then transfer the wires to the tips of your fingers and stretch, hands pointing to the ceiling, at full extension from the tips of your fingers to your toes. After a moment, transfer the wires back to the tops of your hands and drop the wrists as your body begins the descent to a flatfooted stance, arms hanging naturally in your basic stance as the soles of your feet touch the floor. Always return to your natural, connected stance through these exercises.

Maintaining the original natural stance, imagine a change in gravity that is pulling your entire body into a closer contact with the earth. Feel your body *settle* (you're still standing) to the floor. Make no conscious muscle effort to do this; simply visualize it. Now alternate this with a gravity that allows your body to float. Never allowing the soles of your feet to lose contact with the ground, let your body float upward. Try walking in both of these gravitational conditions. Later on you may want to try a lighter or heavier gravity for the individual stance of a character you are developing.

● ● ●

The point of working on stance is to allow your body to be in an easy, natural relationship to the surface on which it is standing, moving, sitting, or lying. Physical tension can make an actor's body seem to be lifting itself from the floor, perhaps forcing the arms to rise slightly from the sides in a tense, unpleasant fashion. Work on stance until the natural one for your body is automatic.

THE BODY IN MOTION

Once you can maintain a good natural stance, you can work on feeling relaxed and centered as you move. Try watching cats because these animals are very economical in their use of energy when they move. If a cat is licking its foot, only the muscles needed to get the tongue to the foot are used; the rest of its body is completely relaxed.

Of course, when you are working on a role, much of your actual movement will be given to you by the director in those first blocking rehearsals in which the overall movement pattern of the play or scene is established. Still, a good deal of movement is left to the individual actor. The point in *preparing* for character movement, however, is so that you, the actor, are able to execute any movement given to you by a director, or that you devise for yourself. An important note: movement exercises are not designed to build up muscle, but to make your muscles pliable and elastic, capable of assuming character movement patterns instead of the movement habits that you have developed over the years. Let's see what happens when you put your basic relaxed stance into motion.

● ● ●

EXERCISE 5

STANCE AND MOVEMENT

Find your basic stance and establish your point of concentration at easy eye level. Walk around the room, keeping good contact between the soles of your feet and the floor. Keep checking your alignment as you walk: remember how it felt to be in a centered, connected-to-the-floor posture when you stood still at the end of the stacking vertebrae exercise, and maintain this as you move. It may help to take steps that are a little longer than usual, even using a gliding, skating motion. Keep your head centered and easy by maintaining your point-of-concentration focus straight ahead at easy eye level.

Maintaining point-of-concentration focus and keeping good contact between the soles of your feet and the floor, walk to a chair and stand in front of the chair, facing away from it. Now lower your bottom onto the surface of the chair, disturbing none of the stance's balance. Keep your body relaxed and aligned. Go slowly! It may help to visualize ropes attached to the points of your shoulders that are lowering your body into the chair, thus taking pressure and focus off the muscles you're actually using, allowing them to relax. Allow your forearms to settle into a natural, relaxed posture on your legs or by your sides. Record in your mind how this sitting stance feels. Stand up, leaving the chair the same way you sat in it, just reversing the process.

Standing again, lean forward, stopping yourself from falling (at the last moment!) by extending one leg or the other, alternately, forward in an easy, relaxed lunge. Use only the muscles that are necessary to keep yourself from falling.

● ● ●

Once you have been able to make an easy connection between stance and movement, let's begin to work on that centering process we talked about briefly. Remember that the natural center of your body is the internal source of mental energy and the focal point of all concentration. Remember also that movement coming from this center will not only be better balanced and more finely focused, it will have a point of origin and completion that will help make it more consistent. Don't think of this center as something mystical. Just visualize it as a focus point of movement, energy, and concentration.

● ● ●

EXERCISE 6

CENTERING EXERCISE

Lie on the floor and do the basic relaxation exercise. When your body is completely relaxed and you've established a deep and easy breathing pattern, allow your mind to focus on the deepest point that the breathing process reaches, probably about two inches below the navel. This is not necessarily where the diaphragm is—it's higher, separating the rib cage from the abdominal area—but is the point from which the deepest breath *seems* to come. Place your hand over this point, perhaps pressing lightly with one finger to help you locate it. If you are maintaining visual contact with a point of focus, you may want to close your eyes at this point, moving to a mental point of focus, just to help concentration. Now imagine that the center point you are visualizing inside the body has physical actuality: it makes no impact on the inside of the body, no sensation (certainly not discomfort), it simply exists at the point you are visualizing. Try making this focal point about the size of a good-sized marble or golf ball. Experiment with color and temperature and substance: make it red or blue or green; let it warm up or cool down; let it become very light or a little heavier. See what impact these changes make on how you feel inside your body as you lie, relaxed, on the floor. When you think you have established a center point, visualize moving from it. Don't actually move the body yet, just imagine movement: imagine it originating from this center point and affecting various parts of your body. Visualize your arms, hands, fingers, legs, feet, moving from the center you have found. Then, still relaxed, still focused, gently move your arms and legs (no big movements yet, just slide them gently along the floor) as you had visualized them. See if you can maintain contact with the center as you do this. Work on making a connection between your body's natural center and the beginnings of movement. Once the center is firmly established and you find you are able to summon and visualize it easily, try moving it from place to place in your body: in the middle of the head, in your knees, at the tip of your index finger. How do each of these positionings of the center make your body feel? How do these changes of the center affect movement? Natural movement should always come from the natural center.

● ● ●

Don't be surprised, by the way, if you feel very little difference at first. You may also feel that these visualizations are silly or time-wasting games. Just remember they are simply psychological aids. Not the end result, they might help you get there and are effective only if you treat them seriously for what they are. They also often need a fair amount of time to develop before they have an impact on the body. So give them a chance. Moving the center around the body will be more easily felt when you're moving around. Let's work on that.

● ● ●

EXERCISE 7

THE CENTER IN MOTION

Keeping your eyes closed, bend your knees slightly and raise your torso to a comfortable sitting position, crossing your legs tailor fashion as you do so. Use your other arm to help you sit up if you need to. This is not a contest to see whose abdominal muscles are best developed! If you are comfortable in the lotus position, you might want to assume that pose, but don't feel you have to if it causes muscle strain. Remember: slow and easy! At this point, you may have to reestablish some of the relaxation exercise, as the mere process of sitting up may have tensed muscles unnecessarily. Continue to breathe and keep your finger on the point that seems to be each breath's deepest point. Now move your hand away from the center point, as if you are pulling a long thread from it: think of the center as a spool from which this thread is unwinding, projecting off into space. Bring your hand back to your abdomen, tracing the thread as if it were disappearing back onto its spool; now pull it out again. Do this several times: it's just to help you visualize the center point and its extension into the space around you. Allow the thread from your center to thicken with each pull until it is a sizable cord. Now, with any assistance from the other hand and arm that you need—but using as few muscles as possible—grasp this cord firmly and pull yourself forward and then upward into an easy, relaxed erect stance. You might want to open your eyes at this point, but keep your concentration!

Holding the cord, pull yourself around the room. As you do so, continue to visualize the point at which the cord attaches to your center. Vary the way in which you pull yourself around: you may pull quickly or slowly, smoothly or in staccato bursts; you may vary the angle of the cord from straight out to upward or downward at various angles; pull the cord as though it were made of rubber or steel or fragile glass. What is the effect on your body of each of these variations? How does it move as a result of each? Try guiding yourself into sitting or lying positions by pulling on the cord.

Remember how it felt, when you were lying on the floor, to visualize the center moving around to various parts of your body—head, knees, one of your fingers—and observe the impact that this changing of the center's location has on stance and movement. Any time the center is arbitrarily moved from its natural point (about two inches, remember, below the navel) it will tend to throw the body off balance. Visualizing the center anywhere but its natural position is useful only if you wish your character to appear off balance or eccentric in some way.

Work with a partner by pulling on each other's center cord. Tie yours and your partner's cords together in an imaginary knot and see how the dynamics between you change as you pull on each other's center. Always note the effect of these visualizations on actual movement.

● ● ●

Remember that these exercises do not exist for their own sake, but so that you can later characterize movement. Might Caliban, for instance, in *The Tempest* have a center that is pulling him from the pelvis or the groin? Might Ariel in the same play be pulled upward into flight by a center of gravity that comes from the tip of his nose? Find as many variations of centered and noncentered movement as you can.

Eventually you will need to start working with movement and centering without going through the medium of the exercise at all—at least after the initial warm-up. For instance, having found the center through such an exercise early in the rehearsal period, you will need to be able to feel centered while doing a wide variety of movements within your scene: jumping, rolling, leaping in various—safe!—ways. But you will always need to maintain an awareness of where the center is and let all movement originate from it.

Another variant of this exercise is to find the center and transform it into the center of an animal. Allow this new center to move you around the room using, say, the center of a snake or a tiger or a bird as the propelling force. Involve the whole body in this transference of energy. Observe the differences in the movement and retain the difference for future reference and use.

Movement that comes from the center is capable of transporting the body in space in a variety of ways. Continue to work on these variations: moving the center around for specialized movements, animal centers, or centers of your own devising. Where is your center, for instance, if the character is flying? But always know where your natural center is and that most movement comes from a relaxed stance connected to the floor and coming from this natural center.

Hand/Arm Gesture

Centering is the basis of all whole-body movement, and, since the hands and arms are connected to the body, is the point around which the hands and arms also move. But they sometimes have a life of their own, and sometimes that life is a negative one. Beginning actors frequently ask, "What do I do with my hands?" The answer to that question, of course, is whatever you would do in real life. Later, the answer might be whatever your character would do in his or her real life. The acting environment, however, seems to put constrictions on us at first that make us very aware of our arms and hands and create a good deal of tension. Any of the relaxation and concentration exercises here will help with this problem, but there is a further area that needs to be discussed before we can go on: isolation.

Isolation simply means the ability to use one part of the body while leaving the rest relaxed. We have already done some work in this area. When we talked about isolating the head from the body in neck rolls, for instance, or primarily using the muscles of the toes to support the rest of the body in stretching exercises—in both of these cases we were isolating parts of the body from others. But let's find out how we can be easier and more relaxed with our hands and arms by doing specific things with them while the rest of the body is very relaxed.

● ● ●

EXERCISE 8

HAND/ARM GESTURE: ISOLATION

Do the stance exercise, finding the connected, natural stance. Once this is established, pay special attention to your hands and arms as an extension of this stance. Think of the hands and arms as separate agents attached to the grounded stance by muscles and tendons, but possessing a life of their own. Move your hands and arms in abstract patterns around your body for a while. Don't consciously guide them; simply let them move. Try to free them from conscious control. Now watch them as they move, becoming accustomed to the sight and feel of your hands and arms in motion separately from your body. Note how a specific position of the hands and arms alone might communicate an individual thought or emotion. You might find it helpful at first to do this exercise to music, changing the kind or tempo of the music to see how these changes affect hand and arm gesture.

● ● ●

The primary function of this exercise is to let you become aware of your hands and arms in the context of your overall movement pattern. For some reason we tend to be very self-conscious about too much hand and arm gesture, seeing it as expressive of melodramatic or overdone emotions perhaps. To combat this, exaggerate these movements at first: make them much larger than they need to be. Break down the barriers. You can exercise some control later. Have a little fun moving around in the most overwrought, melodramatic ways you can think of. Be free and easy. Get used to feeling the body moving at a high level of magnitude. Once you have gotten used to moving your hands and arms in large abstract ways, begin to do so for specific reasons.

Basically, gestures of the hands and arms have two distinct functions: *description* and *emphasis*. Imagine describing to someone the nature of a spiral staircase or the way a snake moves without using your hands. Or imagine a teacher calling a class of unruly 7-year-olds to order without clapping his hands together to emphasize the nature of his authority. All variants of hand/arm gesture come from these two motivations: description and emphasis. Determining a very specific hand/arm gesture that will work for your character is a function of a later stage of the actor's development. For now, let's consider how to prepare for that eventuality by playing some guessing games.

● ● ●

EXERCISE 9

HAND/ARM GESTURE: DESCRIPTIONS AND EMPHASES

Stand facing a partner and each of you repeat Exercise 8, building up a free pattern of abstract movement. When you feel you are moving your hands and arms freely and without tension, each of you gradually begin to shape the movements into descriptions of familiar, specific objects. Each of you shout out the object as soon as you have guessed what the other is describing. Do this several times until both of you feel very free and uninhibited in your movements.

Now move into the area of emphasis, allowing your hands and arms to move so as to underline and emphasize specific emotions. Each of you guess which emotions are being exhibited and shout them out as soon as you know. Now try doing this in turns, letting your emphatic hand/arm gesture grow from the one your partner just demonstrated.

● ● ●

Before we go any further in the area of isolation, remember that isolation of muscles is a function of relaxation as well as specificity. A gesture of the hands or arms is much clearer if it is done against the background of a relaxed body. Most of the movements of your hands and arms will involve isolation, but all gesture and movement, including that of the hands and arms, comes from the center. Let's work on that by doing some hand/arm movements that originate from the center and then involve the whole body.

● ● ●

EXERCISE 10

HAND/ARM GESTURE: CENTERED EMPHASIS

Do the centering exercise to the point at which the center is found and you are sitting up. Instead of finding the thread, move your hand away from the center as if it were an object separate and distinct from your body. Observe your hand as it sits in space in front of your eyes. Now let it move in an abstract pattern. As soon as the pattern suggests a specific emotion—anger, say—let that emotion flow down your arm, across your body and into the other arm and hand. Now let your two hands and arms work together to emphasize and enlarge the emotional state. As the intensity of the generated emotion increases, let your hands and arms lead the body from the sitting position and into movement. Never lose sight of the fact that your hands and arms originated the emotion from the natural center of your body. Move around the room, being led by your hands and arms as they shape the size and color of the emotional state. Channel your hands and arms into a function of emphasis, building on and intensifying the emotional state through your hands and arms alone.

● ● ●

Let's return for a moment to hand/arm gesture as a function of description and see how that also originates from the center.

● ● ●

EXERCISE 11

HAND/ARM GESTURE: CENTERED DESCRIPTION

Work with a partner on this one. Do a basic relaxation and centering exercise so that the two of you are standing facing each other in a relaxed, centered, erect posture. Demonstrate a physical object for your partner (don't tell what it is!) by using the centered whole body, but without moving hands and arms. You must feel your torso, head, and legs demonstrating (from the center!) this physical object without using the descriptive function of your hands and arms. When your partner has guessed the object, she must show you what it is by using *only* her hands and arms. Finally, describe the object, first using your centered body, then allowing this impulse to infect and spread to your hands and arms. Pass this function back and forth a few times. Do this exercise at a higher level of magnitude by exaggerating these movements: do them on a very grand level; then do the same exercise with the absolute minimum of the smallest possible hand and arm movement. Repeat the exercise several times, passing the functions back and forth.

● ● ●

While the hands and arms are frequently used to express movement that is consciously removed from the body, equally important are the hands and arms when used in direct relationship to the body. These kinds of movements—half stance, half movements—are called body gestures.

Body Gesture

Imagine yourself sitting in your own living room talking with friends. Unless you are describing some object or emotion that is particularly intricate, or you are in the middle of an impassioned expression of personal opinion, your hands and arms are likely touching your own body in some way: you may be leaning your chin or the side of your head against one fist, the other hand resting in your lap; or you may have both hands clasped in your lap; or maybe your arms are folded across your chest. Now picture yourself standing at a bus stop: what are your hands and arms doing? You may be holding books or a backpack in one hand, but the other is more than likely stuffed into a pocket or perhaps a thumb is hooked into your belt or maybe resting lightly on one hip. All of these postures are utilizing the hands and arms in what we call a body gesture: close-to-the-body gestures of the hands and arms in relation to the rest of the body. The body gesture is the way we carry our hands and arms most of the time.

In your everyday life you probably use body gestures more than gestures that describe or emphasize: they are the natural at-rest gestures of your usual stance, and we fall into them naturally depending on the environment or situation in which we find ourselves. Still, as naturally and frequently as we use body gestures in everyday life, you may have some trouble recalling them in the acting situation. Here is an exercise that will help you remember your real-life body gestures and apply them to work as an actor.

● ● ●

EXERCISE 12

BODY GESTURE: INITIATOR/RECIPIENT

Find a partner and stand facing each other. Pick one of you to be the initiator and one to be the recipient. When the recipient is standing in a relaxed connected-to-the-floor stance, the initiator should begin arranging the recipient's hands and arms in a wide variety of body gestures, the recipient easily but firmly maintaining these postures. When the body gesture is established, the recipient should improvise a few words that would be appropriate to this posture and body gesture. Now switch the roles of initiator and recipient and repeat the exercise. Having someone else choose body gestures for you will eliminate some of the self-consciousness you might feel in selecting the postures, and also provides both of you with a wider variety of gestures.

● ● ●

A variant of Exercises 12 and 13 may be found in other books that deal with aspects of improvisation for the theater. This next one is rather like one sometimes called a mirror exercise, except here the image is not reversed. Unlike the previous exercise, the partners don't touch each other. We call the exercise "Doppelgängers."

● ● ●

EXERCISE 13

BODY GESTURES: DOPPELGÄNGERS

Stand next to a partner, with both of you facing a large mirror. The initiator begins to assume a variety of body gestures and stances. Go slowly at first! The other partner sees these moves in the mirror and acts as a doppelgänger, or twin to the initiator, assuming the initiator's moves in as close to an automatic, no-time-lag response as possible. Try not to guess what pose your partner will assume next; just release the intellectual function and get into a free-flowing response to the other person. As you progress, move closer together; finally one of you is standing back of the other, just able to see the mirror. It's possible to be so in contact that it looks like only one person in the mirror. Pass the role of initiator back and forth. It's also fun to have the initiator begin (slowly at first) to add words to the gestures, the other echoing them with as little lag as possible. Again, this is useful for tuning in to other people's rhythms and for establishing an ensemble, which we discuss later on.

● ● ●

These exercises are valuable for building up a repertoire of body gestures, and helping you become more comfortable using them. They are a valuable and effective way to assimilate the hands and arms into your character's stance and movement patterns.

Before we leave the subject of body gestures, there are a couple of related matters I should mention. First, I now and again come across students who have been told by other teachers or directors that certain body gestures are not allowed on the stage. Putting your hands in your pockets is most often mentioned. This prohibition is not true. Any body gesture that your character would do is allowed, and often adds realism and detail to characterization. Put your hands in your pockets!

Also, even when your hands are used for carrying some object—books, purse, jacket, an apple—their use may be defined as a body gesture. In fact, the use of these props is one of the most helpful ways that the beginning acting student can become accustomed to using body gestures in an easy, natural way. So in early improvisations and scenes you may want to use props to motivate body gestures.

Facial Gesture

A very important area for gesture is the face. There are several reasons why students are reluctant to utilize the face as a gesture plane, chief among them fear of what is called mugging in relation to the acting process, and fear of being ''uncool'' in relation to themselves.

Mugging is related to the dread words *commenting* or *indicating*, both of which are to be avoided. We discuss these matters in detail later. For now, let's just say that commenting or indicating relate to the acting process when it is not motivated by thought and therefore not seen as real. Mugging is the kind of faulty acting when it is expressed by (often exaggerated) facial gesture. Obviously all of this is to be avoided: externals must come from motivating thought.

There is something other than the fear of mugging that prevents many people from effectively utilizing the facial plane, however: fear of loss of dignity—of displaying emotion too openly, and subsequently being perceived as uncool. We have often been taught to be constantly on guard against others and not let our faces show what we are thinking; that we must be ''cool.'' This is particularly true of young men, who seem to believe that the demonstration of emotion is somehow unmasculine. Yet it is by definition the actor's task to demonstrate emotion, and the most effective place to do so is very often the face. So there are often social and cultural barriers to be broken down as well as gesture skills to be acquired. Let's start to do that by jumping in at the deep end and taking facial gesture to extremes!

● ● ●

EXERCISE 14

FACIAL GESTURE: STRETCHING

Start by standing or sitting in front of a mirror. Do some neck rolls to be sure your head, neck, and face are thoroughly relaxed. Do some shoulder rolls, too: rotating the shoulders easily, loosely in their sockets, up and down, back and forth. With your upper body relaxed, take both hands and gently but firmly massage the entire face (take your contact lenses out first if you're wearing them), pulling and stretching the muscles of your forehead, cheeks, chin, mouth—the entire facial plane—until your face begins to feel relaxed and pliant, like rubber. Observing the response in the mirror, begin moving your lips in as many ways as possible: purse them, stretch them, smile, and so on. Exaggerate these movements as much as you can. Stick out your tongue as far as possible, letting it work with your lips. Transfer this movement to the jaw and chin: open your mouth as wide as you can, then contract your lips into as small a pucker as possible. Alternate between these two mouth gestures. Now let this movement spread to the rest of your face: involve the nose—wrinkling and relaxing it alternately; expand and contract the eyelids and other muscles around the eyes; wrinkle, unwrinkle, stretch the brow. Discover small muscles in the face that you rarely use and begin to utilize them as gesture participants. Get used to seeing your face doing these grimaces and contortions! Don't let it embarrass you! Now transfer to a partner instead of the mirror. Make faces at each other in as exaggerated a manner as possible, stretching and relaxing the face to its absolute limits. You might want to try doing a version of the doppelgänger exercise described in the body gesture section. Working with a partner as you stretch the face into these sometimes ridiculous facial gestures will help get rid of self-consciousness and will allow you to use facial gestures in a more normal way in your scene.

● ● ●

Though you will only rarely be called on to use such extreme facial gestures in a realistic characterization, you will have the capacity. Just remember, the face needs to be used as a gesture plane, but (as with any physicalization) *facial gestures must be motivated by internal thought!*

Consistency is important in developing any physical ability: you must be able to recall the gesture at any time and maintain it as long as it is needed by the performance situation. Here again is an extreme exercise that will help you do that.

● ● ●

EXERCISE 15

FACIAL GESTURE: MASKS

Begin with the facial stretching exercises. Then look in your mirror, think of an extreme emotion (happiness, say, or grief or rage) and let your face reflect this emotional state (see Fig. 2.1). Exaggerate the facial gesture as far as you can. Now see if you can take it even further. Further. Once you have reached the limits of your facial muscles' ability to stretch, hold the facial gesture as long as you comfortably can. You have created a *mask* of grief or happiness or rage. Now stand up and let the emotion transfer to the rest of the body, maintaining the mask on your face steadily and without letting it change. Let the body move around the room, employing a variety of hand/arm gestures and body gestures that are expressive of the mask, but keep the mask constant.

Figure 2.1 Facial gesture is very important as a reflection of the internal thought. An exaggerated mask of an emotion may help students feel what the thought should look like.

Now work with a partner on this one: one as initiator, one as recipient. Begin with the facial stretching exercises in partnership. Then the initiator should name an emotional state to the recipient. The recipient then assumes an appropriate facial gesture—taken to the limits of the ability of the face to stretch—which demonstrates this emotion. Swap the role of initiator when the first partner has taken the emotional mask as far as possible. When both partners have a mask, both should begin an interaction involving movement, hand/arm gestures, and body gestures that are expressive, in a give-and-take situation, of their individual masks. Add dialogue to the situation if you wish, and don't worry at this point if—because of the mask—the words aren't clearly articulated. See how long you can comfortably maintain your mask while doing this exercise. At the completion of the exercise, thoroughly massage your facial muscles to relax them, a good exercise any time. Just remember: don't force it! Take it easy!

● ● ●

So far, you have been given a series of exercises to help you prepare the external, visible parts of acting, those involving your body. Yet to come—in the next chapter—are the equally important exercises that will build your capacity to think the character thoughts which will motivate all these external actions. It is very important to continue doing the physical exercises described in this section as you go on to other tasks. You must develop the ability to relax and find certain gestures just as you would if you were learning dance steps or an athletic skill. Make these exercises a part of your daily routine and they will gradually become second nature. Build each new skill on the basis of one already mastered.

All of these skills are interdependent. While working on the body for gesture patterns, you will also be building a physical instrument to use as the basis of your vocal skills. Vocal quality, for instance, will be affected by relaxation and centering. Slowly develop the body as a relaxed vehicle, and you will also find the basis of good vocal production, which is the next area we discuss.

THE BODY AS PRODUCER OF SOUND

Once your body is relaxed and centered, good vocal production can begin. It is not within the scope of this text to discuss voice production in any but the most general way: you will be given some very basic information and exercises that will serve as a foundation for good stage voice production and speech. You will, in other words, be able to make some headway in discovering your natural voice for use in performance, but will want to invest a considerable amount of future time—both in course work and daily exercise—developing and sharpening your vocal skills.

There are major disagreements among teachers of acting, voice, and diction over how natural the actor's voice should be, particularly when acting in those plays we have labeled classics. I do not propose to try and settle these arguments. For our purposes, let's simply say that the natural voice usually has the following characteristics:

1. develops from proper breathing,
2. travels through a relaxed and unconstricted upper body and throat,
3. is placed properly for resonance and tonal variety,
4. is effectively articulated,
5. properly pronounces words, and
6. projects clearly and naturally to the audience.

You may be surprised to discover that the voice you use on a daily basis is, more than likely, not a natural voice. First of all, you have probably not been breathing naturally, and, in addition, you have likely been applying a considerable amount of muscle tension, particularly in the throat, to produce your vocal quality. You have also probably been producing resonance almost exclusively in the nasal and throat cavities, thus ignoring at least 50 percent of your body's resonance potential. We have discussed some of the aspects of the first two problems, and have talked briefly about the necessity of good natural breathing. Now let's go on to the essential foundation of good vocal production: diaphragmatic breathing. We begin with an exercise that will help you breathe naturally and correctly.

● ● ●

EXERCISE 16

BREATHING FROM THE DIAPHRAGM

Do the first relaxation exercise until your whole body is relaxed and breathing is easy and natural. You should be lying on your back on the floor in a completely relaxed posture. Place your hand on your belt buckle (if you're not wearing a belt, put your hand where the buckle would be if you had one). Under your hand is the approximate location of the diaphragm muscle, a slightly dome-shaped sheet of muscle that controls the natural breathing process. The diaphragm pushes down toward the abdominal cavity as you breathe in, and expands upward to allow air— the power source of speech—up through the esophagus, past the vocal cords, and through the mouth cavity and out. Feel the abdomen expand (your hand on your belt buckle will rise) and relax (the hand will sink) as your breathing process becomes natural and centered. In fact, as air is allowed in and stored, you will be able to feel the expansion not only of the abdomen, but of the lower back and rib cage. This stored air will eventually be allowed to escape and produce speech, but for now, just allow the breathing to become regular in a relaxed body. Continue to allow your body to loosen as you lie on the floor. Now open your eyes and watch your hand as you breathe: as you allow air in, your hand will rise as the air expands the abdomen; as you let the air out, your hand will sink as the air escapes through the windpipe. Don't try to control this process: let it happen. This is the way you breathe when you sleep and it's natural for the waking hours as well. As you continue to breathe in this manner, begin inhaling through the nose, if you can, exhaling through the mouth (in the martial arts, the purification breath). As the natural process asserts itself, begin filling the lower body with breath, holding it for a short time, then allowing it to escape completely, getting as much air as possible out of the body. Continue this exercise until this new natural diaphragmatic breathing is firmly established.

● ● ●

Now that you're able to store a good quantity of air (the power source of natural speech), let's use that power to make some simple subverbal sounds.

● ● ●

EXERCISE 17

BREATHING FROM THE DIAPHRAGM: SOUNDS

Repeat Exercise 16 several times. Gradually establishing natural breathing, you can begin to voice open vowel sounds on the exhaled breath. Start with a soft, relaxed "ah" sound, then go on to "oh," letting both these sounds seem to come from the chest or stomach. Move to "ee" and "aee" (as in "say"), sounds that seem to come from the head. Don't push these sounds or try to make them particularly loud or forceful. Just let them begin to happen. Sustain them as long as you comfortably can; then let them naturally die out. As these sounds begin to come easily from the right source, you will begin to hear more resonance and depth to the sounds. Begin to develop these various vowel sounds a little: try for a fuller, deeper sound on the "ah" and "oh" sounds, a purer, clearer sound (without screeching or nasality) on the "ee" and "aee" sounds. Again, don't force these sounds. Just listen to them and develop them from the easy, natural source of diaphragmatic breathing. Your voice courses will take you much further in the process of producing good sound.

As you learn to breathe from the diaphragm, you will not only be establishing the basis for future exercises that take voice production into more advanced and specialized areas, you will also have made a good start on relaxing your whole body. Once you are on your way to making satisfactory progress in the producing of good basic sound, the next step is to pay some attention to forming and pronouncing the sounds correctly: articulation and diction.

Articulation

Articulation is the formation of sound with the lips, tongue, lower jaw, and soft palate. If you are a beginning actor who has grown up in the United States, you will probably need to consciously overarticulate at first, since one of the less desirable characteristics of everyday American speech is articulatory sloppiness. Think back to the number of times your parents told you not to mumble, and you'll realize you have spent many years perfecting speech that sounds appropriately "laid back" or "cool" but may be largely unintelligible. In order to correct this, you must set aside a few minutes of each day to practice good articulation until this habit is as firmly established as the habit of lazy slurred speech. If you are lucky enough to speak fluent French, Spanish, or Italian, you probably have an edge on your peers, as these languages generally require more active articulation. As you begin to work on articulation, your speech will probably sound a little self-conscious at first: words may tend to be visibly overarticulated; keep it up, though—eventually your new clear, precise speech will start to sound natural and will finally be second nature.

Where to begin? Perhaps the first thing to do is to enroll in a course that most schools call "Voice and Diction." It is always best to work in the company of others who are struggling with the same problems; and, too, having a teacher present has obvious advantages as someone to evaluate your progress and set new goals for you. But I believe that an ongoing individual discipline of simple daily vocal workouts will be the most important factor in ultimately transforming your voice and speech patterns. Don't get the wrong idea. Study on your own is essential, but take the courses by all means! They are very important in providing standards and measurements of progress and in introducing you to accepted speech. Also work on your own on a daily basis. This is what accomplishes the miracle.

What to do in these daily workouts? Many of the old tongue twisters that may be familiar to you from your primary school playground are excellent examples of perfectly appropriate articulation exercises. Here are some familiar and not-so-familiar ones. Repeat them over and over again at different rates—from slow to fast—paying particular and detailed attention to each individual sound. Work on this daily.

● ● ●

EXERCISE 18

TONGUE TWISTERS

This old standby is particularly good for initial and final consonants. Pay attention to all those initial *p*'s and final *k*'s and *d*'s:

Peter Piper picked a peck of pickled peppers. If Peter Piper picked a peck of pickled peppers, where's the peck of pickled peppers Peter Piper picked?

This one is excellent for the neglected final ''s.'' Make sure not one is omitted:

He thrusts his fists against the posts and still insists he sees the ghosts.

These are good for exercising the articulatory muscles. Exaggerate the movement of the tongue, lips, and jaw as you repeat them:

Toy boat, toy boat, toy boat, toy boat . . .

Unique New York, unique New York . . .

Rubber baby buggy bumpers, rubber baby buggy bumpers, rubber baby buggy bumpers . . .

And this one is great for distinguishing between the unvoiced ''th'' sound and the ''s'' sound. Leith (pronounced as if it were spelled *Leeth*) is a town in England. Go slowly at first; it looks simple, but it's a killer:

The Leith police dismisseth us.

● ● ●

There are many more of these simple tongue twisters, and you will want to add to your collection as you move along. Just remember that in order to correct articulation problems it's taken you years to develop, you will probably have to work with these exercises (and other more advanced ones as you acquire them) for almost as long, as often and as regularly as possible. Most actors practice them or ones like them all their lives. Get used to a regimen that you'll follow for many years to come.

Diction

There are many disagreements over what is and what is not good diction in American speech. Diction is, simply, the correct (or at least the most generally accepted) pronunciation of all the individual sounds that make up the words of American speech. The British have their standard English—similar to the speech of those who read the news on the BBC—but it may be true that there is no such thing as standard American speech because the regional diversity of our speech habits have never quite combined into a common standard. But actors, no matter what regional pattern their everyday speech springs from, must find a clear, unaccented speech that they can use as a basis of their characterized stage speech.

Before we proceed, let one thing be clear: characters in plays speak with the voice their authors gave them, not in some dreary, neutralized, sterile good stage speech that the actor may have, unfortunately, learned in a class left over from the nineteenth century and often called expression, declamation, or public speaking. Certainly, the spoken word on the stage must be heard and understood clearly by the audience, but its color and shape must be the character's, complete with the character's regional, educational, and cultural background. This is true no matter whether the play was written in the fifteenth century or the latter part of the twentieth, whether in patterned language or in prose. I believe that every actor needs to develop a clear, unaccented speech over which the speech of the character can most easily be superimposed.

The best way for the beginning actor to approach this clear speech is probably by learning the International Phonetic Alphabet (IPA). The IPA is not only the most detailed and comprehensive system of pronunciation of these many sounds, but it is also, as its name suggests, truly international: words from any language may be analyzed using its symbols. So it would be well worth your time to use it for determining the most accepted pronunciation of various words. Having said that, I am aware that many of you may not have learned the IPA, so I have used a simple "rhymes with" scheme in the exercises to show correct and incorrect pronunciation.

● ● ●

EXERCISE 19

COMMON DICTION ERRORS

Here are some of the most frequent diction errors made by American acting students. Are you guilty of any of them?

Correct	Incorrect
get (rhymes with *pet*)	git
just (rhymes with *must*)	jist or jis (rhymes with *mist* or *sis*)
pen/men/send (the "e" sounds like the "e" in *bet,* not like the "i" in *tin.*)	pin/min/sind
couldn't/wouldn't/didn't	could-UHnt/would-UHnt/did-UHnt

To pronounce these words correctly, keep the tongue pressed against the roof of the mouth for the second syllable. This is one, I believe, that originated in California's "Valley Girl" speech pattern:

could you	cuh-joo
would you	wuh-joo
can't you	can-choo
won't you	won-choo
did you	di-joo
bet you	beh-choo

(Keep the final "d" or "t" sound separate from the following initial "y" sound.)

Final *g*'s are also a problem, of course. First, don't drop them: say *getting*, not *gettin*, and second, don't attach them to the following word (as in *Lon Geyeland* for *Long Island*). Sloppy speech also sometimes produces the omission of whole syllables from a sentence. Learn to listen to your own speech and the speech of others for bad diction. Only your own awareness and constant repetition will unlearn bad habits it's taken you years to acquire: don't expect to lose them overnight.

● ● ●

There are countless other examples of bad diction in American speech. The ones just listed are some of the most frequent. From your classes and from just plain listening, you must discover others you may have in your own speech. Many of these are the result of regional pronunciations (see *Lon Geyeland*) and, increasingly, cultural slang. While each person must be free to speak the way he or she wishes, the acting student must realize that speech is a tool to be kept honed and polished.

Vocal Placement

What is vocal placement? Musical instruments with strings would sound small and flat if they did not have some sort of resonator box. For example, an acoustic guitar's bulk is mostly made up of the hollow body that magnifies and resonates the sound of the plucked strings. Similarly, the human voice must be placed in the resonating chamber of the body that will produce the most effectively vibrant tone of the desired sound. The most frequently mentioned of these chambers are the chest, the throat, and the nasal and sinal chambers of the head. Some voice teachers also speak of throat and abdominal placement. Because sound is produced through relaxed breathing and the vibration of the vocal cords, practice placing the sound in these areas in order to produce specific and well-resonated tones.

The chest tone is a fuller, deeper tone that is usually—though not necessarily—of a lower pitch than the others. Some voice teachers refer to it as the abdominal tone, though this is more than likely a tone resonating in the lower chest. Visualize the chest cavity filled with dark bass sound.

The throat tone (including the mouth, the pharynx, and the larynx, and sometimes called by these names) is a medium tone of medium pitch. It resonates in the esophageal and oral cavities. Be careful that the throat does not constrict when producing this tone.

The head tone resonates in the nasal and sinal cavities. This is a high, bright tone that should sound clearly and without shrillness.

● ● ●

EXERCISE 20

PLACING THE VOICE

After finishing a stacking vertebrae and neck roll series, stand in an easy, erect posture, hands by your sides and with a medium stance. Establish good diaphragmatic breathing. As your breath rises from the release of the diaphragm, visualize sound filling the chest cavity and use an "ah" sound to produce chest resonance. On the next breath, send the breath into the esophageal cavity. Use an "eh" sound to resonate in the throat. Be careful not to let the throat constrict. Breathe again, and make an "ee" sound when practicing resonance in the head. Head tones should be high and clear but not shrill and strained. Now physicalize these tones: when producing the "ah" chest tone, gently but firmly push your hands down toward the earth, palms parallel to the ground; when producing the "eh" throat tone, push the hands, palm outward, toward the wall; when producing the "ee" head tone, point the index fingers sharply to the sky. Give these physicalizations full value and they will help you relax, isolate, and concentrate. You may wish to substitute words for the sounds. Just for fun, my students enjoy saying "I" for the head tones, "need" for the throat tones, and "help!" for the chest tones. Keep your physicalizations vigorous and experiment with alternately sharp and softer explosions of sound as you produce the words. Try this exercise facing a wall and visualize bouncing the voice off it, like a basketball bouncing off the backboard. This will help later on when you work on projection. Try going from stomach to head, too.

● ● ●

The variety of sound produced through proper vocal placement will acquaint you with one of the bases of good vocal color—the ability to infuse a word or phrase with vocal energy that is expressive of the meaning of the word—or variety.

Projection

Once the sound is produced, articulated, and correctly pronounced, it must, if spoken on the stage, be projected to the audience in the theater. Projection is perhaps the least understood of the vocal skills of the student actor, and projection problems among the most pervasive.

Projection is the ability to speak at what appears to be a conversational—or even whispered—level and still be heard by the audience member sitting furthest from the stage. Projection is accomplished by combining several techniques:

1. proper breathing, storing the breath and releasing it steadily enough to produce a strong, consistent tone;
2. strong and precise articulation;
3. psychologically focusing speech, which entails maintaining a clear mental image of the words and visualizing directing them to the audience.

The first two of these can, as we have seen, be technically learned and practiced. The third technique involves both imagination and experience. There is nothing of the psychic in this ability of mentally directing speech to the audience; it is simply a matter of firmly visualizing the intellectual and emotional meaning of the words and building the *need* to communicate the means to the people listening. Projection is related to volume or loudness, of course, but only peripherally. Shouting is not projection, but will produce the undesired effect of alienating the audience and deadening their listening capacity.

● ● ●

EXERCISE 21

PROJECTING THE VOICE

You will need a partner for this exercise. Stand at either end of a large room and each of you alternate speaking a short phrase to the other (the tongue twisters used in the articulation section would help you work on two problems at once!). Start the exercise at the level of an unvoiced (not using the vocal cords) whisper, then progressing to a voiced (using the vocal cords) whisper, then to quiet, intimate speech, then to normal speech, then to magnified (louder than normal) speech. Be sure you don't wind up shouting at each other. If you feel any scratchiness in your throat, then you are merely shouting through throat muscle tension—not projecting. The first thing to remember is that the breathing must be regulated, strong, and consistent, utilizing breathing exercises you have already learned. Second, you must correctly and clearly articulate your words. Third, you must feel the need (particularly on the whispered phrases) to communicate with your partner. You must direct your words to your partner. After you have worked this exercise face to face, turn your backs to each other and try it that way. Increase the distance between the two of you as the exercise goes on. Don't try for impossible distances (about thirty or forty feet should be your maximum at first).

● ● ●

This chapter has introduced you to the fundamentals of relaxation, centering, and the application of the physical externals. You must continue to work on these techniques for as long as you are an actor, and you must exercise them on a daily basis, doing some form of them before every rehearsal.

Physical warm-ups, as we will discover later, are an indispensable part of the rehearsal and performance environment and will provide you with a way in which to prepare the body for both. But you must go beyond that if you want your body to be completely ready for the jobs it must do. Your own physical regimen will vary in length and intensity depending on what problems you are dealing with and on what level, but it is extremely important that one be established and practiced daily. If you want to start developing an individual warm-up routine now, then you might want to look ahead at Exercise 34, which describes a typical group of exercises I suggest young actors do at the beginning of any rehearsal.

You must not think, when you have read and worked on the exercises in this chapter, that you have accomplished what you need to in terms of voice and movement. Far from it! You must now go on to new courses in these areas, and, as noted before, to develop these skills by dealing with them daily. This is just the very beginning! Other, more advanced, learning situations will broaden the scope of your vocal and physical work and take you into areas not even discussed in this book. Further development and advancement beyond these first basic principles is up to you.

At this point, however, you are ready to go on to work that deals with the internals: intellectual and emotional understanding—the essential thought process that provides the foundation for and must always motivate the external manifestations we've been discussing.

CHAPTER 3

• • • •

DEALING WITH INTERNALS

In the preceding chapter, we had to learn how to relax the body before the physical disciplines of voice and movement could be exercised. So, too, there is a skill that must be developed before we can work on the internal process. That skill is concentration.

CONCENTRATION

The first thing to understand about concentration is that it must be invoked by positive, not negative, energy. If you try to relax a muscle by forcefully commanding it to do so it will tense; if you order your mind to concentrate on some task it will immediately wander to a thousand distractions. You have probably all had the experience of sitting in the library trying to study for a final exam for a subject in which you are not really interested. Every noise, every passerby, every stray thought all demand more attention than the book in front of your eyes; even a slight flaw in the table where you are sitting will force you to gaze at it with rapt intensity instead of assimilating what you're reading. Did it just happen to you? Do you need to reread the preceding sentences? Perhaps, fi-

Figure 3.1 Most students understand how difficult concentration is to maintain at times; yet it is one of the actor's most important tools.

nally, a jingle from a television commercial will come into your head uninvited . . . and stick. There the senseless tune will stay, circling endlessly from beginning to end and back again, dominating your mind and forcing out all other thought (see Fig. 3.1). No matter how many times you tell yourself to concentrate on the textbook in front of you, your brain refuses to cooperate: the commercial jingle wins. Why?

You can learn two things from this example: first, it helps to be truly interested and involved in the subject matter on which you are focusing, and second, you must find a positive and easily visualized aspect of the material on which to direct your attention. In this case, the course for which you are studying is obviously not one that commands your interest, and the jingle is cleverly designed by the advertising agency which produced it to be easily recognized and absorbed. It is a positive, if unworthy, focus of concentration.

So the first thing you need to know about actor concentration is this: you must invest everything your character says and does with the same interest and importance that you do with the events of your real life. Since theater is based on conflict, most scenes and plays you will work with find the characters in them at some critical point in their lives; they are, for the most part, dealing with matters that are very important to them. You, the actor, must feel the same way about these issues: you must focus on the events of the play as if they were happening to you in reality. Right from the beginning, think of acting as involving yourself in actual events, not as a game you are playing. Remember, if you go on to become a working actor, rehearsing and performing a play will become the way in which you earn your living: serious business. Start by thinking of it that way now. This simple leap of the imagination is the first essential step in concentration: when you are in character, be as seriously interested in the life of your character as you are in your own!

Second, focus your mental energies in a positive way: don't try to clear your mind of distractions—that effort will become a distraction in its own right. Instead, focus directly and actively on the immediate elements of your scene: the text, your partner, and the physical environment of the play. We discuss and work on each of these in more detail later, but for now let's associate them with three ways of thinking about concentration that I call the three circles of concentration. Use these circles as positive concentration aids (see Fig. 3.2).

The first circle of concentration involves the private thought process that the text of your scene indicates your character is thinking and which is motivating the character's speech and actions. When we discuss intellectual and emotional understanding of the text we will find out how to discover and analyze these very thoughts, give them labels and identity, and find out more thoroughly how they produce words and movements. For now, let's begin by seeing if you can become accustomed to thinking somebody else's (your character's) thoughts in an uncomplicated, direct, private way. In a way, this is the core of all acting: the invasion and assimilation of another personality. First we discover that the thinking is private, yes, but this intensely private act will be accomplished in front of others: an audience! So here is our first lesson in that basic activity mentioned at the beginning of this book: isolation in public.

● ● ●

EXERCISE 22

CONCENTRATION: THE FIRST CIRCLE

Sit in a chair in the middle of the room. Take a book and put it down on a table by you. If you are in class, the other members of the class will be sitting around you. If you are working on this exercise outside of class, do it with a partner so there will be at least one person observing you. Now just sit: do absolutely nothing. This may seem easy in the beginning, but as time goes on, you will find it can become very difficult indeed. After a few moments, you will find your thoughts straying to many other things: above all, the fact you are being observed will probably be a constant source of distraction. The point of this exercise, however, is to focus your mental energy on positive, not negative, points, in this case private thoughts in public. But there are all those distracting, intrusive public thoughts! How do we get rid of them? Begin by thinking of yourself as surrounded by a cone of light as if projected from a lamp above your head. The cone of light forms a circle on the floor which is, say, six feet in diameter, disappearing to a point in the air above your head. Like all psychological visualizations in this book, take some time to invest this one with as much reality as you can: think of yourself as isolated and protected within this cone of warm surrounding light. Once you have succeeded in creating this cone of light and isolating yourself in it, forget about it—let it stand on its own, enclosing you, but don't consciously think about it. Instead, raise your hand in front of your face and look at it. Don't think about looking at it! Really look at it. Examine its color and shape; flex it, move the fingers, observe how the muscles

Figure 3.2 In ordinary life we all go from isolation to shared experiences to memory without conscious thought. The acting student must learn to enter these circles of concentration at will.

work to make different configurations: a fist, an open-palmed stretch, a cupped receptacle. Concentrate positively on your hand (always within your protective cone of light) until you are effectively alone within this public situation. For a moment become aware of those observing you; then go back to concentrating on your hand. The paradox of this exercise is that you must break the circle of concentration in order to become aware of your public position, but you should be able to go back to your positive activity more and more efficiently the more often you do it. This ability to jump back and forth quickly and easily from isolation to awareness of observation while doing as little damage as possible (none, ideally) to the level of concentration is one of the basic skills an actor must learn. Complete this exercise by picking up the book you brought with you, opening it, and reading from it. Read silently at first—but *really read!* Don't pretend to read; don't just look at the pages and move your eyes! *Really read the words on the page:* comprehend them, become actively interested in what they have to say. Now read the words aloud, as you might, perhaps, if you were alone and wanted to emphasize what you are reading. This is all done *not to demonstrate to the observers that you are reading; it is done because the character is really interested in the contents of the book.* Work on this exercise until you read aloud from the book with no awareness of the audience, or as little as you can manage. Keep the cone of light on some unconscious level as a shield.

● ● ●

Once you are more relaxed with your ability to become isolated in public, you are ready to go on to the second circle of concentration: involving the other people of the play and its physical environment in your circle of concentration.

I believe that the other person in your scene is your most valuable and important focus of positive concentration. First of all, in addition to being the most immediate object on which to direct your thoughts, your partner is (or should be) actively seeking your focus. She is concentrating on you just as much as you are on her. Second, she is returning energy to you. In the previous exercise the book was the motivating thought, but it did not change as a result of the energy you gave it—your partner's ever-changing attitudes toward you are a direct result of your input and will motivate you to change in turn. Make direct contact with your partner: such contact is an invaluable tool for concentration and a constant source of motivating energy.

We are often unwilling to look other people in the eye and sometimes very unwilling to touch others. In this exercise you should concentrate on your partner the same energies you invested in your hand and in the book in the previous one: *really look at them—right in the eyes!* Give them energy! Dare to touch them!

● ● ●

EXERCISE 23

CONCENTRATION: THE SECOND CIRCLE—PARTNERS

Repeat the previous exercise. When you have gotten to the point where you are holding the book and reading from it silently, your partner should enter the scene.

You should not be aware of her entrance until she breaks the plane of the cone of light that you have created as the environment of the scene. As soon as she does break that plane, though, you must concentrate on her with all the positive energy you invested earlier in your own hand or in reading the book. When you find yourself sharing the circle of concentration with another person, the circle itself expands. It was a circle of light about six feet in diameter and now it will expand to include the environment you and your partner share, and you must enlarge your area of concentration as the circle expands. In a play, this larger circle would be the stage set, the entire environment of the play. As your concentration grows and you are actively focusing on your partner, look at her with the same interest and care that you looked at your hand or read your book: observe everything about her, starting with the face, then including the entire body. Get used to really looking at someone. Remember, of course, she will be doing the same to you: returning energy! After the two of you have come to the point where you are totally at ease with observing each other and are concentrating on each other well, extend the exercise by reaching out and touching hands. Get to know your partner's hand as well as you got to know your own earlier. This exercise can then go on to include further physical and vocal involvement if you wish. Maybe review a doppelgänger exercise focusing on concentration. Keep your concentration within the cone of light that illuminates your physical environment.

● ● ●

The second circle also involves the environment as a positive focus on concentration. In its way, the set and the objects in it can be almost as valuable to an actor as the other characters in the scene. Often they can provide very positive activities on which you can concentrate. The great Russian director/teacher of the last century, Constantin Stanislavski, talks of giving his students an exercise in the reality of concentration by hiding a piece of costume jewelry in the room in which they are working. Told to find it, at first the students pretend to search, turning the exercise into a game. Stanislavski invests the exercise with serious intent, however, by telling the students that if they do not find the brooch they will be forced to drop the class. Instantly, the search becomes real: concentration becomes immediate and intense because all the students want, above all, to stay in the class and learn. When the pin is found, Stanislavski explains that the difference between the two searches is the difference between good and bad acting: good acting is as urgent and important as a real-life situation. Sometimes focusing on an object in the stage set, the physical environment, can help make your concentration positive, the performance itself real, for the actor and therefore for the audience. Let's try working this idea out in an exercise.

● ● ●

EXERCISE 24

CONCENTRATION: THE SECOND
CIRCLE—ENVIRONMENT

Repeat the first circle concentration exercise until you are reading your book. Let the thought cross your mind that the subject matter of the book is of no interest to you. Let the book drop, and, still seated, allow your eyes to wander around the room, looking for something new to occupy your attention, allowing the first circle cone of light/concentration to expand as you do this. The search itself is a positive concentration device. Don't skimp on it: really look for something to do! Finally, you see several objects on the table where you found your book. The book was a real prop, but these are imaginary. Pick each of them up and examine each carefully. Try communicating the identity of the objects to your audience by the way you handle each one. Don't think of the audience while you do this, though: think of the object. This involves something called *sense memory.* We discuss this skill later, but for now see how effectively you can create each of these objects when the object isn't actively there. Don't show off! You are not a street mime, demonstrating a wall or the wind to your audience. All you are doing is handling an imaginary object with such concentration that it becomes real to you and there- fore to your audience. Always remember you are in the first, or private circle of concentration. Cultivate your public solitude. Now, *keeping this expanded first cir- cle, which has now become the second circle,* stand up and allow the cone of light to expand to include the entire set. You are still alone; your isolation is still complete. The only difference is that the circle is larger. Walk around the physical environment: sit in chairs, handle objects, turn on a television set, wash dishes, do any activity you wish. The important thing is to keep your concentration focused— just as when you are alone in your own room or apartment—on the activities you are involved in. Use the objects you handle as the positive focus of your concen- tration. You can change this exercise into a slightly different kind of second circle exercise by having a partner enter the set. Now you are in the shared second circle of concentration, but both of you can use objects as a positive concentration exer- cise: have a pillow fight, play a game of cards, wash the dishes together. Or just talk, using your partner as she moves about the room as an object of positive focus. The circles of concentration are a device to aid concentration. In a real scene or play, they will mix and blend just as they do in real life.

●   ●   ●

The third circle of concentration that we explore is one we call the *infinite* circle. It is invoked when your point of concentration needs to go beyond the environment of the set, either in time or in space. For instance, your character may be remembering something that happened in the past, daydreaming about something that will happen in the future, visualizing an object or a place that exists in a geographically remote place (across the street or across the ocean), or the character may simply be allowing thoughts to wander for any of a variety of reasons. At any rate, in all these cases the character's eyes are focused on a point beyond the walls of the set and the concentration is directed to that focal point. We call this focus the third circle of concentra- tion. A change to the third circle can happen while you are already in the first or second circle of concentration, slowly and gradually or quickly and abruptly. You must become adept at switching from circle to circle, from focal point to focal point. The trick is to make each point of concentration as real as you can.

● ● ●

EXERCISE 25

CONCENTRATION: THE THIRD CIRCLE

Repeat the first circle exercise to the point where you are reading in your book. At a certain point in your reading, allowing something in the words to trigger a real memory of your own in your mind. Raise your attention from the book and focus straight ahead and visualize the environment of your memory. Build up a detailed picture of where you were when this event took place: shape each blade of grass, or texture of the rug, or switch on the car dashboard. Wherever you were, recreate it in detail! As you are remembering an event outside the confines of the room you are sitting in—either in time or space or both—your point of focus will extend beyond the room to an infinite point. (Your eyes will actually move when this is successfully done, spreading slightly farther apart. Check it in a mirror.) Focusing on this past and/or remote event is putting your concentration in the third, or infinite circle. Like all the circles, this one will combine with others in the scene. Try going from second circle involvement with a partner and objects—playing a card game, perhaps—to third circle. In the middle of the game something triggers a mutual memory and both of you focus on that past and/or distant event. See what happens to the activity in the second circle. Does it slow down? Stop? Continue in a different way? Let memories and other third circle thoughts alternate with the second circle activity. Take turns with your partner leaving the set and going back to first circle: reading or finally just sitting and thinking.

● ● ●

These visualized circles are simply convenient focal points that you can use as aids in developing the skill of effective concentration. After a while, if you work on them enough, they will become automatic, and you will be able to go from one to another smoothly and easily. You will need to be able to do so, because in the scene or in a real performance of a real play, you will have to switch back and forth among these three circles very quickly and very often.

Concentration is needed to meld an entire cast of a play together in a closely functioning unit. We may speak of the ensemble acting of a particular cast in a particular play. What this means is that everyone in that cast is concentrating, at various times in all three circles, on the thoughts of their characters and the other characters around them: listening and interacting as if the thoughts, words, objects, and people of the play were happening on an actual level in real time. Real listening and seeing produce real concentration, which produces real energy. The audience, then, feels as if it were witnessing an actual event and is more successfully drawn into and—in some way—included in the circles of concentration of the cast on the stage. Ensemble acting is a great pleasure, as any actor who has been fortunate enough to participate in a production in which that level of concentration and energy sharing was present will testify. It's the closest thing to reading minds that most of us are likely to experience.

Concentration, then, is the basis and starting point of all the activity that we have labeled as internal. Continue to work on these exercises in concentration on a daily basis so you can build up the mental muscles that are so necessary if you are effectively to explore and understand the play and your part in it.

Understanding the play is a process that happens on many levels. To begin, let's start with the simplest, most obvious level: understanding the words, actions, and ideas of the play intellectually.

UNDERSTANDING THE TEXT

In a play there are three primary sources of factual information: the words the characters say, the parenthetical directions the playwright has seen fit to include, and comments added by possible editors in introductions, footnotes, and the like.

Getting facts from the dialogue itself can be tricky because, just as in real life, characters can exaggerate or even lie, so, somewhere along the line, you'll need to decide whether or not the character is telling the truth as you go through the play. You'll also want to compare what the character you're playing says about himself with what the other character or characters say about him, both in his presence and when he's offstage.

Parenthetical stage directions in an original script are always written by the playwright, but if you are working from an "acting edition" issued by one of the large publishing houses, some of the stage directions may be the blocking and other notes from a previous production (usually the first Broadway or important commercial production) of the play. All stage directions are useful in establishing factual material, and you should understand them thoroughly and give them serious consideration as you build your character. There may be times, however, when these stage directions don't fit: when you're working with a director who has a very specific concept, for instance, which is different from the one your acting edition is based on, or when the physical **stage environment**—the set—is very different. In those cases stage directions may certainly be changed or even ignored after careful and judicious consideration. For now, though, since you're working on your own without a director, just accept the stage directions pretty much at face value.

Later on, when you're working on a classic, or a more modern play published in an anthology, you will find information in various sources outside of the text of the play. An editor's introduction, footnotes, and other explanatory material can be very useful, sometimes essential. You won't get these in the exercise scene, of course, or in many contemporary plays. When you do run into them, utilize them but don't feel bound by them, particularly when you're working with a director. There are also sources of information outside the play that you will want to consult in understanding your character. We discuss these in the chapter on the readthrough.

Now let's look at a specific example of text and see what information we can find. The following scene was written especially to give you practice in understanding a text intellectually and contains specific problems in that regard. The scene can readily be worked on by men or women: there are no gender pronouns and the names are not gender specific. (See Fig. 3.3.)

Exercise Scene for Understanding the Text and Subtext

A Mountain Holiday

(*The kitchen of a small mountain cabin in the Cascades. The furnishings are very simple: a table, two chairs, a wood stove, some cabinets, two beds. TERRY stands in front of the sink twisting a faucet back and forth. JAMIE sits at the table reading a newspaper with intense concentration and a sense of urgency.*)

TERRY: (*Suddenly slamming a hand down on the top of the faucet.*) Something's wrong with the water.

JAMIE: What?

TERRY: I said something's wrong with the . . .

JAMIE: Look at this.

TERRY: No! (*Twists harder at the tap.*) I can't get this . . . ow! (*The faucet breaks off in TERRY's hand.*)

JAMIE: (*Looking up, taking spectacles off.*) What did you do that for?

TERRY: I didn't do it on purpose.

JAMIE: So what's wrong?

TERRY: There's no water.

JAMIE: Of course there's no water, you just broke off the faucet!

TERRY: No, there was no water before the faucet broke!

JAMIE: Well, what'll we do?

TERRY: Fix it, I guess.

JAMIE: How? We can't!

TERRY: There's nobody else to do it.

JAMIE: (*Wailing.*) But we don't know anything about plumbing!

Figure 3.3   Even the simplest tasks in a scene must be prepared for and thought about.

TERRY: We'll have to learn, won't we?

JAMIE: How?

TERRY: Is the modem hooked up?

JAMIE: How can it be? There's no electricity.

TERRY: Doesn't matter. The computer runs on a battery.

JAMIE: It does?

TERRY: Yeah. Go try it.

JAMIE: Where is it?

TERRY: I don't know! Try that cabinet.

JAMIE: Okay . . . where are my glasses? Oh, here . . . (*Picks them up but does not put them on, opens a wooden cabinet.*) Yeah. Here it is.

TERRY: Turn it on.

JAMIE: Where's the . . .

TERRY: Look for it!

JAMIE: Okay, okay! Don't be so . . .

TERRY: And hurry up!

JAMIE: It's on! Stop yelling at me!

TERRY: See if you can get a directory.

JAMIE: Okay . . . (*Sits down, puts the glasses on, and types on the keyboard.*) There's just this list of names and . . .

TERRY: Stupid idiot! You've got directory assistance. We don't need that, we need . . .

JAMIE: Well, we could call somebody for help and . . .

TERRY: There's nobody to call! We're *it*! We're all that's left!

JAMIE: How do you know? There could be somebody in . . .

TERRY: Shut up! We need water! Get the emergency repair directory on the screen! Now!

JAMIE: Okay, okay . . . (*Types again.*) There it is.

TERRY: Find plumbing.

JAMIE: (*Types.*) All right, I've got it.

TERRY: Check the water supply index.

JAMIE: Okay . . .

TERRY: Hurry!

JAMIE: Okay! (*Types, squints at the screen.*) It says it wants our zone code.

TERRY: So, type it in.

JAMIE: What is it?

TERRY: Don't you know anything? It's 6754329.

JAMIE: (*Typing.*) 6 . . . 7 . . . 5 . . .

TERRY: (*Impatiently.*) 4329!

JAMIE: (*Typing.*) 4 . . . 3 . . . 2 . . . 9 . . . (*There is a pause. JAMIE gazes blankly at the screen.*)

TERRY: Well? What does it say?

JAMIE: It says . . . it says there isn't any.

TERRY: What?

JAMIE: It says there isn't any water. It says the reservoir for this area is empty. It says . . .

TERRY: (*Slumping into a chair.*) All right, all right, I heard you. (*Pause.*)

JAMIE: What will we do?

TERRY: We'll sit here.

JAMIE: How long?

TERRY: Until we die.

JAMIE: No!

TERRY: Yes! Like everybody else!

JAMIE: No!

TERRY: Yes! Now shut up! (*Pause.*)

JAMIE: You going to wear that hat until you die?

TERRY: Shut up!

JAMIE: Stop telling me to shut up!

TERRY: I'll keep telling you to shut up as long as you keep whining!

JAMIE: I don't whine! Stop telling me what to . . . (*JAMIE is cut off as TERRY rises and slaps JAMIE hard on the face.*) Oh! (*JAMIE collapses, sobbing. There is a long pause.*)

TERRY: Everything's going to be all right. We just have to keep calm . . . keep . . . we just have to keep . . . a tight hold on . . . ourselves . . . we just have to keep . . . we just have to . . . (*TERRY stops talking, sits looking down, twisting a ring on one finger. JAMIE'S sobs gradually diminish and there is silence. At last JAMIE looks up at TERRY, who does not meet this gaze. JAMIE wipes tears away with the back of a hand.*)

JAMIE: Terry . . . (*Voice still choked with tears.*)

TERRY: . . . what?

JAMIE: I'm . . . thirsty.

TERRY: That's what they all said, Jamie. That's what they all said . . .

JAMIE: And now they're all . . .

TERRY: Gone, Jamie. They're all . . . gone.

JAMIE: It's just . . . us?

TERRY: Yes. (*Takes off hat and throws it on the floor.*) Just us.

JAMIE: Oh . . . (*Silence. They both sit with bowed heads. Jamie begins to cry again. There is a knock at the door. They look at the door, then at each other. The lights fade to black.*)

THE END

● ● ●

EXERCISE 26

UNDERSTANDING THE TEXT

Now answer the following questions about this mini-play, the answers to which will begin to form the basis for understanding it:

1. Who am I?
2. Where am I?
3. What am I doing?

These questions are, of course, much more complicated than they seem. There will be some information in the script that is definite, specific, and easily recognized. Other things may be harder to spot, or may be missing entirely, in which case you'll have to create facts out of whatever information you're given. Let's look at these three questions more closely and construct some possible answers:

1. Who am I? Your name is either Terry or Jamie, but the text gives no further personal information, so you'll have to provide it yourself. Start with the most obvious: gender. Let's make it easy. If you're female, so is the character; if you're male, so is the character. How old is your character? Does the dialogue give any hints? Apparently not. Very well, since age does not seem to be a pivotal issue, again let's make it easy: make the character your own age or close to it. Nationality or ethnicity is not stated in the stage directions or indicated in the dialogue and is not an issue in the scene, so let's not worry about that at all. What clothes is your character wearing? Look at the dialogue again and you will discover that Jamie wears glasses and Terry has a hat on. Begin to decide what effect these have on characterization. In the stage directions you will discover that Terry also has a ring on one finger which she or he twists. Why do you suppose she or he does this? The playwright obviously found it important enough to mention, so take it into consideration as you develop your character.

2. Where am I? The stage directions say you're in the kitchen of a small mountain cabin in the Cascades. The Cascades are a mountain range in the Pacific Northwest. Does this bit of geographical information make any difference to the actor? What sort of climate might this location dictate? Since there are apparently power disruptions in the area, does that mean the characters might be cold? Understanding such things are important, as you will want to create the environment in which your characters exist, including weather, temperature, and so on. The description of the set indicates the presence of a wood stove. Does it have a fire inside it? Is the air thinner than usual because you're on a mountain? Does that mean the characters might have some trouble breathing? Does this affect their mood? See if you can find other geographical factors that might affect the performance. For instance, there appear to be no near neighbors. What effect might that have?

3. What am I doing? This is a very large complicated area that must be examined in great detail. You must be sure you understand what the basic problem is from scene to scene and for the whole play. Later on we explore underlying meaning or philosophy of the scene. For now we're just trying to determine the more obvious problems that need solving. Among the tasks or actions we find in this scene are dealing with the faucet at the sink and working a computer/telephone of some kind. Most people can figure out the physical actions involved in dealing with a kitchen tap (one thing to decide, though, is whether a tap and a faucet are exactly the same thing: both terms are used, and you should never take anything for granted) but the computer/telephone is another matter. What exactly is this instrument? Is it the same as a modern telephone except with a computer attached? What is a modem? Where do you go to find out? Can you, the actor, type well enough to *seem* to perform the action as if you are accustomed to it? What sort of situation have these two characters become involved in? Why is the water turned off? Has there been a natural disaster of some kind? A war? Is this an end-of-the-world situation? If so, who is knocking at the door at the end? Should the characters be relieved or afraid when they hear the knocking? You must know the answers to these questions! See what other actions and problems you can find in the text. You and your fellow actor (and, in later plays, your director) must come to some clear understanding of all these problems before you can tackle the underlying meaning of the play. There are no editor's introductions or footnotes here, so you don't have to worry about these things. You might, however, give some consideration to the title. What does it mean? Does it indicate that the two characters originally set out on a holiday and met trouble? Is it irony? Make a decision on this that fits your concept.

● ● ●

The questions in this exercise are just some of the ones to ask when you are trying to understand a text. There are other questions posed by other texts, and other ways of answering them, other approaches. Answering these basic questions is a way to begin.

Once the text is understood, and all questions relating to who you are, where you are, and what you're doing are answered, the next step is to understand and assimilate the underlying thoughts that produce the character's speech and action. Now we must determine what all these factual matters add up to in terms of characterization: what emotions are motivating the characters and what does this play mean?

UNDERSTANDING THE SUBTEXT

Over the last hundred years, much has been written about the internal life of a character, most notably, perhaps, the schools of thought that developed out of the work of Constantin Stanislavski at the Moscow Art Theatre. Stanislavski did a great deal of work with plays—particularly those of Anton Chekhov—which came very close to paralleling the uneventfulness of daily life, so he developed detailed and specific ways of expressing this reality. Stanislavski wanted his actors to explore the creation of characterization in exactly the same way that the actor's own mental life was created: by connecting a series of spontaneously occurring thoughts. The actor's process, of course, is much more accelerated: whereas it has taken the actor the sum total of his or her years to develop a personality, the character must be developed within the limited time (usually weeks or months) of a rehearsal period. In order to do this properly, the actor must build the character—in a careful but somewhat compressed and accelerated way—from the words and actions the playwright has written and the underlying thoughts that connect and motivate these words and actions.

Every time these thoughts change, adherents of the Stanislavski school say that a new motivational unit is created. These motivational units, connected by the transitional thoughts which take us from one thought to another, are what the Stanislavski school calls the subtext. Stanislavski compares this process to that of eating a turkey in very small bites as opposed to attempting to eat the entire bird in one gigantic mouthful. A motivational unit perhaps most commonly occurs with each line of dialogue, but it is very important to remember that this is not always the case. A line of dialogue may contain multiple motivational units, particularly if the line is a long speech. Several lines of dialogue—interrupted by other characters' speech or actions—may be motivated by the same unit of thought. Just remember: there is a new motivational unit every time the reason for speech or action changes.

Once these motivational units are determined, they are put together by the actor into the spine. The **spine** is the direct through-line of the character's life as it contributes to the overall meaning of the play. The spine helps the actor visualize the progress of the role from beginning to end. Some actors like to chart the progress of the character's spine graphically in the margin of the text. We talk more about that later when we discuss the scoring of a script. Discovering the spine takes you a step forward in actualizing the subtext, making the emotional understanding practical. It also leads you toward comprehending the overall meaning of the play, what Stanislavski calls the superobjective.

The **superobjective** is, simply, a concise statement of meaning that expresses what the director and her actors believe the playwright intended for the play to express. It is absolutely necessary that the director and the actors have a thorough and complete understanding of the subtext—motivational units, spine, superobjective—before going on to the next step. This understanding is the first step toward good characterization.

Motivational Units

Let's go back and look at our exercise scene again and determine the motivational units, the spines for each of the characters, and the superobjective of the play. All of these things, taken together, make up the subtext. Let's begin our work on subtext by talking about motivational units.

● ● ●

EXERCISE 27

SUBTEXT: MOTIVATIONAL UNITS

To begin this exercise, I go through the first page of the exercise scene, giving you some suggested motivational units for both characters on the first page. After that, you go through the rest of the dialogue and make similar decisions for the rest of the motivational units. Remember that a motivational unit is the reason for the speech or action, not merely a paraphrasing of the line which it motivates, and that it may change within a line or not change for several lines of dialogue.

Motivational Units for Terry

Line: ''Something's wrong with the water.''
Unit 1: This first one is fairly straightforward: Terry has been twisting a faucet and no water is coming out, so the line is spoken to inform Jamie of this and to express how Terry feels about the lack of water. Since the line is accompanied by a stage direction indicating that Terry slams a hand down on the faucet, we must presume that Terry's very frustrated, perhaps very angry about this failure of the water system. You should always feel free—within reason—to interpret the line as you see it. Few lines will be so specific (either within themselves or in accompanying stage directions) that they can only be interpreted in one way or to one degree of emotion.
Line: ''I said something's wrong with the . . .''
Unit 2: This is fairly obvious, too. Terry is repeating the first line because Jamie has not heard it. This repetition, however, would probably include an increase in anger or frustration, so it's a separate motivational unit.
Line: ''No!''
Unit 3: Here we have a change within the line. The first word, *no,* comes from a preoccupation with the water problem and increasing anger and contempt at Jamie's unawareness of the problem and wanting to change the subject. Terry's probably also angry that Jamie has interrupted the repetition of the problem. It's quite a strong emotion by now, so it produces a pretty strong negative response to Jamie's interruption.
Stage direction: ''Twists harder at the tap.''
Unit 4: The stage direction is motivated by increasing frustration and a desperation to get the water on.
Line: ''I can't get this . . .''
Unit 5: Here the motivation is a return to trying to explain the problem to Jamie. It's probably accompanied by another increase in anger.
Line: ''. . . ow!''
Stage direction: ''The faucet breaks off in Terry's hand.''
Unit 6: Both the exclamation and the stage direction are motivated by the faucet's breaking off. Remember that Terry's anger has been steadily increasing, so the faucet's breaking will indicate quite a strong verbal reaction. Note that there were four separate motivational units in one of Terry's lines of dialogue.
Line: ''I didn't do it on purpose.''
Unit 7: This is almost certainly sarcasm. Because Jamie has been so unwilling to listen to Terry, and since Terry is so preoccupied with what is considered a very important problem, Jamie's statement of the obvious would no doubt produce a very strong cynicism. Note that interpreting the motivational unit in this way allows for a change in Terry's building emotions. Going stronger and stronger on the same emotional level has definite limitations, and a change of tactics must soon be indicated.

Motivational Units for Jamie

Line: ''What?''
Unit 1: Jamie has not heard what Terry has said. Jamie is totally involved in the newspaper, which the set description stage direction indicates is being read with ''intense concentration and a sense of urgency.''
Line: ''Look at this.''

Unit 2: There is apparently something in the newspaper that Jamie thinks is as important a problem as Terry's preoccupation with the sink. As you read the rest of this exercise play, you will note that we never learn what it is in the newspaper which is so urgent to Jamie. You have to create something, then. It should relate to your defining of the overall problem of the play.

Stage direction: "Looking up, taking spectacles off."

Line: "What did you do that for?" Both the line and the stage direction indicate that Jamie's attention is now focused on Terry. The fact that Jamie apparently thinks Terry has broken the faucet on purpose might indicate to you that Jamie is either very unobservant, not very bright, or not thinking very clearly.

Line: "So what's wrong?"

Unit 3: This indicates that Jamie's emotions, like Terry's, are now becoming stronger. Perhaps Jamie is a little angered at Terry's cynical response.

Now go on with the rest of the scene and find motivational units for all of your lines. Try to find out as much as you can about your character as you do so. Just remember that the purpose of determining the subtextual motivations is to discover exactly what the character is thinking and how these thoughts produce speech and action.

● ● ●

Remember that motivational units do not occur with the same regularity as the line: there may be more than one in a line or several lines may be motivated by the same thought. Defining a motivational unit is not the same as paraphrasing the line of dialogue. Find the underlying reason for the line: why does the character say those particular words or do those particular things? Be specific and as detailed as you need to be. Don't write a book, though: a motivational unit needs to be succinct enough to be easily remembered and charted.

Spine

Let's go back to the beginning and find out how all these motivational units hang together to form the character's spine.

● ● ●

EXERCISE 28

FINDING THE SPINE

Using the exercise scene, put the motivational units you found for your character together into a direct through-line of action. What is the motivational path your character follows from the beginning to the end of the scene? Let's look at the motivational units you were given for the two characters at the beginning of the scene and plot the beginning of the spine for Terry.

Charting the Spine for Terry

Right from the beginning Terry is involved in the solving of a problem and is frustrated and irritated. Jamie's apparent indifference to the problem of the faucet merely increases Terry's anger, to the point where Terry hurts a hand and yells at Jamie. Almost immediately, however, Terry seems to subside into a quieter acceptance of the situation. In fact, with a slight adjustment to unit 6 for Terry—a little less sarcastic, a little more deflated—and we would find Terry beginning a new cycle that makes the character seem rather overwhelmed by the situation. You probably noticed a new wave of practicality in Terry when, in the middle of the second page, Terry asks the question, "Is the modem hooked up?" Certainly you spotted this as a brand-new motivational unit, and I'm sure you did your research and found out what a modem is. For the next few units, Terry seems to be reenergized, and, although still impatient with Jamie, is deeply involved in trying to solve their problem. When there is no answer to their call, Terry is plunged into something like despair again. When Jamie breaks down there is a return to a kind of energy in comforting Jamie. At the end Terry seems lost and overwhelmed. Go over your own list of motivational units for Terry and—if they indicate something different—plot your version of Terry's spine. Do the same thing for Jamie.

● ● ●

The spine for your character gives you a direction in which the emotional values of your character proceed. When you're doing a longer scene—and especially when you do a full play—the spine is very useful in giving you a sense of direction. It is always a good idea to visualize in some way the progress of the spine. Later on when we learn about preparing the script, you'll want to develop your own system of visual shorthand to chart the direction of your character's spine from page to page.

Superobjective

Thus the motivational units are the smallest unit of subtext and, when put together, form the spine. In their turn, when the spines of all the various characters are understood and charted, they can be put together to lead us to the play's superobjective. Please understand that when you are working on a full play the director will be very much a part of determining and understanding the subtext. Usually actors decide on motivational units by themselves and see if they meet the director's approval when tried out in rehearsal. Actors also chart the spine for their characters by themselves, adjusting them as they meet with those of other characters and with the changes that will inevitably come as the director guides the cast through the early rehearsals. In most cases, the director will decide the superobjective and work with the cast to understand it and fit their characters into it. You need to be able to understand what a superobjective is, though, and be able to determine one because it is part of the process of reading and understanding a play. Also, of course, you will not—at first, certainly—be working with a director. So let's see what we can discover about the superobjective of our exercise scene.

● ● ●

EXERCISE 29

FINDING THE SUPEROBJECTIVE

Let's restate the definition of superobjective that was given earlier: a concise statement of meaning that the director and her actors believe the playwright intended for the play to express. Here are some questions you might ask yourself as you try to determine the superobjective of the exercise scene:

1. Why are Terry and Jamie in a remote mountain cabin? Have they come there to get away from some kind of global catastrophe? Or are they simply on vacation as the title seems to indicate?
2. Is everybody else on earth dead? Is that what is meant when Terry says, "Gone, Jamie. They're all . . . gone"? If that's true, who's knocking on the door at the end?
3. Is the play set in the future? Certainly, the telephone/computer/modem seems to be from a technology not yet attained. Does this make any difference in the superobjective?

As you work on the superobjective, remember that it should be brief: it's not an essay, merely a succinct statement of meaning that you can refer to as you work on your character's spine and units of motivation. Here are some possible superobjectives for the scene:

1. In some future time an ecological disaster has robbed the world of all its supply of water. Two people in a remote mountain hideaway believe they are the only survivors and are in despair, unable to do any more about their situation, until a mysterious knock at the door indicates to them that there are other survivors.
2. Two vacationers in the mountains find themselves without water. One, Jamie, is so trusting of the other, Terry, that Jamie believes Terry's statement that there is no water because everyone else in the world is dead. A knock at the door brings Jamie back to a more rational assessment, however. Jamie now believes Terry to be insane.
3. Two hikers are lost and stranded in the mountains and break into a cabin where they find that there is no water. A computer keyboard and telephone modem seem to be working, however, and they try to reach the outside world but can't. This leads them to believe that the other members of their party have been lost and are all gone. At the end, however, a knock at the door leads them to believe that they have been found.

As you can see, there are many ways in which a play can be interpreted and summarized into a superobjective. Now, on the basis of your own motivational units and spine, come up with one of your own.

● ● ●

Understanding the text and the subtext thoroughly and completely are the first necessary steps in building a characterization in a scene. Without this understanding, nothing the actor says and does will seem based in reality for the audience. Later, in discussing working rehearsals, we discover that finding the correct reading for a line of dialogue is one of the actor's tasks at this time. This term does not mean that the actor is literally reading from the page. A **line reading** is simply the term used to indicate the way in which an actor will speak a certain group of words: what words will be stressed or emphasized, what inflection pattern will be used, what force and intensity will be applied in speaking the line. Understanding the correct motivational unit is the basis for determining the line reading.

Understanding the subtext is also the most effective means of avoiding commenting or indicating. Commenting is difficult to define, but let's begin by saying that it is anything an actor does that is not based in real thought and emotion, but is done for superficial reasons. Commenting is also anything physical done to call the audience's attention to the actor's internal process. It is sometimes called indicating because these signals to the audience indicate what the actor is thinking. Because this is a somewhat difficult concept to understand we refer to this problem several times throughout the book.

The problem of commenting usually arises when the actor does not trust the internal process to produce a satisfactory external manifestation. In an exaggerated form, commenting might also be defined as showing off or ornamenting the performance. Children, playing among themselves in a backyard, assume roles in a natural and unornamented way, but if they sense an adult is watching them from the kitchen window, they may begin decorating their role playing with obvious and often exaggerated vocal and physical differences: they are showing off to the grown-up. The most obvious examples of commenting or indicating often have to do with age. When you are playing a character who is very young or very old, you may be tempted to indicate the character's age by (if the character is very young) standing pigeon-toed and speaking with a lisp or (if the character is very old) walking bent over, limbs trembling, and speaking with a quavering, whispery tone. These are all simple clichéd indications of characterization and should be avoided.

As we saw earlier, mugging is commenting as applied to facial gesture: exaggerated, artificial facial gestures are not the result of thought, but of an attempt to convince the audience that thought is taking place.

The internal process must be trusted to produce the appropriate external manifestation. This external physical response is not a spontaneous, changing phenomenon: several external manifestations should be generated by thought and the appropriate one for your character consciously chosen, approved by your director (if you have one), assimilated into your characterization, repeated, projected, and given to an audience. If you have gone through the process of understanding your text thoroughly and have analyzed your subtext completely and in detail, arriving at valid motivational units, spine, and superobjective, then you are ready to go on with rehearsals and the continuing process of building a character. The next stage in rehearsals is usually the readthrough of the script with the director and the rest of the cast.

As you go on to these stages, many of which involve the external manifestation, always trust the internal process we have just discussed: it is the indispensable basis of all that is to come.

CHAPTER 4

• • • •

THE
READTHROUGH

The readthrough rehearsal is usually the first time that a director and the entire cast—most often with a stage manager and, perhaps, an assistant director—come together. The readthrough has two main purposes: for everyone to have a clear and shared understanding of the text of the play and to provide the director with an initial opportunity to discuss any ideas that will govern the overall production. These ideas of the director are collectively known as the production concept or director's concept. This idea of a concept is frequently misused. A good director will not try to superimpose too many extraneous elements onto a production, but correctly and sparingly used, such a concept can be very useful, providing the entire ensemble with a general vision of the final effort. Production concepts can encompass a wide range of ideas and theories—particularly if the play in question is a classic drama—such as the time framework in which the production is to be presented, all aspects of design, and any matters relating to interpretation of the text, including acting style.

As you read this book and work on the exercises in it, you are most likely not working on a fully mounted production, and probably do not have a director (unless you consider the classroom instructor as fulfilling that role). This chapter, however, refers to both kinds of work—the classroom scene in which there is no director and the fully staffed production. If you're working on a scene, see how clearly you can imagine this theoretical director, and, for the moment, try to function in that role as well as that of actor.

Before you attend a readthrough rehearsal of a play for which you have auditioned and been cast, or before you first read through a scene you're working on with a partner, you will want to prepare your script so it can function effectively as a workbook.

PREPARING THE SCRIPT

Scripts will come to you in various forms. There are hardbound published editions that are usually found in libraries and are primarily for individual reading or play analysis coursework. If you are cast in a fully produced play, though, you will probably be given what is called an acting edition, scripts obtained from the large publishing houses that specialize in plays which have received major productions in New York or a regional theater in, say, Los Angeles, San Diego, Seattle, or Chicago. These scripts (as we noted earlier) will probably have stage directions, blocking notations, and cuts in the text that were initiated in this original production. Your production will probably change much of this, adding a good deal of its own notation: blocking to fit its environment, new cuts, perhaps even some textual additions. All of this will need to be entered into your own script. Unless you are advised otherwise by the director or stage manager (ask if you're not sure), the script you are issued belongs to you; you not only may write in it, you should. Your script, whether you use it for a classroom scene or in a fully mounted production, will eventually contain a huge amount of information added by you during the course of rehearsals.

An acting class scene, however, probably comes from a copy of the play that is borrowed from the library or the instructor: obviously you can't write in a borrowed script. Even if the script does belong to you (as this text and the included scenes you'll be working on very likely does), you may want to keep it intact. An acting edition is usually a compact 6×8-inch paperbound edition with limited marginal space for your own notes. So you will need to put the script in a form that is convenient to use as an active journal and workbook, a way to transfer the text of the play or your scene into a format with much wider margins.

First obtain permission to duplicate the pages of the text for your own exclusive use. Be aware that copyright laws prohibit the photocopying of much published matter. However, laws vary when the photocopy is for your exclusive use, so you need to find out whether or not you are allowed to do this. If you can, the photocopying method is very satisfactory. Since an acting edition is small, this duplication process (onto $8\frac{1}{2} \times 11$-inch pages) will usually leave some nice wide margins. If you have doubts about the legality of the photocopying or can't do this for other reasons, an alternative is to cut a rectangular hole (a little smaller than the printed text of your script) out of the center of some blank notebook sheets, disassemble the pages of your text (be sure it belongs to you!) and paste or tape the pages onto those sheets. The holes in the pages let you read both sides! Put binder holes in these pages with a three-hole punch and put them into a sturdy notebook. Add some blank pages at the beginning for notes and a daily journal of rehearsals. If your binder has pockets in the front or back covers, you'll have a place to store rehearsal schedules and other notices. Another good idea is to include a plastic pouch for pencils as well. You will always want a good supply of writing implements for the rehearsal process, and pencils should be used so that frequent changes can be erased. Keeping the pencils with your script makes them handy if the point breaks.

After your script is installed in its notebook and is therefore ready for work—all the space you need for notes and plenty of writing implements—the next step is to find a way to guide your eye to your character's lines, physical actions, and cues. **Cues** are simply the indications that it is time for you to speak or perform some action. The most usual cue, of course, is the end of the line preceding yours, but cues can also be a sound, an action, or a change in the lights. These cues will usually be your signal to speak, but you will also have cues to move or perform other tasks. We'll discover later, too, that cues can come earlier in the preceding line than the last word. For now, though, let's just assume that your cues are the end of the preceding line.

An efficient way to make all the information that relates to your character plainly visible and organized is to use felt-tip markers of three different colors to highlight your lines, your cues, and your business. For instance, you might highlight all your spoken lines in yellow, the cues in orange, and business that concerns you or actions you perform in green. Not only does this make it easier for you to locate your place in your script, it will help you in the process of learning lines.

LEARNING THE LINES

Perhaps no other part of the acting process is more fundamental, more vital, and more onerous than learning lines. I believe in getting this drudgery over with as quickly and as efficiently as possible, beginning to learn the lines as soon as you are cast or as soon as the scene is assigned to you. If possible, you should have your lines learned prior to the first reading with your partner. In a full, directed production you can certainly begin to learn your lines as soon as you are cast, as long as you realize that directors sometimes make cuts in the text. Usually those are given at the first readthrough, though, and I think it's worth making an early start, even if some of the lines you learn are eventually cut. Certainly you will want to be well along in memorization by the first blocking rehearsal.

You may be asking at this point, "Why is it called a readthrough if I already know my lines?" Well, first of all, you probably won't really know them, you'll just be at the point where you're beginning to learn them. And the readthrough is not a test of how well you've memorized the lines; you'll actually read from the script and will be paying attention to other matters. But I still think you should begin the memorization process as soon as possible.

Memorizing lines is the most basic and mechanical step in working on a role and, at the same time, this task is vitally important to everything that follows in the creative process. You must know your lines as well as you know your own name, or the alphabet: they must be learned, it seems to me, on something like the autonomic level. Why? Because your brain, as much as humanly possible, must be preoccupied with *character* thoughts, not *actor* thoughts; you must be dealing with the internals that we discussed in Chapters 1 and 3, thinking the thoughts that the character should be thinking and not the thoughts that you, the actor, are thinking. "What is my next line?" is definitely not a character thought; it is decidedly an actor's thought.

At this point, let me say again that I don't believe it is possible to rid your mind completely of all of your own thoughts and think exclusively the thoughts of the character. During the 1950s and 1960s, the onslaught of what was referred to as the Method dominated the theory of acting to an alarming degree. This school of thought was a derivation of the theories of Stanislavski about whom, you may remember, we briefly talked in Chapters 1 and 2. Many advocates of the Method believed that the actor was supposed to be in character to such an extent that he or she literally became the character. While I firmly endorse the idea that you should think in character as much as possible, it is an absurdity to try to do it exclusively. In the first place it is impossible, and in the second place it is undesirable because there must be a part of the actor who is conscious of and, to some degree, controlling some of the circumstances of the performance. Holding for laughs, for instance—which is a motivated, in-character waiting for the audience's responsive laughter (if there is any) to start to subside before the next line is spoken and any that might have been unheard because of the laughter repeated—is a function of actor thought, not character thought; yet it is essential to a good performance. No, you don't have to be in character to the extent that all of *your* thoughts are suppressed: just the ones you don't need. "What's my next line?" is, as we have noted, definitely not needed. So let's just say that you must know your lines so well that you don't have to think about them.

Remember, too, that learning your lines is never done in rehearsal. Memorizing lines is done on your own time. How? you may be asking. What is the best method of learning lines? My students frequently ask me this, and I tell them that I think this technique is very much up to the individual. The technique involved is one of rote memorization, after all, and each person has a favorite method of accomplishing such a dreary but necessary task. Let's talk about what I perceive as the two most common ways.

Open your script to the first page where your character has a spoken line. Note the cue of your first line, and then memorize the line that comes after the cue. Cover the line with a piece of paper or a 6×8-inch file card, look at the cue, and say the line you've just memorized. Look at the next cue, memorize the line that comes after it, then cover both lines with the card, go back to the first cue, say the first line, look at the second cue, say the second line . . . and so forth through that page. Review the first page. Do the same thing for the second page; then review pages 1 and 2. As you memorize a page, always go back to the very first page and review from the beginning each time you add a page. In this way, go through your entire script. Once you've memorized all your lines, go back and memorize all your cues. You'll probably find that most of them are lodged in your memory by now, but check to be sure.

Learning lines, by the way, is a maturation process. Don't be surprised if you wake up the morning after you've spent several hours memorizing a scene only to discover that you really don't know the lines. As you rememorize them that day you'll find things go much more quickly and easily. Finally, a day or two after you began—if you're reviewing, as you should, on a daily basis—you'll find that the lines are firmly in your brain. Daily review is an indispensable part of the process: go over all your lines every single day of the rehearsal and performance period.

Of course, you will always find the rare person who needs only to look at a page of dialogue in order to memorize it accurately and fully. While you may envy these people their facility, go about the process in your own perhaps slower but nevertheless thorough way. Don't skimp on this process: it is the root and basis of everything you subsequently do.

There is a second method I think of as a supplementary technique. Once you have memorized the lines (and your cues: remember that you don't know your lines until you know when to speak them!), you may want to record all your lines onto an audio cassette that you can carry around to use on your personal tape player. (See Fig. 4.1) To use this technique most effectively, speak your cue, leave a space long enough for you to say the following line, then speak and

Figure 4.1   The process of storing the words your character speaks in your memory is time consuming, but must be repeated as often as possible during the run of the play.

record your line. This way, when you play the tape back you'll hear the cue, and have blank tape time to speak your line live before you hear the recorded version. This is a good way to check for accuracy. Carry this tape with you in your car and use that otherwise wasted commuting time in the mornings and evenings to work on lines. Other drivers may give you strange looks, of course, but don't mind them: a lot of people talk to themselves. And be careful! Don't let all your concentration go to your script. Your main thoughts when you're operating your car should be on driving safely!

Remember that you must always learn your lines word for word as the playwright wrote them! Do not rearrange or paraphrase your lines in an attempt to give them immediacy or reality. Reality is certainly the goal you must strive for, but not at the expense of the written line. Learn your lines exactly as written and find the reality in them during later rehearsals.

As long as you are working on this part, don't stop the line-review process. Even when you are in the performance process, with rehearsals far behind you, do not stop reviewing your lines: do it every day!

DEALING WITH THE DIRECTOR'S CONCEPT

When we discussed the internal process in Chapter 3, we answered some preliminary questions about our exercise scene in a section called "Understanding the Text." Go back and look at your answers for that section as they related to *A Mountain Holiday* with Terry and Jamie. Review what choices you made when you decided (1) who you were, (2) where you were, and (3) what you were doing. Also, in that same chapter, in a section called "Understanding the Subtext," several choices for a superobjective were given: which of those choices (or other alternatives you might have come up with on you own) did you choose? Once you have reviewed your choices in answering these questions and have reminded yourself why, based on the text of the exercise scene, you made those particular choices, see if you can apply the principles by which you chose them to another situation. Let's look at how these issues might come up (and they will) at a readthrough in which a director's concept might affect many of your decisions.

Suppose, for instance, you are cast in a production of *Romeo and Juliet*. Since this is very likely your first part in a real play, it is not very likely that you are playing either of the title characters. Anyway, analyzing such large and complex parts in such a complicated play is beyond the scope of this book. Let's say, rather, that you've been cast as either Samson or Gregory (we'll make a leap of faith and assume that these parts would be open to both sexes), the two servants who appear, briefly, in this opening scene of the play.

Romeo and Juliet, Act I, Scene i.

(*Verona. A public place. Enter Samson and Gregory, of the house of Capulet, swords and bucklers on.*)

SAMSON: Gregory, on my word, we'll not carry coals.

GREGORY: No, for then we should be colliers.

SAMSON: I mean, an we be in choler, we'll draw.

GREGORY: Ay, while you live, draw your neck out of collar.

SAMSON: I strike quickly, being moved.

GREGORY: But thou art not quickly moved to strike.

SAMSON: A dog of the house of Montague moves me.

GREGORY: To move is to stir, and to be valiant is to stand. I will take the wall of any man or maid of Montague's.

SAMSON: That shows thee a weak slave, for the weakest goes to the wall.

GREGORY: 'Tis true; and therefore women, being the weaker vessels, are ever thrust to the wall; therefore I will push Montague's men from the wall and thrust his maids to the wall.

SAMSON: The quarrel is between our masters and us their men.

GREGORY: 'Tis all one; I will show myself a tyrant. When I have fought with the men, I will be civil to the maids—I will cut off their heads.

SAMSON: The heads of the maids?

GREGORY: Ay, the heads of the maids, or their maidenheads; take it in what sense thou wilt.

SAMSON: They must take it in sense that feel it.

GREGORY: Me they shall feel while I am able to stand; and 'tis known I am a pretty piece of flesh.

SAMSON: 'Tis well thou art not fish; if thou hadst, thou hadst been poor-John. Draw thy tool; here comes two of the house of Montague . . .

This scene goes on for ten or fifteen more lines and contains all that we hear of Samson and Gregory. It is short, but it amply serves to illustrate our purpose here.

We'll assume that, as with the exercise scene in the mountain cabin, your dedication to acting leads you to study your part very thoroughly. You know you must understand the text (deciding who you are, where you are, what you are doing), analyze the subtext, and learn the lines. Moreover, your enthusiasm for this, your first part, leads you to construct a superobjective for the entire play based on your own reading and understanding of the text before the readthrough by the entire cast.

Let's start with your superobjective. You surely saw immediately that this play was not about Samson and Gregory, no matter how much you might wish that it were. You probably understood it was a play about the two title characters and how they fall in love, marry secretly against the wishes of their two sets of parents, and die as a result of a series of unforeseen circumstances, undelivered messages, and complex plans that don't work. But you may, because of your enthusiasm for your own small part, be led to believe the play has a good deal to do with the fights that erupt between the two families; you may construct a superobjective which sounds something like this: "The play concerns the tragic love affair between Romeo and Juliet as a symbolic representation of the ongoing conflict between the Capulet and Montague families *and their servants*. This conflict is representative of many such conflicts that existed between wealthy Renaissance Italian families. These feuds between these two commercial tribes eventually lead to the development of powerful crime families.'' (See Fig. 4.2.)

Would this be correct? Well, it might be, given a director who agrees with you. What happens, though, if you get to this first readthrough of the production in which you are cast to discover that the director's superobjective is this?: ''The play concerns the plight of two teenagers who fall in love in spite of the ongoing feud between their two families. Their love might end the conflict, except the immaturity of the two young people leads them into a pattern of noncommunication that results in their tragic death. Such patterns exist in the twentieth century, and, in order to emphasize this modern parallel, this production will be costumed and set in the 1990s.'' What becomes of your superobjective with its allusions to Renaissance Italian commercial dynasties?

Obviously, the lesson to be learned here is to begin, as soon as you are cast, to try and understand the play of which you are to be a part, but wait until you have heard your director's concept before you form a definite superobjective. In a classroom scene, where there is no director, you and your partner need to discuss superobjective (both for the play and for your scene) at your own small first readthrough: you can't be working at cross purposes with your partner. If you have trouble with this, ask your instructor for help.

What, however, about understanding the text? If you are going to learn your lines you must know what they mean, of course, and one glance at the short scene from *Romeo and Juliet* will convince you that this process is going to be

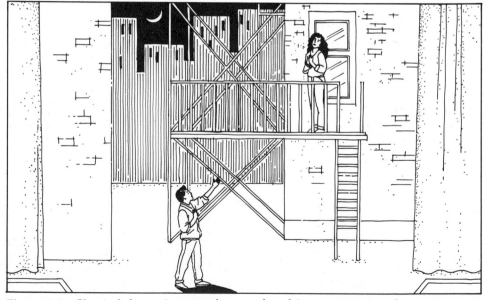

Figure 4.2 Classical drama is very often produced in contemporary dress, giving the young acting student an opportunity to relate very directly to these characters from another age.

much more complicated here than it was in the exercise scene with Terry and Jamie. What on earth are bucklers? And what's all this talk about coals and colliers and collars?

Understanding a Complicated Text

Of course, most of the scenes in which beginning acting students will be involved are not going to be as complex as a scene from Shakespeare, with its dialogue written in Elizabethan verse. But if we begin with a difficult problem you'll surely be able to solve simpler ones on your own. A good edition of Shakespeare will provide you with notes—usually on the facing page, sometimes in the form of footnotes—which explain Elizabethan English words and phrases that you might not readily understand. Such an edition is essential if you are to understand the words. In some cases, these notes might make the Shakespearean scene easier to comprehend than a complex modern play. In any case, the first thing you need to do is to refer to those notes. You may, of course, also want to consult a variety of outside sources. There are many books on the plays of Shakespeare as well as a wide variety on more modern plays. Now let's work on the Shakespeare scene.

● ● ●

EXERCISE 30

UNDERSTANDING A COMPLICATED TEXT

Let's look at the first four lines of the opening scene of *Romeo and Juliet*. What does Samson mean when he says " . . . we'll not carry coals"? What does this have to do with anything in the play? Might you not decide that these two characters are carrying baskets of charcoal around? Would this lead you to believe they are husky dockworker types? Let's hope the notes in your edition tell you, first of all, that these opening lines are merely banter between two young friends and the many references to " . . . coals . . . colliers . . . choler . . . collar . . ." are puns that Shakespeare intended to establish Samson and Gregory's joking mood and their irritation (choler/anger) at the rival family. There are many other hidden jokes and comments (some of them frankly and crudely sexual) in this short scene that will help you play one of these parts. Check the notes carefully. Other questions you might ask yourself are: What does Gregory mean when he says ". . . the weakest goes to the wall." Is that bad or good? What did the Elizabethans mean when they used the word *tyrant*? Was it always bad? Does Samson mean it to indicate a negative meaning? Who is "poor-John"? What "tool" does Gregory wish Samson to draw? To complete this exercise, see how many of these problems and their solutions you can find: be sure you have a good understanding of every word in the scene. Keep working at the scene until you are certain you have understood all the lines clearly and completely and are therefore able to interpret them correctly. Once again, don't try to do this on your own. Find an edition of Shakespeare with good notes and consult it. There are plenty of them in your library. You will also find many works there on Elizabethan history and Shakespearean criticism, volumes on *Romeo and Juliet* alone. Do as much outside research as you need to obtain complete textual understanding.

● ● ●

So perhaps it is obvious by now that the superobjective of a play is allied to the director's concept, and complete understanding of the text sometimes is a matter of research. Consult your director on lines which, even after outside research, may not be clear to you. The director may also want to reinterpret some lines that you thought you understood: perhaps the director has an alternate version of the meaning of the line. Every line has more than one interpretation.

If you are working on a classroom scene with a partner, discuss the first reading thoroughly as you do it and when you finish it. You and your partner must act as director, and it is only by working together and testing each other that you will both arrive at a complete understanding of your scene. Feel free to make suggestions to each other about line interpretation and about possible outside sources that could help you work on the text. Both of you, of course, must come to mutual agreement on a superobjective for your scene and for the play from which the scene is cut.

READING ALOUD

In the actual readthrough, the problems of understanding, background, and concept are complicated by the fact that this is the first time you've read the text aloud in front of the director and the rest of the cast. So you may feel a certain amount of pressure that may cause you not to read very well. Remember that the purpose of the readthrough is to understand the text, and no one is expecting a polished performance. Concentrate on the tasks at hand.

Many times, however, my students ask me for hints on cold reading, or sight-reading either because they are faced with a readthrough, or because they are auditioning for a film or television role (which media often require sight-reading a script) and feel nervous at their lack of skill as a reader. My answer to this is always the same: if you want to learn to read aloud well, then you must practice reading aloud. Most of the current generation is not, unfortunately, very accustomed to reading in any form. Over and over again, students tell me they are part of the visual or computer generation, and that such skills have not been an important part of their lives. Acting students, however, must frequently read aloud, and the only way to learn to do this effectively is to set yourself a regimen of exercises.

Pick a passage from Shakespeare, perhaps one of the sonnets, and study it for meaning. Once you've understood it, read it aloud once or twice a day. Gradually expand your repertoire of reading, spending ten or fifteen minutes a day reading aloud. Listen to yourself as you read, making sure you are reading for sense and meaning as well as verbal skills.

At the readthrough itself, as we said, you will be concentrating on specific tasks of understanding and assimilation, but you can also work on reading skills at the same time. First of all, relax. Don't allow the situation to make you tense. Slow down. There is a compulsion, sometimes, to try and read very fast. Resist the temptation to perform. Take the text phrase by phrase (word by word if necessary) and comprehend what you're saying. And listen to the others! It is never too early to begin the process of listening and response. And *never* hesitate to ask questions. Remember that the readthrough is an information session, not a performance.

It is in this first rehearsal, then, the readthrough, that these things and others like them are discovered and discussed. If you go into the readthrough with as much understanding of the text as you can manage, with your script well organized and marked, with your lines and cues on the way to being memorized, and with some idea of what the play is about and how your part contributes to that overall meaning, then you will be ready to hear what the director has to say regarding concept and adjust your thinking to that. Don't feel you have wasted time, for instance, if you find that some of your hard-memorized lines are cut. This editing is not only one of the director's prerogatives, you must assume that it will ultimately be to your advantage by making the text cleaner and more understandable to the audience. Certainly at this early point, you must trust your director's overall view of the play.

It is also at the readthrough that you will gain other very important information. Be a good listener! Listen carefully to all that is said. If you are not sure of the director's concept, ask questions. Why is the production in modern dress? Or medieval dress? Or futuristic dress? What does this costuming concept do to enhance the meaning of the play? Think about your own character and how you fit into the overall scheme of things. Once again, ask questions if you need to. The readthrough is a time of information demonstrated and understood. Don't leave this period in the rehearsal process until you feel you have a thorough and complete understanding of the play's superobjective and a preliminary understanding of your character's place in it (character spine). More time will be spent on this idea when we discuss the working rehearsal in Chapter 6, but the readthrough is the beginning point of understanding your character's direction as it relates to director's concept and superobjective.

If you have prepared and organized your script, memorized your lines, gained all the information that you need from the readthrough, then you are ready to begin to put your performance on its feet in the blocking rehearsal.

CHAPTER 5
• • • •

THE BLOCKING
REHEARSAL

The readthrough is likely to take place somewhere other than the stage itself. Since its primary purposes are literary and abstract rather than physical and practical—the understanding of the script and the establishment of the concept and superobjective—it is usually more appropriate for the reading to be held in a room where the cast, the director, and the staff can gather around, say, a large table that will enable them to read and write comfortably. Blocking rehearsals, however, are directly concerned with the space within which the play will eventually be performed and are usually held on the stage itself or, if that is not possible, in a rehearsal space which is comparable in size. In either case, some approximation of the set will be available for the rehearsal.

In the readthrough, the director most likely spent a certain amount of time helping the cast to visualize the set and talking about the costumes, lighting, music, and other complementary attributes of the fully mounted production. All of these things are important, of course, but at this crucial point where the production begins to find its feet, it is the set—the physical environment of the play—that is the most important. And the set very much depends on what kind of theater—performance space—is being used for the production.

UNDERSTANDING THE SPACE

What kinds of theaters are you most likely to be working in? In the latter part of the twentieth century, live theater in the United States and Europe probably takes place in one of three general types of performance environments: (1) the proscenium stage, (2) the thrust stage, and (3) the black box space. The precise configuration of these types of theaters varies widely, but let's look for a moment at what you can generally expect to find in each of them and how each tends to affect an actor's performance.

The *proscenium stage* (Fig. 5.1) has a long tradition of use in the history of Western theater. The word *proscenium* comes from a Greek word that literally described the space on which the episodes of early Greek tragedy were performed. Visualize a simple platform in front of a small building for the actors to dress in and you will come close to defining the very early Greek stage. This simple stage house and the platform in front of it survived in Roman theaters and went on to form the basis of the traveling players' simple stages during the Middle Ages. These crude platforms, often nothing more than the folded-down side of a wagon, eventually developed into the theaters of seventeenth-century Europe. From there, the tradition of the proscenium theater descended, virtually

Figure 5.1   A theater with a proscenium stage is often quite large and gives the audience a "picture frame" view of the play. Actors must often think about keeping "open" to the audience, and must be able to "project" emotion as well as voice and gesture in a larger space.

intact, to the modern era. Today the proscenium stage is usually contained within the enclosed rectangular structure we call a theater. The slightly curved rows of audience seats typically rise—for better spectator visibility—up the long axis of the rectangle from a platform stage separated from the audience area by an arch, the proscenium arch, which serves the same function as a picture frame: isolating and framing the play in its own, frontally viewed environment.

Modern proscenium theaters tend to be large, seating between five hundred and several thousand people. With their front perspective, usually ample backstage, and *fly space* (the area directly over the stage itself from which scenery can be raised and lowered: "flown"), they are ideal for large-scale spectacles with lavish sets, lighting, and costumes. Most traditional musical theater pieces are well suited to the proscenium theater.

For the actor there are some drawbacks to performing in a large proscenium space. While it is true that the size of these theaters provides some actors who need—or think they do—the large spaces on which they can create performances of a great size and magnitude, the scale of these spaces can force an actor into vocal and movement patterns that are less than—or should I say more than—real. Projection in a theater that seats some two thousand people must be constantly on the actor's mind, so reality in intimate scenes is sometimes beyond the modern actor's grasp. Of course, most large theaters in these technologically advanced days are seeded with microphones that solve the audibility problem. Still, there has remained a tradition, particularly in musicals, of outsized and not very real acting that stems from the size of these proscenium spaces.

The picture-frame frontal perspective also forces the actor into a somewhat artificial awareness of being visible to the audience. The old adage of "not turning your back on the audience" is, of course, no longer practiced, but, still, it is the face of the actor that most easily reveals emotion, so you must develop an awareness of sitting, standing, and moving in ways which share frontal visibility with the audience while appearing to be aware only of the other people and objects on the set. This idea of facing the audience as much as possible can be taken to absurd lengths, however. Basically, if you remember to keep as open to the audience as possible—not to stand in complete profile or with your face hidden any more than is needed for specialized reasons—you will be all right.

Incidentally, it is from the proscenium stage that the idea of upstaging another actor originated. Upstaging is when one actor stands farther away from the audience than another actor, thus forcing that actor to look away from the audience. The theory is that the actor doing the upstaging is then the major focus of the audience, more easily seen, the primary object of the audience's attention. This practice has become something of a joke in today's theater, certainly only done by the most egotistical and artificial of actors. It has, of course, no place in a performance that hopes to create the illusion of reality, and is always to be avoided.

The *thrust stage* (Fig. 5.2) is much friendlier to actors. It was in the time of Shakespeare, the period in which a renewed interest in theater as an art form was reborn after the hiatus of the Middle Ages, that such a configuration for theaters came into its own.

Figure 5.2 A "thrust" environment brings the audience closer to the action, involving them more directly and giving them a variety of perspectives on the play, but the actor must adjust the size of the performance to the more intimate space and remember to share the action with all areas of the audience.

The Elizabethan period in England—roughly the latter half of the sixteenth century and the first half of the seventeenth—saw the first theater building constructed specifically for the performance of plays in more than a thousand years. There had been a strong resurgence of interest in all kinds of literature during the preceding hundred years, and suddenly there was an explosion of talented men—alas, few women were involved in any profession during this time and certainly not the theater—who were writing poetry that was meant to be spoken aloud: performed. When theaters were built in which these new plays could be heard, a good deal of attention was paid to the perfect environment for listening to as opposed to watching a play. Certainly the visual element was important to the Elizabethan playgoer, but the way in which the theaters were constructed makes it clear that the spoken word was of paramount importance. The audience sat or stood around a platform that pushed aggressively into their midst, providing an intimate, almost collaborative environment for the performance of plays. This was the beginning of the thrust stage in theater architecture, currently enjoying a revival of use.

In our own time, the thrust stage is an increasingly popular design and has been constructed in new theaters of varying shapes and styles. The Tyrone Guthrie Theater in Minneapolis, Minnesota—perhaps the first important thrust theater in this country—has a large wedge-shaped stage extending out into an irregularly shaped auditorium. Because of the success of this theater, thrust stage theaters began to appear all over the United States beginning in the 1960s, and, with the spread of the regional theater movement—whose companies often emphasized the classics, particularly Shakespeare—the plan gained in popularity. The Old Globe Theater in San Diego, California, is an example of such a theater.

The thrust stage has many advantages for the actor. First of all, such theaters are frequently much smaller than proscenium theaters, requiring less effort in vocal projection and making actor visibility less of a problem. Your performance need not be of such magnitude as to tempt you into artificiality, and the emotional distance to the audience is less, making intimate scenes, in particular, easier to perform believably. There are some problems though: maintaining frontal visibility is more complex on the thrust stage because the audience is sitting on three sides of the performance area. Acting in the proscenium setting, you only had to worry about facing in one direction in order to be frontally visible, whereas on a thrust stage you must think of three points of focus. Of course, it is primarily the director who must take this into consideration when blocking the play and be sure that each actor is moved around more frequently or, if the actor is standing still for a longer period of time, that he or she is standing well toward the back wall, where there is no blockage of the audience's view and the actor need worry only about facing forward. But the actor, too, must be aware of this problem, and, even when put by the director in an advantageous position, must find the motivation for more small movements and stance adjustments so as to be visible to the largest number of audience members at any given time.

There is also a problem concerning quick exits on a thrust stage. The distance to the backstage area from the point of the stage closest to the audience can be considerable. Most theaters with thrust stages solve this problem by making use of a device that comes to us all the way from the times of the Roman Empire. Under the audience in a modern thrust stage run two (sometimes more) ramps that open at the foot of the stage. If an actor needs to make a quick exit from one of these spots, she need only duck into this ramp, rather than crossing the entire stage to get off the performance space. These ramps are usually called by the somewhat unattractive but vividly descriptive name that the Romans called them: one is a *vomitorium*; two are *vomitoria*.

The third form of staging today is perhaps the one most frequently used by small struggling groups and is often found in university theaters (there is probably one in your department): it is the *black box*.

This name probably originated because the architectural form is too varied to lend itself to a single descriptive term, and because the walls are usually painted black to be as inconspicuous as possible. The typical black box theater (Fig. 5.3) is a large rectangular or square room with no permanent stage, but platforms that can be arranged in many different ways to accommodate audience seating. In probably its most frequent arrangement, this seating encloses what is sometimes called an *arena* or *theater-in-the-round* performance space: square, rectangular, or, sometimes, round. But the flexibility of most black boxes allows for a

Figure 5.3 The "black box" theater environment will usually provide the most intimate of all actor/audience relationships. The actor must be very aware of sharing the performance with all of the audience.

wide variety of acting spaces, some with the audience seating scattered among the actors for maximum direct contact.

While the relationship between actors and audience in most of these flexible theaters is very intimate and direct, providing maximum potential for actors to give low-key performances that are very close to reality, there are some problems. First of all, frontal visibility is much more complex. In most cases, with an audience seated on four sides, you must find motivated ways to move and adjust position even more frequently than on a thrust stage. Again, the director's blocking will deal with the broad patterns of movement, but you, the actor, must be aware of making your face as visible to as many people as possible at any given moment, while maintaining believability. One positive aspect of such a theater—the test of good high-level-of-reality acting—is that the audience is so close, any artificiality or fakery on the part of the actor is easily and immediately visible. Acting in a small flexible black box is a test of the actor's skill.

There are other configurations for the shape of modern theaters, but the three we have described are by far the most common. Each offers the actor advantages, and each presents performance problems to be solved. You must learn to find your way around each of these stages, adjusting the size and scope of your vocal and physical performance to the demands and freedoms of each. It is likely that your first acting class scene will be in a plain classroom in which the instructor has arranged the chairs of the other students, the audience, in rows facing the area where you will perform—in other words, a miniature make-shift proscenium. But by the time you have finished another acting class or two you will no doubt have experience with all three of these staging types, plus some that combine aspects of all three. Many times when you audition for roles, you will have to adapt to a wide variety of rooms with many different kinds of performance conditions. The more flexible and adaptable you train yourself to be, the better.

SCORING THE SCRIPT: WRITING BLOCKING DOWN

So far, you should have two sets of notes written into the script you've prepared for use in rehearsals: you have marked your lines, cues, and actions as they are indicated in the edition of the script you're using, and you have taken notes during the readthrough and written them in the script as needed. Your notes should concern a clear understanding of the script, pronunciations and mean-ings of words, and any preliminary interpretation notes or information regard-ing concept that the director has given during this part of rehearsals. These notes are the beginning of the process known as *scoring* your script.

Each actor will find his or her own individual style for scoring, and there is a wide range of choice concerning the kind of information written down. Cer-tainly, there is wide variety in the manner in which lines are marked, and the kinds of notes written during the readthrough depend entirely on what is valu-able and necessary to the individual actor. In terms of blocking, as we will see, there is less individual choice: all blocking the actor receives should be written down in quite specific ways. No matter what information written into the script, however, or by what different techniques, it is all a part of the scoring process.

Look at scoring as if you were a musician. If you are a violinist sight-reading a piece of music, you are able to take advantage of the many words and signs the composer has written into the musical score indicating the composer's wishes regarding your interpretation of the piece. For instance, the composer might write "f" or "p" under a certain sequence of notes, indicating that they should be played *forte,* or loudly, *pianissimo,* or softly. If the music is to be played very loudly or very softly, then "ff" or "fff," "pp" or "ppp" might be written. Com-posers also write notes in words (often in Italian) that indicate the speed at which a passage is to be played, how the instrument itself is to be used, or perhaps compare the passage to a human voice singing or a dance being danced. Composers also draw long open triangles lying on their sides to indicate that a passage becomes gradually louder or softer (depending on which way the point of the triangle is pointing), how long a note is to be held, and a variety of other miscellaneous signs that indicate a broad spectrum of directions to the musician. Most playwrights, of course, dislike being this specific regarding the interpre-tation of the lines in their plays, wanting the actors and directors to be as free as possible in finding their own ways of saying the words and performing the actions. So as you, the actor, in conjunction with your director, come up with these interpretations, *you* must be the composer and write in the words and symbols that indicate the way they are to be performed: you must score your script.

Scoring will be very important later on for the running rehearsals where the actors work on the rhythm of their delivery. In that section we use various markings that resemble the ones used by the composer to indicate rate, pace, build, and so on. But at this point we have just begun the rehearsal process, barely started to score our scripts with notes regarding the mechanical work of learning lines and the intellectual understanding of the play. You might want to go back and review those notes at this point in the rehearsals to confirm your understanding on everything you have covered, and be sure that your prepared script is well organized and not cluttered.

Once you are secure about your place in the process, be sure you have plenty of sharpened pencils and lots of room in the margins of your script, because one of the most important parts of the scoring of your script is coming up: writing down blocking.

At the beginning of this chapter we noted that the director or the stage manager will probably bring to a first readthrough some device that will enable the cast to visualize the set on which the play will be performed. The most common of these devices is the *ground plan* or *floor plan* (Fig. 5.4), which is a map of the set as seen from above, showing the walls, doors, windows, and architectural features of an indoor set, and any trees, hills, bridges, streams, or any

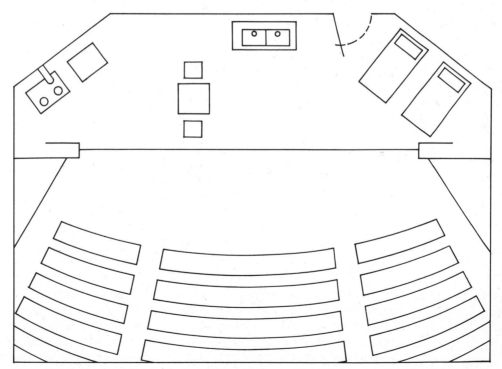

Figure 5.4 A ground plan, such as this one for our exercise scene, *A Mountain Holiday*, is a symbolic representation of the set seen from above.

other feature of an outdoor set. A ground plan is drawn to scale and shows the boundaries and major features, particularly those that affect actor movement, of any performance environment. You, the actor, need to learn this ground plan as thoroughly as you can; in blocking rehearsals the director will be giving you your major movement patterns based on this plan, and you need to be able to follow these directions accurately and to supplement them with smaller movements and adjustments of your own. Before you can do that, however, you must know the language the director will use to communicate these directions to you. Let's begin to learn that now.

A Mountain Holiday is to be performed on a proscenium stage for this exercise, and the ground plan describes what is sometimes called a *box set,* or an enclosed interior. The areas of a proscenium stage are typically divided into a grid that allows the director to communicate very specific parts of the stage in which the actor must move (see Fig. 5.5).

To begin with, *upstage* is the direction away from the audience, *downstage* is the direction toward the audience; *stage right* is the actor's right as she faces downstage, *stage left* is the actor's left as she faces downstage. The imaginary *center line* divides the stage into two equal portions left and right of that line, and a horizontal center line similarly divides upstage and downstage portions equidistantly. So there are already four major areas to the grid. Using just these four major areas, blocking areas can begin to be divided into these general grid areas: upstage right, upstage left, downstage right, and downstage left. You can also visualize areas that are closer to the center line and would be called upstage center, right center, center, left center, and downstage center. For speed and convenience in writing these areas into your script, they are usually abbreviated as UR, UC, UL, RC, C, LC, DR, DC, and DL. If you want a further narrowing down of these areas, you can divide them into up right center (URC: between UR and UC), up left center (ULC: between UL and UC), down right center (DRC: between DR and DC), and down left center (DLC: between DL and DC). If needed, you can continue to divide these areas into even smaller units if you are working on a particularly large or complicated set and therefore need finer distinctions; in fact, you can adjust the areas and the language that expresses them in any way which is useful to you. These are simply the accepted terms in most American theaters today. The blocking you write into your script is for your own use, though; if you find another version of these terms and their graphic expression convenient, quick, and useful, by all means use it.

In the first blocking rehearsal, you will need to follow the director as she indicates where she wants you to be at any given moment and write these directions down clearly and concisely, so that when you run the scene again you can follow them easily. It is worth pointing out at this juncture that blocking rehearsals should be used just for that: getting, writing down, and understanding the blocking. You probably know your lines fairly well now (although you will still be carrying your script in order to write the blocking down), so you should not use this rehearsal to work on memorizing lines. Remember, anyway, that work is done on your own time. Nor should you be looking ahead and thinking about the tasks you will be dealing with in future rehearsals. This

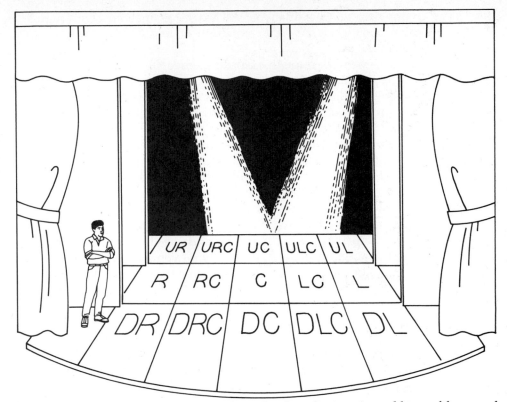

Figure 5.5 Blocking on a proscenium stage involves the actor in problems of focus and movement that will maintain high visibility and believable action. The space grid uses standard abbreviations for stage directions to provide reference points that simplify communication of these movements between director and actor.

period of time when the director tells you where to move and you are writing her directions into your script is just for that: concentrate on understanding the physical environment and your place in it at any given moment.

Here are a few hints about how to conduct yourself in the blocking rehearsal. While both you and the director will want to accomplish the task of blocking as quickly and efficiently as possible, don't let the situation (or the director) rush you. Get your blocking written down clearly and concisely so that you can go back and study it later. If you scribble it so rapidly or carelessly that you can't read it in the cold light of a later private work session, then you won't be able to memorize it (memorizing blocking is, of course, as necessary as memorizing lines), you won't be able to duplicate the moves at a blocking runthrough (usually the next step), and therefore the process will be interrupted for you, the rest of the cast, and the director. So take your time, within reason, to write your blocking down clearly and accurately. If the director is going too fast and you need more time, ask for it. Better to be a little slow—and thorough—now than to accomplish the task in a sloppy fashion. Use a pencil! Blocking frequently changes, and you don't want to clutter your script with blots, scratches, and obliterations. All markings in your script should be clear and clean: they're all important as signposts, and you should be able to read them at a glance.

As you walk through a blocking rehearsal, the director will talk to you about where he wants you to stand or sit or walk, and you will move in those patterns, writing the directions down in your script as you go. For instance, let's suppose you are playing Terry in the *Mountain Holiday* exercise scene. In the description of the set at the beginning of the scene, the playwright indicates that Terry is standing at the sink working on a faucet. If the director agrees with this arrangement, then he'll tell you so and you will write that in your script. Keep in mind, however, that the director may not proceed with all the playwright's stage directions. He may want Terry at some other point in the room, having the character move to the sink as the lights come up for some reason. Any such modifications of the script's stage directions are well within the prerogative of the director. Of course, both you and the director will always want to have a definite and firm motivation for *any* movements, whether or not they are indicated by the playwright or originate from the director. Movement, just as speech, must always be motivated. We talk more about motivation in the section on the working rehearsal. Just remember for now that whether movement directions are from the script or from the director, your job in a blocking rehearsal is to get them clearly and graphically into the notes in your prepared script.

How? Let's suppose the director is sticking with the script's directions: you might want, simply, to underline or bracket the sentence that describes Terry's position. Don't highlight it: again, these directions tend to change and highlighter is not erasable. If the director gives you a new direction for the rise of the curtain, then cross out the printed stage direction, and write the new one in the margin, as close as possible to the moment in the script where the action happens, with a clear arrow indicating precisely when the stage direction begins. For example, your opening note might be "Terry crouching in front of stove DL. At rise, X URC to sink. Try to work faucet."

At rise means when the curtain rises or opens or, perhaps more usually nowadays, the lights come up. *X* means "cross to."

And so your first stage direction is written in. Try always to write the stage direction into your script so it fits into the sequence of speech and action. As we said, this first direction might be written in the margin, or, if there's no room there, at the very top of the script, before the set description, with an arrow running from it to the point where it fits into the other action. Suppose, though, that action needs to fitted to a specific sentence or even to an individual word?

Look a little further down into the body of the exercise scene. Terry is apparently working at the faucet for the first few lines; then Jamie asks Terry to come down and look at the newspaper; Terry stays at the sink, however, twisting at the faucet until it breaks off. The director might suggest that you move down to the table on the line "Fix it, I guess" with a broken handle in your hand, throwing it down onto the table in front of Jamie with some forceful frustration. How do you write this in clearly and concisely? How about this: draw a clear arrow just before the word *fix* out to your ample margins and write "X DLC to table, bang faucet down." Make a mental note that if your blocking requires you to make a loud noise—such as throwing the broken faucet down—it doesn't happen as you say the line. The noise will probably make the line inaudible. Try to time the noise so that it happens before or after your (or the other character's) line is spoken. You might motivate a small pause during the line to do this.

If you agree with the director's notion that the throwing down of the broken faucet is indicative of the frustration that Terry feels, then you might want to make a brief note about that; but remember you don't want to clutter your script unnecessarily. Might the word *bang* not be enough to suggest that motivation? You will be making a lot more motivation notes at the later working rehearsals, so for now keep them minimal.

Directors vary widely in the way they give directions at this (or any other) point. Some may, as we indicated, *suggest* blocking to you, being very careful not to intrude on the possible choices regarding your character's reasons or motivations for moving. (Again, more on this in Chapter 6.) These directors may give you only suggestions: "Move around in the area of down stage right on this speech . . . " or "Work center here . . . " or "Stay around the stove for this. . . ." Others may be more forceful and detailed in their blocking, making very specific demands instead of requests. These directors will often tell you exactly how to stand or walk or sit. Getting along with your director is an all-important task for an actor, and how to deal with the delicate matter of who decides what is right or wrong for the character or the scene is outside the scope of this text for the beginning actor. I hope it is enough, for now, to suggest that you should be developing a good objective sense of how to work with people in all situations. Rehearsing a play is just one of a multitude of human working environments where you will need these skills. Remember that while the creative input of the actor is an extremely important part of the rehearsing of a play and all good directors will regularly consult the actor's opinions, the director's position in the theater is, for generally good reasons, a fairly autocratic one. If you trust your director, then go ahead and trust her instincts for blocking. The time for debating these choices may be later, anyway, when the question of motivation comes up in the working rehearsals. Of course, any blocking that you strongly feel invades your own personal safety or integrity must be discussed and, if necessary, refused right away.

Let's look at another example of writing down blocking. Look at the line in the exercise scene that comes later on: "I don't know! Try that cabinet." Let's suppose the director indicates that he wants Terry to express something like despair at this point by sinking into one of the chairs at the table. You might write down "X to US chair, sit, lean on table, face in hands." When? Try it at several points during that line and draw your arrow from the word which seems to work best as the beginning of this action.

Look at the line "4329!". Notice that the author has put in a stage direction that reads "Impatiently." I tell my playwriting students to be very sparing in writing such directions that tell an actor how to speak a line. Here is one, however, that seemed necessary. You might ask your director if, to express this adverb, you may pace energetically back and forth. If he agrees, then you might write "X, pacing, between sink and UL bed." The arrow that indicates when this pacing starts probably comes just before the line "4329," though it could certainly happen as the character says the line, in which case you might circle "4329" and have the arrow come out of the circle to the marginal notation.

Let's look at one more example. There is one indicated stage direction that requires some explanation and a good deal of caution. We have reached the point in the play where Jamie's panic is increasing, forcing Terry into some drastic action, which on the stage must be very carefully planned and staged so as to be very, very safe, while appearing to be spontaneous and violent (see Fig. 5.6). Go back and look at that page and study these lines:

TERRY: I'll keep telling you to shut up as long as you keep whining!
JAMIE: I don't whine! Stop telling me what to. . . . (JAMIE *is cut off as* TERRY *rises and slaps* JAMIE *hard on the face.*)

The slap is a very special stage direction. No actor should ever hit or perform any violent physical action on another actor unless both actors have been thoroughly trained in attack and response safety measures by a responsible expert in stage combat. For very simple actions (and this slap may be considered one), your director may feel competent to deal with instructing the actors in performing them. If the actions require it, the good director will call in a trained stage combat director who will instruct the actors in safety procedures and work with them until they are able to perform the action safely and with the illusion that it is real, spontaneous violence.

Your stage direction here might read as follows: "Face J., slap US cheek, right hand. See fight (or combat) instructor for work." The arrow indicating

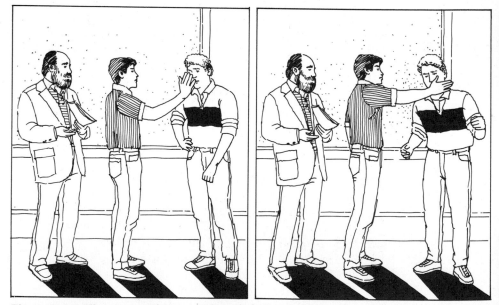

Figure 5.6 All stage combat must be carefully planned, rehearsed, and executed for maximum safety as well as reality and effectiveness.

when this action takes place might come from the words *me* or *what* in Jamie's line that is interrupted by the slap. Always when a line is interrupted, the cue will probably need to be backed up in the line to allow time for the action to take place. In all subsequent rehearsals until the action can be safely executed, the slap is merely indicated, not actually performed.

Now let's see what you've learned about writing down of blocking.

● ● ●

EXERCISE 31

WRITING DOWN BLOCKING

Now that we have talked about some of the indicated and implied actions in the exercise scene *A Mountain Holiday,* let's block the whole scene and write the blocking down (Fig. 5.7). Get a partner, and decide or have your instructor decide, who's playing Jamie and who's playing Terry. Determine specifically what the set looks like: where the various items of furniture, doors, windows, and so on, are located. Use the indications in the script as your guide. For the purposes of this exercise, each of you should alternately function as actor or director: the actor playing Jamie should direct the actor playing Terry, and vice versa, providing each other with blocking. If you're the actor, of course, your part of the exercise will be

---

A Mountain Holiday

(The kitchen of a small mountain cabin in the Cascades. The furnishings are very Standing *simple: a table, two chairs, a wood stove, some cabinets, two beds.* TERRY *stands* Standing *in front of the sink twisting a faucet back and forth.* JAMIE *sits at the table reading* URC *a newspaper with intense concentration and a sense of urgency.)*

TERRY: *(Suddenly slamming a hand down on the top of the faucet.)* — Stepping back
Something's wrong with the water. — Pushing chair back DC

JAMIE: What?

TERRY: I said something's wrong with the . . . x ——x DR

JAMIE: Look at this.

TERRY: No! —— XURC

(Twists harder at the tap.) ✩

I can't get this . . . ow!

(The faucet breaks off in TERRY'S hand.) Terry *falls to floor*

JAMIE: *(Looking up taking spectacles off.)* What did you do that for?

TERRY: I didn't do it on purpose. —— Rises, XDL

JAMIE: So what's wrong? — Stands

Figure 5.7 Here is a page of *A Mountain Holiday* showing sample blocking for the actors playing both Jamie and Terry. Your own script, of course, contains only your blocking.

to write that blocking down clearly and concisely. If you're directing, you may want to experiment with methods of blocking you suppose directors with varying temperaments might use: one of you might work as an extremely meticulous and demanding director would, giving very detailed and specific blocking directions; the other might block as a much more permissive and even vague director might. One of the perils of actors is to have a director who has not done his homework or doesn't seem able to give blocking, indicating to the actor to "do whatever you want with blocking. . . ." Check each other's scripts to see how each has written down blocking. Try moving around the set as directed by the blocking written down by the other student. Does it accurately reflect where to move? Is it clear? Concise? Does it do the job? Block the whole scene in this way and check each other's work.

● ● ●

Before we leave the subject of writing blocking down, let's look at other types of stages and other kinds of physical environments and sets that would affect the process of writing blocking down.

Go back and look at the opening scene from *Romeo and Juliet*. The first thing you might notice about an edition of Shakespeare's plays is the near-complete absence of stage directions. We don't know, with any accuracy, how many of the interpolated directions in Shakespearean editions were actually written by Shakespeare: probably very few, if any. But most editions, from whatever source, will have one or two. In the version used in this text, the only indication of environment is the terse "Verona. A public place." Stage set designers often enjoy the problems that staging Shakespeare present them: there are usually so many shifts from place to place that almost never is any attempt made to represent these places in any kind of realistic manner. Then, too, there may be inherent in the director's and designer's concepts an element that changes the nature of these places considerably. First of all, both are quite likely to stage this production in an environment more like the one Shakespeare would have known: a thrust stage. Moreover, the director and designer of this *Romeo and Juliet* may have decided to set the production in modern times, say, the mid-1990s. It is immediately evident that the thrust stage environment is going to affect the blocking process considerably, but so is this time change. A concept that involves a change of time affects your performance in ways of speech, movement, and motivation, and it is going to change the physical environment drastically: costumes, props, and set. Those problems will have to be dealt with when you encounter them in a real play. For now, however, what blocking problems does the thrust stage present?

Moving around a thrust stage on a set of this kind is quite a different task. The set designer's floor plan and *rendering* (the picture the designer presents the director of what the finished set might look like) of a thrust stage "Verona. A public place." might look very different from those designed for a proscenium stage, because the basic shape of the performance area dictates that major parts of the set be placed for optimum audience visibility and focus. Actors must adjust to these differences. A thorough director makes decisions concerning the blocking grid of a thrust stage and informs the actors of her decisions so that the blocking as it is given and written down will share the same vocabulary and spatial designations.

Since a thrust stage is usually a wedge-shaped extension of a basic proscenium stage, some directors use the same grid as for the proscenium process, extending "downstage" to the lip of the thrust closest to the audience (Fig. 5.8). If this is done, it will make for bigger blocks of space on the grid, so your director may divide them further, having downstage 1 (D1) and downstage 2 (D2) zones, with the downstage 2 area as the major body of the thrust space, from the proscenium line to the downstage edge of the thrust.

Using this plan, downstage right in zone 1 would become DSR1 and upstage left center in zone 2 would become USLC2, and so forth. If this becomes too

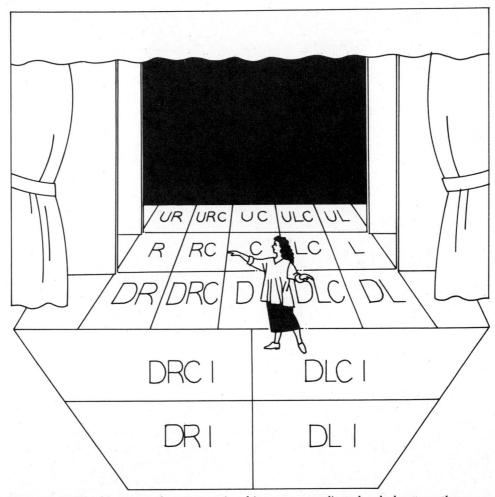

Figure 5.8 Blocking on a thrust stage is a bit more complicated only because there are more audience points of view for the actor to think about. The grid is again based on standard stage directions.

complicated, the director may decide to stick with the proscenium grid and try to orient more detailed and specific blocking toward major fixed set pieces.

Let's visualize a sample set for this play on a thrust stage. The designer might put a sizable two-level building at stage left with a stairway to the upper level offstage, behind the facade of the building. Let's have this building run on its long axis from URC to DL. We'll have the designer put a door just about exactly at LC. Let's locate two small round tables at DLC and almost exactly at the crossing of the center line. The ground plan might also note some changes in the height of the stage floor where steps lead up to the door in the building: 6″ in a circle means the floor rises 6 inches from the permanent floor; 12″ in a circle means a rise of 12 inches from the permanent floor, or 6 inches higher than the previous step. Let's also put a series of low platforms UR and URC that move down to the main stage floor in three 6-inch increments. Every one of these factors influence the way you move on the set and how you write blocking down.

At the beginning of the play, for instance, Samson may be at the railing of the balcony on the upper level of the building as the lights come up; a number of other actors ("Montagues") may enter from URC, standing on the upper levels of the stage shortly after rise. Gregory may enter through the major door of the building, using a cue from Samson: a whistle or a cry indicating the enemy.

If you're the actor playing Samson, you would write in your script at the top of the scene "In black: up escape stairs to gallery, lean rail LC," indicating that you climb the offstage stairs in the blackout and are in your place at about left center as the lights (or the curtain) come up on the scene.

If you are the actor playing Gregory, you write in and circle Samson's sub-verbal response to the appearance of the Montagues. A subverbal is a noise made by your character that is not in the form of a word. With permission of your director, these can and should be inserted by the actor when appropriate. The arrow coming out of this circled subverbal indicates "Enter through main door LC. X table DLC." When writing down blocking on a thrust stage set, you probably will want to use objects on the set as an orientation point as much as possible.

Let's do an exercise in blocking such a scene on a set like this one.

● ● ●

EXERCISE 32

BLOCKING ON A THRUST STAGE SET

Repeat Exercise 31, using the *Romeo and Juliet* script instead of *A Mountain Holiday*. Imagine the very simple set I have described. You might want to make a rough sketch (don't worry about being artistic, just clear) of the major set elements (Fig. 5.9). Take turns being actor and director. Remember, for purposes of this classroom exercise at least, that Samson and Gregory are played by either two men, two women, or a man and a woman. Be as specific as you can in writing your blocking down: this scene not only involves a minimal thrust stage set, but there are levels to consider.

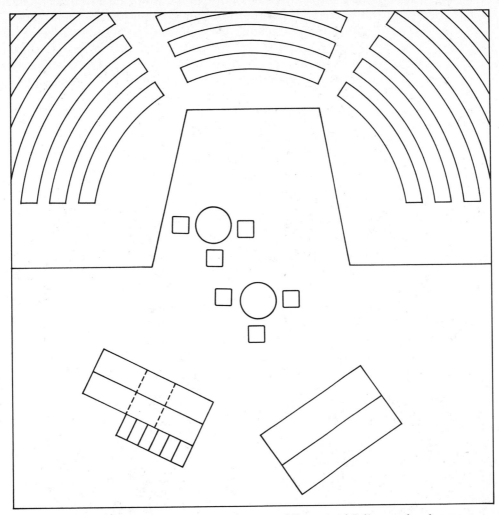

Figure 5.9 The ground plan for a production of *Romeo and Juliet* on the thrust stage. Remember that the circled numbers indicate how high (in inches) a platform or level is from the *stage floor*.

Here are some questions you might ask yourself as you do this exercise: What is an appropriate line for Samson to come down from the upper level? How early in the scene does this have to be accomplished? On Gregory's line which begins "'To move is to stir . . .'" what movements might make the line more meaningful? In what parts of the stage? Where on the stage will the Capulets and the Montagues meet for a confrontation?

Remember that working on a thrust stage puts you in closer contact with the audience, but you also have the responsibility to share frontal visibility with the people sitting to either side of the thrust. Motivate a number of small movement and stance changes in order to do this. Don't just do them: motivate them!

Blocking on a set in a black box theater can be very different from either the proscenium or thrust stage. Remember that such a flexible theater can be arranged in many different configurations: the relationship between audience and playing space can change to match concepts that any director and designer can imagine. For now, however, let's start with the simplest, the audience seated around the action on four sides in a rectangle, a staging method frequently called arena staging, central staging, or theater-in-the-round.

When you are involved in a blocking rehearsal in a production using this kind of staging, you must first be sure of what kind of reference points the director is using to orient the actors to the set. There are several such systems in common usage: (1) the clock system, (2) the compass points system, and (3) an adapted version of the system used for the proscenium stage.

In the clock system, the director simply has the cast visualize a clock face superimposed on the floor of the set. One direction is established as 12 o'clock, and the corresponding sides of the rectangle that will become 3, 6, and 9 o'clock automatically fall into place. Thus the director asking you to move to, say, 5:20 would be giving you a fairly specific location.

In the compass points system, the points of the compass substitute for the numbers on a clock dial. When a direction for north is established, the east, south, and west follow as a matter of course. This system is perhaps a little more detailed and specific than the clock system, as you can use directions such as NW, SE, NNW, and SSE to pinpoint areas toward the center of the stage.

Some directors—I am among them—find it easiest of all simply to superimpose the proscenium stage grid pattern onto the rectangular arena. All you have to do is establish which direction will be upstage, and the regular proscenium blocking vocabulary can be used: UR, UL, DR, DL, and so on.

No matter what the method of giving blocking directions in an arena theater, the director will be setting movement with two major considerations in mind:

1. to see to it that more distance than usual is maintained between the actors
2. to keep the actors moving more than in other staging methods.

If you, the actor, are aware of the director's need to do this, then you will be able to cooperate in both these areas: keep your distance so that audience visibility is maintained, and, since there is apt to be more movement than usual, be ready for more blocking directions than you would normally get in proscenium or even thrust staging. Both the actor and the director have to work together to make sure that each actor is visible to the maximum number of people in the audience at any given moment. If you're too close to the other actor, you block each other. If you stand or sit in one place too long, you are not visible to the people behind you for too long a period of time. Of course, there are going to be times when you must be very close to other characters, but your director will try to minimize those moments, and you should be ready to cooperate in that. Actors should also be aware of making more small adjustments of their position when standing or sitting for any length of time, sharing with as much of the audience as you can. Remember, of course, that any moves you make, no matter how small, must always be motivated. Never allow movements to seem as if the director *told* you to move. If you must stand for a long time, you will probably be placed in a corner entrance so as not to obstruct anyone's view.

● ● ●

EXERCISE 33

BLOCKING IN ARENA STAGING

Repeat Exercise 31, blocking *A Mountain Holiday* as the scene might be played in four-sided black box staging (Fig. 5.10). Create your own floor plan, using the script as a guide to where the major items of furniture, doors, and the like, would go. One of the differences you'll note right away is that doors and windows are all imaginary, since there are no walls. Otherwise, in a scene like this, the set can be very similar to the proscenium one, except that items of furniture can be ranged around all four walls (Fig. 5.11). Use either the clock or compass methods, or you might try just

Figure 5.10 Blocking in a "black box" space can be communicated in many different ways. Here are two of the most common techniques: the "clock" grid and the "compass points" grid.

Figure 5.11   The ground plan for a set in a "black box" space usually contains only furniture as the audience could not see over walls or other high levels. Audience position is often indicated in such a ground plan.

superimposing a proscenium grid on the floor of the black box performance space, simply making an arbitrary determination of upstage and downstage.

● ● ●

Remember that in four-sided staging, the actor must remain visible to all four sides of the audience as much as possible, so more small movement and focus adjustments will have to be motivated. Keep your distance from the other performer unless close contact is necessary. Such close contact should always be purposeful and brief in four-sided staging, though, so good audience visibility can be maintained.

Your blocking notes are very important and must be written carefully and clearly into your script so that they may be memorized and followed with ease.

Don't just jot obscure notes down; remember you'll have to read and study them later. Take your time and be clear: effective movement depends on blocking clarity.

So far, the scoring of your script has included these elements: the marking of your lines, cues, and actions as the edition of the script indicates them; the notes you took in the readthrough that deal with a clear understanding of the script: pronunciation of words, meanings, and interpretational indications; and now the blocking notes. The scoring of the script will continue right through the rehearsal period. Be sure you deal with each step in the proper order: don't rush through the process or anticipate the next step before the present task is completed.

The blocking rehearsal can be a stressful time, particularly for the director, who is involved in the very complicated task of balancing a stageful of actors and organizing a pattern of movement that will work for this particular production of this particular play. As an actor in a fully produced play, you will want to be as cooperative as possible with your director as she gives you blocking. At the same time, you need to be as forthcoming as possible with any beginnings of information you might have about the character you are working on. Especially if the director asks your opinion about stage movement, be ready and willing to talk in a clear and intelligent manner about your character and how he would move. Blocking certainly can be discussed if you disagree with something any director gives you. It might be advantageous, however, to try it first, then express whatever doubts you might have, together with suggestions, at a note session or other appropriate time. In the theater, as in any other human activity, cooperation, intelligence, and sensitivity to other human beings are all exceptionally useful qualities for everyone to develop.

While blocking is the prerogative of the director, you will probably frequently find yourself—as you no doubt do in this beginning acting class—faced with the task of preparing a scene, including blocking, by yourselves: you and your partner. In such cases, the process should be followed just as it is outlined here, except you and your partner will share the task of developing the physical environment and fitting your characters' movements into it. Take turns trying to be an objective eye, looking at and critiquing each other's moves. You might also want, presuming your instructor allows it (most will), to find someone to look at your scene from the point of view of blocking, just to be sure that everything is visible and focused. This process is very valuable to all acting students as— believe me—you will find many directors, even in the profession, who leave a good deal of character movement up to the actor. You should develop a good sense of where you are on the set in relation to the other cast members and to the audience. In fact, it is always a good idea to review and evaluate your performance as objectively as you can immediately following every rehearsal, including blocking sessions.

Blocking is a major part of your performance. In a very vital sense, if we include all the variations of gesture and stance in blocking, it is the entirety of the visible characterization. Treat it seriously: receive, write down, memorize, and rehearse blocking with great care, concentration, and thoroughness.

CHAPTER 6

• • • •

THE WORKING REHEARSAL

The working rehearsal is at the heart of the actor's task. It is during this period that the most important decisions are made by the actor—in conjunction, of course, with the director—regarding the subtextual framework of the role. Remember the opening sentence of Chapter 1? "Acting is the external manifestation of an internal process."

So far, we have talked in some detail about the internal process, and I have described how each actor must prepare his body in order to express those internal thoughts externally. We have also discussed these ideas in the context of your performing a real part in a real play (or a real classroom scene). In doing this, you have gone through some very definite steps: you have prepared a working script, memorized the lines, and, with the director and the rest of the cast, read through the script to be sure that everyone has thoroughly understood the text and is clear on how the director's concept affects that understanding. You have also been given the broad pattern of your physical movement from the director in the blocking rehearsal. Now you are ready to work your way through the entire play, exploring the subtext in great detail, and deciding what, precisely, the external manifestation of that internal process will be.

On your own, you have probably already been exploring the subtext, beginning to understand your character and that character's various motivating impulses. This early work on the subtext is certainly natural and to be encouraged, but it should not be your major focus until these working sessions. Each stage of the rehearsal sequence should concentrate on its own specialized tasks. Try not to anticipate the next steps or think about the end result: keep your mind on the immediate task, and, as each new level is mastered, the characterization will accumulate layers of meaning, acquire dimension, and develop naturally toward completion.

This is particularly important in the working rehearsal. The internal questions to be answered in these rehearsals are the very real basis of everything that follows, and you should never try to move on from this working period without having fully mastered the subtextual levels. I recognize that it is tempting to want to rush through the hard detailed work of this period, to get to the satisfying running rehearsals where it all gets put together, or even to begin to savor the excitement of performance. In fact, you may now and then have a director who will put some pressure, subtle or direct, on a cast to begin at too early a stage to work on problems of pace and rhythm or even on performance-level energy. Resist this tempting pressure. If it comes from a director, you may have to be tactful; if it comes from your own eagerness to speed up the process, then make yourself be patient and thorough. Of course, it's perfectly all right for you or the director to begin sketching in some tentative observations of where scenes are likely to speed up or slow down, where builds might likely develop; but at this stage, stick primarily to the work at hand: concentrate on making these very important choices, and work persistently on each stage of the process as you come to it. And at this stage of that process, the working rehearsal, you must take great care to construct a firm subtextual framework, completely exploring the varying mental and physical options that the underlying motivation for the text offers you.

WARM-UPS

To prepare yourself for the working rehearsal, begin the habit of doing warm-up exercises. Warming up the voice, the muscles of the body, and focusing your concentration are essential preliminaries to any rehearsal. Most people don't warm up physically before a readthrough because they know they'll be sitting for several hours. In blocking rehearsals, where no characterization energy is required and there is much stopping and starting with no attempt at continuity, there probably is still no need for warm-ups. Even in those situations, however, some concentration or relaxation exercises are helpful before starting, so a great many actors begin a warm-up routine right from the beginning of the blocking rehearsals; certainly by the time you begin the working rehearsal sequence, warm-ups are necessary.

The working rehearsal, like blocking rehearsals, will be conducted (if done properly) in very slowly developing segments, with much repetition and pauses for discussion of motivation, so a long warm-up session is probably not called for. Tailor your routine to your own needs and the demands of each particular rehearsal. In a working rehearsal, not only will you want to focus and concentrate on the work to be done, but you may want to begin exploring the effect certain thought and emotional choices will likely have on your body in terms of movement, and you need to be ready for that. By the time you are at the next stage, the running rehearsal, the warm-up habit should be firmly established and the routine almost automatic, so it's a good idea to begin your warm-up routine no later than the start of each working rehearsal.

It is worth noting at this point that promptness in the theater is an absolute necessity. First of all, when you become a member of the actors' union—Actors Equity Association—promptness becomes a part of your contract. In many production companies, fines are charged for every minute an actor is late. Equity rules state that cast members must be in the theater one half hour before curtain. In the profession, promptness is part of the job. As a student of acting, develop the habit of arriving at rehearsal well ahead of the call time, allowing time for your warm-up routine.

For performances, the union half hour rule is a minimum amount of time prior to performance curtain to arrive at the theater. However, you will almost certainly want to allow more than this minimum amount of time in actual practice. Not only do you need plenty of time to get into costume and makeup, you will need extra time to prepare yourself for the job to be done. In rehearsals, whether in the profession or at the university, you will want to arrive at least a half hour before the posted call time. The stage manager or an assistant—and probably the director—will be there preparing the rehearsal set and furniture, so you can probably get into the rehearsal room. You will need this time to do your mental and physical warm-ups. Since this early part of warm-ups in individual—your director may later organize group warm-ups—begin by developing a sequence of muscle stretching exercises.

Some productions will have a staff or cast member specifically designated as warm-up leader. Ask him or her to show you some simple exercises to loosen up the muscles of the legs, arms, back, neck, and jaw. If you're working on your own, go back to Chapter 2 and look at some of the early exercises there and see if any of those seem appropriate. These exercises should be simple, nonstressful movements that loosen and relax: don't try to force your body to respond. The point is to avoid stress, not induce it.

If your cast has a warm-up leader, she will work with the group on relaxation and concentration exercises at the beginning of the posted call time for rehearsal. You should do some stretching exercises before this. If you are working on your own, do your routine before the rehearsal starts, so you are ready when the director is. You will learn a good deal by watching others warm up, and gradually you will build a routine that works for you.

● ● ●

EXERCISE 34

AN INDIVIDUAL WARM-UP ROUTINE

If you do your own warm-up routine before a rehearsal begins, be sure to arrive at the rehearsal room in good time. Dress in comfortable working clothes that allow you to move easily. Beginning in the blocking rehearsal stage you may start to wear special rehearsal clothes that approximate some item of your costume. Shoes, particularly, are very important items of apparel. Right from the beginning, wear the kind of shoe you will wear in performance (hard soles, etc.) so you can get used to their effect on your movement. Don't wear any of these rehearsal items as you do your warm-up, but have them ready for the beginning of the rehearsal. Loose jogging sweats and sneakers or soft dance shoes are good for easy movement. Don't go barefoot (the floor may not be swept when you warm up) and don't wear just socks, which allow your feet to slide. As soon as you arrive at the rehearsal, begin to focus your mind on the task at hand. There will, of course, be some social activity on the set, particularly in the period before the rehearsal begins, but try to keep this to a minimum the closer you get to the start of the working situation. Too many students look upon being involved in a play as exclusively social, and this is a very dangerous attitude that inevitably produces sloppy work and the displeasure of the director. Most serious acting students will not expect you to cut down on your preparation time by too much social chatter, so don't think you're being rude if you isolate yourself and begin stretching and concentrating. As you focus your concentration and begin to work on loosening muscles, try to feel how your body is responding: focus your concentration on your body and on relaxing individual muscles. You might begin by doing a short version of Exercise 1 until you are sure you have relaxed the whole body. Now sit on the floor with your back straight in an easy, erect posture and your legs extended in front and parted to form a V. Easily and loosely bend from the hips, reaching with your hands, extending, alternating right arm, left arm, as far down each leg as you can—don't worry if you can't touch your toes, take it easy!—pulsing the upper part of your body downward (gently!) toward your legs. Do this a few times, until the back muscles seem looser and limber. Begin work on breathing at this point, inhaling through the nose as you straighten your back and exhaling at each extension of the torso down toward the legs. Sitting up straight, clasp your hands lightly in front of you, gently touching the chest, elbows out to each side, and, leading with each elbow in turn, twist the upper body (gently!) first to the right, then to the left, pulsing your torso from side to side. Keep the legs in contact with the floor as you do this, but don't lock your knees. Once the muscles in your sides are relaxed by this process, stand up and shake any tension out of the body. Bounce gently in place (maintaining floor contact with your toes), shaking your arms and hands, rotating shoulder joints, and easing jaw muscles. Then find an easy stance and move into a stacking vertebrae routine (Exercise 2), giving even more controlled relaxation to the upper body. Now do some neck rolls as shown in Exercise 3. Take it easy! Don't push! Always be very gentle with these neck rolls. Never let the head snap or rotate too strongly—the purpose is relaxation, remember, not developing muscles. Shake out again. Now put your hands over your face and scrub your face with your open palms. Don't press too hard on the eyes! If you wear contacts, skip the eyes. Gently massage the muscles of the face so they're loose. Now make some exaggerated faces: loosening the jaw with wide-open stretches; stretching the brows, the nose, the lips, the cheek muscles. Now shake out again. At this point, you might want to do some form of centering routine, similar to Exercise 6, which will focus and refine concentration and balance. As you go through these loosening, concentration, and relaxation exercises, begin to pay some attention to your breathing, focusing on correct diaphragm breathing and keeping the throat relaxed (review Exercise 16). Now make some gentle sounds to warm up the articulatory mechanism (Exercise 17) and move on into some tongue twisters (Exercise 18). Shake out when you need to, and repeat any part of your routine any time you feel you need it. You will find, as you develop your own regimen of warm-ups, that you will begin to tailor the exercises to your own needs. Never start to work without doing this exercise or some version of warm-ups.

● ● ●

Just remember: your body, your voice, and your mind must be relaxed, focused, and concentrated, ready to go to work when your director and the rest of the cast are. Whether your routine is individual or done in a group, you are the best judge of whether or not your body is relaxed and your mind ready to concentrate as the working rehearsal begins. Don't skimp on these warm-ups. If your body and mind aren't ready, then the rehearsal will not be as effective as it should be and you will not be focused on the choices you must make in a working rehearsal.

SCORING THE SCRIPT: MAKING CHOICES

In a continuation of the script-scoring process, we come now to the single most important internal step for the actor: determining individual motivational units for your character within the ensemble (the rest of the cast or just your scene partner), deciding how to externalize these subtextual units, and writing these decisions into your script.

In Chapter 3 we discussed the motivational unit and its place in the subtext, and in Exercise 27 we determined and analyzed the motivational units for the two characters in *A Mountain Holiday*. You might want to go back and review this chapter and exercise before you go on, but the important thing to remember is that the motivational unit is the smallest unit of subtext. Your director has discussed the largest subtextual unit, the superobjective, in the readthrough, or you and your partner—if you're doing a classroom scene without a director—have discussed the superobjective of your scene (and the play) in your first meeting when you read the scene together. Later on, as a transition between the last working rehearsal and the first running rehearsal, you will need to work out the spine, the intermediate subtextual level that links the motivational units into lines of action that support the superobjective. During working rehearsals, however, your task is to be sure that your individual motivational units are correctly stated within the ensemble and to make choices about the impact of these subtextual decisions on the external process.

Making choices is a phrase you will frequently hear from experienced actors. If you sit and listen to conversations between actors in the green room (the waiting room or lounge in all theaters where actors wait to go on stage) or at parties after rehearsals or performances, you will hear them endlessly discussing whether or not they have "made the right choice" or that they like what another actor is doing but they "question his choices" or that they feel the director is not properly appreciating "the choices I've made" in this or that scene. Why are these choices so important? As the preceding paragraph indicates, they are internal decisions made about subtextual thoughts and the way these decisions are reflected in the body (blocking, stance, gestures, facial expression) and in the voice (volume, pitch, inflection pattern, emphasis of certain words). These subtextual thoughts are the principal mental activity of the actor, and the external manifestations are not only the main physical activity of the actor but, significantly, the only visible and aural evidence the audience has about what the character is thinking.

Do not underestimate the importance of making choices at this point in the rehearsal process or skimp on the time to make them and record them in your script. It is very important to continue experimenting with both the internal and the external process throughout the working rehearsal period.

What are some of these choices? In the readthrough and blocking rehearsals you found out (1) who you were (various details about your character, mostly from the text itself, but you probably have also begun outside research and talked extensively to your director about characterization), (2) where you are (the director showed you a floor plan in the readthrough, and you familiarized yourself thoroughly with the set in the blocking rehearsal), and (3) what you are doing (the director included general information about the major actions in the blocking rehearsal). Now you need to go further with all of this, particularly with much more specific information about what your character is doing and how it is expressed. Explore the smallest units of action, asking yourself (and your director and/or your scene partner) very specific questions about each line or action as you go along. These questions are going to be different from scene to scene, from play to play, but here is a list of some of the choices you might make in a working rehearsal:

1. Why does my character say this line? Why did the character choose those specific words? How do I say the line to get that meaning across?
2. Why does the character perform those particular actions? How do I perform them to get that particular meaning across?
3. What is my character thinking while the other character is speaking? What sort of actions, if any, do my character's responsive thoughts produce?
4. What transitional process takes my character from one thought to another and how is this shown?

Here is another exercise scene (Fig. 6.1) to use as practice in answering these questions and making choices based on them, both internally and externally.

Once again, nothing in the scene is gender specific, so it can be worked on by any combination of men or women.

Exercise Scene for Making Choices

Shopping Around

(*A small sidewalk café in a shopping mall: two white metal tables, two white plastic chairs at each. At one table is SAL; LOU is at the other.*)

LOU: I'm sick of this mall.

SAL: Yeah. Me, too.

LOU: You work here?

SAL: Yeah.

LOU: Yeah. Me, too. (*Pause.*) The drugstore.

SAL: Excuse me?

LOU: I work at the drugstore.

SAL: Oh. Burton's.

LOU: No, the drugst . . . oh. You mean *you* work at Burton's?

SAL: Yeah.

Figure 6.1 Sal and Lou in *Shopping Around* present acting students with a wide variety of motivation unit choices as well as many changes in direction of the "spine."

LOU: Yeah? Oh, I thought you meant . . . yeah, Burton's. I buy my shoes there sometimes.

SAL: You buy there?

LOU: Yeah, I . . .

SAL: I don't know why. Stuff stinks.

LOU: Sometimes. *Sometimes* I buy there. Usually I . . .

SAL: Old people's shoes, most of it. Jerky stuff. For old people.

LOU: Right. When I buy there, it's for my mother.

SAL: You buy shoes for your *mother?*

LOU: Yeah. Right. Or my father. When I buy for them, I buy at Burton's.

SAL: Why?

LOU: Well, just like you said, they sell old folks' shoes, right? And so . . .

SAL: No. I meant, why do you buy shoes for your folks?

LOU: Because they . . . they don't get out of the house much. They . . . can't walk.

SAL: Oh, yeah? What do they need shoes for, then?

LOU: They . . . like to look nice.

SAL: Yeah? Weird. (*Pause.*)

LOU: Yeah. Well, I guess I'll . . .

SAL: I like that.

LOU: Huh?

SAL: I like that your parents are weird.

LOU: You do?

SAL: Yeah. You're probably weird, too, right?

LOU: Well . . .

SAL: I like that.

LOU: Oh.

SAL: Come on over here. I got something to tell you.

LOU: Huh?

SAL: Come on over here and sit, why don't you? Let me tell you something.

LOU: Oh. Okay. (*LOU moves to SAL's table. There's an awkward pause. LOU seems to be struggling to think of something to say.*) So . . . what did you . . .

SAL: Yeah. I thought you were weird. You don't look weird, but there was something about you. I can spot it, most of the time. Yeah . . . (*There's another long pause. LOU seems to wait for SAL to speak again, but SAL just stares at LOU.*)

LOU: Yeah. Well . . . I don't think I'm . . . I mean I'm not all *that* weird. Not really . . . I . . . (*Another pause.*) You know, I think I better . . .

SAL: By the way . . . what I wanted to say was . . .

LOU: . . . yeah?

SAL: What I wanted to tell you was . . .

LOU: Yeah? What?

SAL: I was born on Mars.

BLACKOUT

Before we go on to the next exercise, let's answer the questions that would have been discussed in the readthrough and blocking rehearsals for the exercise scene, *Shopping Around:*

1. **Who am I?** The director, in discussions with you, has told you that she sees these characters as young college students who work at part-time jobs while they go to school. Neither of them, she says, is at all remarkable looking.
2. **Where am I?** The director has told you that, as the text describes, you are sitting at two tables in an outside eating area at a typical shopping mall in any American city. She has also said it is a weekday, late in the morning, no one else is around: a sunny, warm day in spring.
3. **What am I doing?** The director has blocked the scene so that, at the beginning, the two characters are having coffee, not paying much attention to each other. Sal is reading a newspaper; Lou just sits. As the scene begins, she says, neither is paying any particular attention to the other.
4. **What is the superobjective?** The director has indicated that she thinks the scene is about loneliness: how some people seek human contact, and how others have retreated into fantasy and isolation.

We presume you agreed with your director regarding these questions (or that you and your partner have agreed if this is a classroom scene without a director), and you are ready to begin the working rehearsal; so let's go on to the exercise and explore the scene in detail, making individual choices about the subtext and its external manifestations.

● ● ●

EXERCISE 35

MAKING CHOICES

We begin this exercise by going about halfway through the scene, making the necessary choices for both characters. Then you can go through the rest of the scene by yourself, making choices for the character you're playing, or you can go through the rest of the scene with your partner, making the choices for both characters at the same time. In a working rehearsal for a real production, you will have gone through the script on your own, reviewing your lines and blocking and making some preliminary choices; then you, the director, and the rest of the cast will make these choices together during the actual working rehearsal. We need to go through both characters' lines and actions in great detail, line by line, so be sure you have prepared your script for the scene and have plenty of sharp pencils!

First Stage Direction

The script indicates the barest essentials, two tables and simple chairs in a shopping mall. The director has also stated that it is a weekday morning and the mall is nearly empty. It was also established that, while Sal was reading, Lou was "just sitting." We must decide if Sal is really interested in the reading matter or reading to avoid Lou. Is Sal reading a book, magazine, or newspaper? Let's choose a magazine. Which one? What kind of magazine would Lou (the way you want to play Lou) be reading? Let's say it's *Rolling Stone,* and we'll assume that Sal's reading it because it's interesting, not to avoid Lou. What is Lou's physical attitude? Is Lou bored? Restless? Does the character slump in tiredness or does the physical attitude seem to indicate a readiness to engage Sal in conversation? Lou has the first line, so before we decide that, let's look ahead to it.

Line 1: Lou: "I'm sick of this mall."

Let's take this at face value, text accurately reflecting subtext: Lou is bored, tired of the job, tired of the mall, wants company. So the choices for both the attitude of sitting expressed in the stage direction and the vocal reading of this line should reflect these things. You might also decide, however, that Lou is shy, so there could be a considerable pause while courage is summoned to make this conversational overture. Also, think about whether Lou blurts the line out once the decision is made to speak. Or is there an attempt at sophistication, as if Lou makes remarks like this all the time? Does Lou's voice squeak with nervousness? Or does it sound assured and practiced? An alternative here would be to play Lou as a bore who bothers strange people with unwanted conversation. If you try that, you might find it causes Lou to speak very slowly and deliberately. Try a number of alternatives like this, but for now let's go on the presumption that this first line is spoken after a pause and a bit breathlessly from nerves.

Line 2: Sal: "Yeah. Me, too."

The line is short and sounds unresponsive. Since we decided earlier that Sal is really interested in *Rolling Stone,* let's take this at face value, too: Sal doesn't want to be interrupted. Is the magazine shaken a bit in annoyance to show this? Does Sal turn away a little to avoid Lou? Is the line reading abrupt, colorless, completely disinterested? Or is it obviously angry? Let's say that Sal isn't totally rude, just doesn't want to be bothered, so the line reading is flat and colorless to discourage further conversation, and Sal does turn slightly away so as not to be bothered further.

Line 3: Lou: "You work here?"

There is no indication of a pause before this line, but, since Sal's answer to the initial question has been very low on energy, obviously signaling to Lou that Sal doesn't want to be bothered, you might take a pause anyway. Lou, as you have decided to play Lou, would need to build up the courage to speak again. You might also choose, however, for this second conversational attempt of Lou's to be stronger than the first, out of either desperation or a stab at bravado.

Line 4: Sal: "Yeah."

This is even more noncommittal, and it is even more obvious that Sal doesn't want to be bothered, isn't it? Is there another choice? Maybe Sal is just so involved in the magazine that Lou is barely heard. How would that make the reading different? Think of further variations in choice. For now, though, let's assume the most obvious: Sal really doesn't want to talk to Lou. Does Sal's physical attitude change? What if there is an even more pronounced turn away? An angry glare? Maybe Sal hunches over the magazine for privacy.

Line 5: Lou: "Yeah. Me, too." Pause. "The drugstore."

Note that the playwright writes the first word, "Yeah," as a separate sentence, not as a part of a phrase with "Me, too." Doesn't that lead you to believe that "Yeah" is read with some definite acceptance of defeat? Look for hints like this in the writing—even in the punctuation—to help you make your choices. Certainly, it would be hard to be eager and joyful after Sal's response. So let's assume Lou has gotten the message that Sal doesn't want to talk. Lou does, in a last forlorn hope, provide a little more information: Lou works at the mall, too. But there is no hint of a response. Lou then has a pause indicated in the text. Is this another chance to build up courage? Or is it despair? Courage, it would seem, because when Lou speaks again, with specific information about a job at the drugstore, it must be said definitely enough to provoke a response from Sal.

Line 6: Sal: "Excuse me?"

Sal's response could be aggressive, in which case there might be a sharp turn back in the chair toward Lou and a strong and intimidating tone to the voice. Or the response could be the vague neutral response of someone who really has not been listening. Let's presume the former: Sal has reached the end of patience and moves around to confront and bark at Lou. Sal has had enough of this invasion of privacy.

Line 7: Lou: "I work at the drugstore."

Since Sal's line was so strong, the first impulse would be to make Lou's line weak and timid in rebuff, but need it be? Perhaps Lou feels like there has been some ground gained in making friends with Sal, even if it was expressed in anger. The line might then be read with something like eagerness, face brightening and body straightening. Of course, this response, in the face of Sal's rejection, makes Lou look pretty naive and certainly not perceptive to others. Is that the impression you want to give? Let's say you and the director like that choice for the character of Lou.

Line 8: Sal: "Oh. Burton's."

If Lou's previous line is delivered with the eagerness of the truly naive, then how does Sal respond? Certainly Sal has not demonstrated naivety so far, rather the reverse, so why does the character not simply walk away in anger at having been disturbed? Well, because that's not what the script says Sal does. So, at this point, the actor playing Sal might well want to discuss the point at which the character has arrived. Have the previous choices been good ones and is there a reason for Sal's response now? Or does the actor feel that previous choices have now painted Sal into a corner: no motivation for the line the play gives the character to say. As a director,

I might ask the actor playing Sal to see Lou's persistence and simple eagerness to talk as so extreme that it suddenly seems rather amusing to Sal. Is that a possible choice here? Perhaps there is a small laugh to indicate "Oh, well, why not talk to this simple soul?" and the character of Sal might just settle down, put *Rolling Stone* on the table, and see what this conversation holds. Remember that this exercise is *suggesting* choices. Ultimately, you and your director and the rest of the cast must all agree on these decisions. So Sal decides to finally engage Lou in talk and responds with an amused "Oh . . . " and then settles back (resignedly?) to provide some starting information. An alternative choice here (which might be mixed in with the decision we just made) is for Sal to take a first real look at Lou and decide that Lou looks interesting enough (for any number of reasons: use your imagination!) to want to have a conversation. If that is true, then appropriate changes in facial gesture and the way Sal sits in the chair are called for. Sal gives Lou the name of the store Sal works at, Burton's, and settles back to talk. Presumably (because of the next line), this motivates Lou to further joy, making Lou, perhaps, edge toward Sal the better to pursue talk.

Line 9: Lou: "No, the drugst . . . oh. You mean you work at Burton's?"

And here is justification for the earlier choice that Lou is a bit simple and naive. The presumption that Sal meant *Lou* works at Burton's is so obviously incorrect that even Lou corrects it very quickly. Externals at this point are probably eager at first, then embarrassed as Lou realizes the error. There may be a shy smile on the words of the correction when Lou realizes Sal works at Burton's. And Lou might be able to relax the stance of aggression and desperation here, since Sal seems to be hooked. This, in fact, might be a major turning point for Lou.

Line 10: Sal: "Yeah."

This seems straightforward in light of previous decisions: Sal is enjoying Lou's confusion a little. There might be an amused, slightly cynical edge to the voice, a bit of a smile.

Line 11: Lou: "Yeah? Oh, I thought you meant . . . yeah. Burton's. I buy my shoes there sometimes."

Here is substantiation of the previous choice. We also get, seemingly, further relaxation of Lou: maybe enjoying Sal's smile, even at Lou's own expense.

Line 12: Sal: "You buy there?"

Based on information from Sal's next line, we know the choice here should be surprise, yes, but some confirmation for Sal that Lou is naive. Sal thinks the merchandise at Burton's is for "old people" so it confirms Sal's impression of Lou. But perhaps Sal is also intrigued, because the scene does not end here with Sal's walking out. Again, sometimes choices are made simply because that's the direction the play goes in. The facial gesture on this line might be condescending and cynically amused. Maybe he's tapping the table with the rolled-up *Rolling Stone*?

Line 13: Lou: "Yeah, I . . . "

Lou does not see the trap, goes right on with enthusiasm to explain that . . . what? That Lou does indeed buy shoes there for Lou's personal use? Is that what Lou would say if Sal did not interrupt him? Remember that all lines ending in an **ellipsis** (three dots: . . .) are either (1) lines that trail off because the character, for various reasons, does not finish the thought or (2) lines that are interrupted by the next line or action. This could be either. If it is a trail-off, it is because Lou realizes that the shoes in Burton's are not up to Sal's fashion standards and Lou does not finish the sentence for that reason; but, given we already know something of Lou's naivety, that seems unlikely. Much more likely, given Sal's aggressive nature, is that Sal interrupts Lou with a devastating response.

Line 14: Sal: "I don't know why. Stuff stinks."

Sal might be playing with Lou, but more likely this is a statement meant to be taken as evidence of Sal's omniscience in all such matters. This is probably read rather haughtily, maybe with a cool examination of the surroundings.

Line 15: Lou: "Sometimes. Sometimes I buy there. Usually I . . ."

This is quick thinking for Lou. You will need to show the audience that Lou is doing some major adjusting to the previous statement. Is Lou trying to think of further cover for the mistake? What effect might this have on Lou's face and body? Lou is already beginning to tell a lie: think of what happens to people's externals when they lie, particularly if they're not good liars.

Line 16: Sal: "Old people's shoes, most of it. Jerky stuff. For old people."

Sal is now hooked in turn. Sal obviously begins to like having an audience for these various pronouncements on matters of taste. What conclusions do we draw from Sal's use of the phrase "Jerky stuff"? What kind of characters use that kind of slang?

Line 17: Lou: "Right. When I buy there, it's for my mother."

And here is Lou's outright lie. All the previous choices let us know it's a lie and substantiate themselves as choices at the same time. Lou seems to be gathering more confidence in the lie, though, so there might be a more aggressive stance. Now, there could be a choice, I suppose, in which this information that Lou provides about buying shoes for Mom and Dad is the truth, but it doesn't seem to fit in with the previous choices we made for both characters. You will learn, as you explore choices in a working rehearsal, that they are based on each other, and, once the first are made, the subsequent ones come from them. You will want to strive for consistency in this process of making choices.

For the remainder of this exercise, continue going through this scene, making choices together (with your director if you have one) for both characters. Remember that internal choices affect your externals: think about vocal and physical choices that result from the decisions you make about internals.

Some questions to ask yourself as you proceed: Why does Sal say: "I like that your parents are weird"? Is Sal mentally unbalanced? Does Sal collect unusual people? Why? What impact does this have on externals? Is Lou telling the truth about the character's parents not being able to walk? Why does Lou become increasingly monosyllabic? Does Lou become afraid of Sal? Does Lou think the situation is out of control? Is Sal telling the truth about being born on Mars? Obviously not (unless you're making the scene a science fiction/fantasy scene), so why does Sal say it? Does *Sal* believe it? What impact does that have on Sal's externals? Is Sal saying it to frighten or confuse Lou further?

● ● ●

Once you have completed this exercise, go back over the scene and see if the choices you have made work well as they progress through the entire scene. You will only be able to determine this, by the way, if you have effectively written your choices down. Score you script well. Remember that you will want to refer back to these choices again and again, so write them down clearly and concisely. The scoring process is very important.

As you review the choices you have scored in your script, be sure they work, that you made the right choice. Be sure they are consistent within your own character and work with the other character's choices. Don't hesitate to change them if they don't seem to flow smoothly into each other. Remember: don't leave this important decision-making process until you and your director and your partner are all absolutely satisfied with the choices you all have made.

It should be fairly clear by now that the decisions you make about motivational units and the effect they and other subtextual matters have on the external manifestations of your body and voice are dependent to a great degree on similar choices being made by the rest of the cast (your partner) and on the guidance and conceptual decisions made by your director. In Chapter 3 we discussed motivational units in some detail and practiced them by using the exercise scene *A Mountain Holiday.* But determining motivational units is a product of the ensemble: you, the rest of the cast, and the director. Everyone involved in putting the scene or the play together is going to have an impact on your choices, and you and your decisions will affect everyone else. So, while you certainly should make some preliminary decisions about your own motivational units on your own time—probably shortly after the readthrough—these decisions cannot be finally made or implemented until you and the ensemble work on them together in the working rehearsal.

Also be sure to remember that those first decisions about subtext you make on your own do not usually involve extensive thought about externals. The working rehearsal, however, is the principal time to make choices about what to do with the voice and the body as well as motivational units. They go hand in hand: the subtextual decisions you and the ensemble make suggesting and producing the external decisions. Both kinds of decisions should be continually examined and experimented with during the working rehearsals: "Acting is the external manifestation of an internal process."

EMOTION MEMORY

As you begin to put your characterizational choices together in the working rehearsal, you will discover the emotional basis of the character's responses to the situations in the play. Many times these motivating emotions—so richly contained in the subtext of a good play—will be familiar to you, will be emotions and thoughts you have experienced yourself. The readthrough should provide you with a clear understanding of these emotions, but giving these emotions depth, validity, and the resonance of reality is done, for the most part, during the working rehearsal. One of the principal tools for doing this is called emotion memory.

Emotion memory operates on two levels. On the first level, the actor recognizes an emotional response of the character as one the actor has experienced in real life; on the second level, the actor recalls the real-life emotion as clearly as possible, contains it in a form that is more easily recollected, and uses it to motivate and deepen the character's emotion. Sounds like a good idea, you say, but how is it done?

● ● ●

EXERCISE 36

EMOTION MEMORY

Go back and look at the subtext of the exercise scene, *Shopping Around.* Have you ever experienced the emotions Lou feels at the beginning of the scene? Have you ever been rather lonely and wanted to start a conversation with a stranger just to have someone to talk to? If you have (and I expect most people have), go back and recall as clearly and in as much detail as possible the situation which produced that emotion. When you have remembered as much as you can, do an improvisation with your partner that comes as close as possible to the real-life situation. When you come to the moments in the improv that produced the emotions in real life, see if you can feel the emotions again, perhaps even increasing their intensity. Your partner, of course, can be thinking of similar feelings (if the actor has had them) that the actor and the character of Sal share. Perhaps your partner has been on a plane or a train and not wanted to be bothered to talk to a chatty person next to them, and so reads a book or magazine with great concentration. As the two of you do the improv from your separate points of view, pass the conversation back and forth between you, thinking about how you reacted in a similar situation. Afterward, discuss with each other what new energies seemed to come out of this improvisation, what emotions were observed, and how strong and real they seemed to be. Then go back and do the lines of the scene itself slowly, trying to find the moments in the scene that fit most closely to the real situation. Once these moments have been established, you might try running the scene without stopping and see if the emotions come easily. When you begin to work with the dialogue of the scene, though, you'll find there's a problem: how do you think the character's thoughts and remember your own experience at the same time? The simple answer is that you can't. You'll need to find a way to contain the memory of the real experience—the emotion memory—in some capsulized form so that it occupies as small a part of your concentration as possible.

Think of it as a bite of information that can be summoned at the point of the character's emotion in a way that will not be intrusive into the life of the character and your concentration on it. Some people like to turn the real-life emotion memory into a kind of snapshot—like a frozen moment in time—or even a second or two of visualized action—like a clip of movie film—that will remind them of what they felt. These condensations of emotion will intrude very little into character thought, and will be helpful in deepening and authenticating the emotional life of the scene.

●   ●   ●

Thus remembering emotional responses from your own life is very helpful, but what if you are dealing with an emotional situation in a play that you have never experienced in real life? What if you are playing a murderer or a drug addict or someone who is very ill? What if you are playing someone like Medea, who murders her own children? Well, I hope you have never had any emotional context for these feelings, so what do you do? How do you find the roots of such an emotion? In a word: research.

Observation is the actor's best research tool. One of the unpleasant side effects of becoming an actor is that you are no longer able to experience natural emotion in your own life or observe it in others without functioning, to some degree, as a recording device: observing the moment of stress, or sadness, or joy, freezing it and cataloging it in some corner of your brain for future use. The actor, in other words, must become a camera: photographing and filing moments of emotion from real life for use in the fictional life of the theater. Keep a journal.

Start today. Carry around with you a small notebook if you don't trust your memory. Every time you feel a strong emotion of any kind, write down how you felt inside and how your body responded to those feelings: how your voice sounded, what your face did, what gesture patterns your hands and arms took on, how you stood or walked or sat. Every time you see another person in an emotional situation, observe it. Do your observing with discretion and consideration, of course; don't be rude or intrude on others, but do it objectively. Take note of what physical responses the emotion brought out in other people. Write it all down in your notebook. Later, privately, see if you can duplicate that response with your own body and voice. The real emotional stimulus will no longer be present, so it will be very difficult. Just remember that the real emotional stimulus will not be present in the performance of the scene or play either. To a great extent, this is the nature of all theater, the recreation of emotion that is as real as it possibly can be under the always artificial circumstances of the stage. Emotion memory is a tool that will help you to recreate emotion accurately and authentically. An actor's journal is an invaluable way of noting and remembering emotional responses.

A note of caution here: while I am recommending you become an observer and regurgitator of real-life emotion both in yourself and in other people, don't let this habit turn you into an objective machine. Of course you must continue to react to all situations in your daily life with humanity and with genuine regard for others. We have all read of the news people who keep their cameras rolling in the midst of tragedy. Without getting into the ethics of such a situation—not the province of this book—it seems to me that dedication to one's profession has limits. Yes, you must observe and note emotion: that is your job. You are also a human being, and must continue to respond to life spontaneously and with care for others.

TRANSITIONS AND PAUSES

We have discussed motivational units—the smallest unit of subtextual emotion that an actor has—in theory and in practice. We have found the various choices that such emotions produce in the actor's body and voice. We know these subtextual units mark the changes of emotion the character feels as the play moves forward. Now we need to talk about transitions, how one goes from one motivational unit to another.

How do you get from one thought to another? Perhaps the most frequent advice I give the students in my class, the remark I make to them most often is, *"Think the thought!"*

Let's take a very simple situation: a child stands in front of a candy counter (Fig. 6.2). The salesperson says: "Which kind would you like?" The child thinks for a moment, then says: "The red lollipop." The salesperson smiles and says: "Are you sure?" The child thinks again and says: ". . . maybe the green one." The salesperson reaches for the green lollipop: "All right." Child: "Or maybe I'll have the chocolate-covered cherry . . ." Salesperson: "Why not both?" Child: ". . . I don't have enough money." Where are the transitions in this exchange? Obviously, the first one is the child making the initial decision (which the playwright

Figure 6.2 Actors have as many choices in building a character as children have in a well-stocked candy store. Choose with care.

might indicate in a stage direction similar to the words here: "The child thinks for a moment." So that's what you, the actor, must do: you must think the thought! You must actually allow the following thought in something like the following words go through your brain: "Which *do* I want? The lollipops look wonderful, but I also like chocolate. Which do I want? *Which?* Oh, I can't resist the red lollipop." Yes, this is a motivational unit, but it is subtextual to a pause; it is the thought that takes the actor from the moment of lights coming up on this simple scene through the salesperson's question to the moment of decision: "The red lollipop." It is a transitional thought, and such thoughts, usually (but not always) taking place in pauses, are as subtextually important as the lines you speak.

The salesperson's second question prompts a second transitional thought. The question is: "Are you sure?" The thought is (and you must *think* it): "Am I? I like lime, too. Maybe I like lime better. Yes. I do." This takes you to the line: ". . . maybe the green one." Incidentally, the ellipsis (. . .) before the line is sometimes a playwright's way of signaling to the actor that there is a particularly important transitional thought here: usually indecision of some kind. Another transitional thought comes before the decision to take a chocolate-covered cherry, and a most important thought, a balancing of monetary accounts before the line ". . . I don't have enough money." Here the thought might be quite long: "I only have a dime. Lollipops are ten cents, chocolate-covered cherries are ten cents. Ten plus ten is twenty. I only have ten. I don't have enough." *And that entire thought must be thought!* Those words, or something like them, literally must go through the actor's brain.

And that, by the way, is the answer to the question: "How long is this pause?" Answer: "As long as it takes to *think the transitional thought*." The younger the child in the candy store, the harder the arithmetic, the longer the pause.

As you go through your scene, writing down your motivational units, it is equally important to write down your transitional thoughts. Many actors memorize them, once the choice is made as to what they are, finding it easier to think the thought that way.

Some plays have more pauses than others. The plays of Anton Chekhov and Harold Pinter, for instance, are considered particularly rich in subtextual thought and contain more than the usual number of pauses. Many young actors find pauses difficult, probably because there are no words (and maybe even no actions) to demonstrate to the audience that they are "doing something." Pauses, however, can be just as full of information for the audience as dialogue or action. Indeed, a pause that is thought through is referred to as a *filled pause*. This filling of pauses with thought is very important and should be practiced and refined along with all your other mental and physical skills.

There is a famous scene in Chekhov's *The Cherry Orchard* in which a group of languid Russian aristocrats sit in the orchard, idling away an afternoon. The one energetic character, a peasant who has worked his way into the middle class, dominates the scene with talk for a while, then stops talking. The others chat in a desultory fashion. Then, little by little, one by one, they fall silent, too. There is quite a long pause. Even if the actors are busily thinking, some in the audience may begin to wonder: "Has something gone wrong? Has someone forgotten the line? What is happening?" Then one of the characters, the old eccentric brother, Gaev, makes the laconic observation: "Ladies and gentlemen . . . the sun has set." The audience sits back, breathing more easily, chuckling, perhaps, at this very familiar scene. "Oh," the audience says to itself, "that was it. That was why they were so quiet. They were watching the sunset. I've done that. And when I did, I was quiet, too. I recognize that pause." The pause is justified, like a tonic chord in music is resolved. We are satisfied. But only if the entire ensemble was really watching the sunset and really thinking the appropriate thoughts!

● ● ●

EXERCISE 37

FILLING PAUSES

With a partner, do an improv that establishes some facts about a sibling relationship you share: discover who is the older, who the other family members are (establish at least one other family member in some detail), how you feel about each other, and so on. Be as free as you can in providing information for each other's reactions. Once the factual basis of the family is established, set up the "who, what, where, when" framework so that the two siblings are in a waiting room in a hospital where they have been waiting for news of another member of the family who has been in a serious automobile accident. Remember, as you begin the improv, that these situations are not filled, usually, with a lot of talk. You have been in the situation for a while, have all the available information, and all that is left to do is wait. See how long you can motivate the silences that will result. See how dialogue, when it does come, is tempered by long pauses. When you have finished the improv, discuss the pauses (and the resulting dialogue) with your partner. Now both of you write down the transitional thoughts and the dialogue, memorize all of it, and repeat the improv the next day (or the day after, depending on your time schedule) as a memorized scene. Try to think the transitional thoughts as spontaneously as you did when you were improvising the scene. Can you use emotion memory? Have you had such an experience? How did you feel? Try to transfer those real thoughts to the improvised situation. When you repeat the exercise as a memorized scene, were the pauses as long as they were in the improv? Work for consistency.

● ● ●

When you have completed this exercise to your satisfaction, go back to either of the exercise scenes (*A Mountain Holiday* or *Shopping Around* or even *Romeo and Juliet*) and find the pauses, writing out the transitional thoughts, memorizing them, and applying them to a working session on the scene with your partner.

Before we leave the subject of pauses, there is a famous one I can't resist mentioning. Before the time of most of you reading this book, there was a comedy actor that some of you may have (should have) heard of: Jack Benny. Mr. Benny's character was based on the fact that, among other things, he was a miser. In one memorable moment (and you must remember that this was on radio, where there was no visual element to fill the eye or the pause), a mugger pointed a gun at Mr. Benny and uttered the familiar line: "Your money or your life!" Mr. Benny's only response to this ultimatum was a pause. As the pause lengthened (and it got quite long), the laughter grew and grew. The thought was obviously "Which do I value most, my money or my life?" and Mr. Benny was thinking it for all he was worth. Most of us, of course, would not have to think about this, which is why the pause was so in character and so funny.

Pauses, of course, are based on listening. You are either listening to the inner voice of subtextual motivation, or you are listening to other people in the scene or play. We have been talking about pauses and transitional thoughts, in which, for the most part, you are listening to your own thoughts; now we need to talk about listening to the ensemble: your partner and/or the other people in the play.

LISTENING IN THE PRESENT TENSE

Like everything else in acting, listening to what goes on in a scene or play has to be as close as possible to the real thing. What is real listening? Think of the last time you were about to take off in one of the big airliners: remember when the flight attendants demonstrated the oxygen masks and other safety equipment? Did you listen? Probably not. You should have listened, but more likely your attention was on the book you were reading, or the conversation you were having with the person sitting next to you, or the nervousness you were feeling as takeoff approached. You weren't really listening to the attendant because you felt no compulsion to do so; this was information you already knew or felt you wouldn't need, so you were mentally in a different place, thinking about something that had already happened in the past or that would happen in the future. Real listening takes place in the present.

For instance, suppose an emergency arose and the plane had to make a forced landing. In such a case, you would listen to explanations about how to prepare yourself for this dire emergency—where the exits are and what to do when you get there—very attentively indeed. You would listen as if nothing else in the world were important, and you would listen exclusively in the present tense: the instructions would be the only things to occupy your thoughts and you would hear them as for the first time. You would not be thinking fuzzily of the past or making plans for the future: nothing would exist but the present moment that is filled with the voice of the flight attendant giving you information vital to your safety and well-being and which you would be concentrating on with all your might. In the performance of a scene, listening to the others in the play must be at such an immediate level.

Of course, not all listening needs to give the impression of a life-threatening situation, or even of any particular urgency; but you must listen with the same concentration as you would if you were faced with an urgent situation. You must not be thinking of the past or of the future. You must really listen to what is being said, and you must do present-tense listening as if the words were being said for the first time.

● ● ●

EXERCISE 38

PRESENT-TENSE LISTENING

Find a partner. Decide on a subject each of you knows well, but that is unfamiliar to the other. For instance, you may know how to play the guitar but your partner doesn't. Give a short demonstration for your partner (with or without a prop guitar) in the techniques of playing the instrument. Use as many of the technical terms that apply to this subject as possible. Now, from memory, your partner should repeat the demonstration, using the language you used wherever possible. Let your partner talk to you—perhaps the subject is quantum physics—for a minute or two; then you repeat the talk. How much did each of you remember? How many of the unfamiliar terms were you able to use in the repeat? The more you remember, the more acute your listening was, the more present tense. Since you knew you were going to be called to repeat what you were being told, your concentration was sharply focused on listening. Now do an improvisation based on two guitar-playing quantum physicists. As you go through the improv, establishing any "what, where, when" you like, try to listen with the same concentration and immediacy as you did to the factual demonstrations. Evaluate each other when you finish the exercises, checking each other for present-tense listening and fact retention.

● ● ●

This first part of this exercise—listening to a recital of factual information—is not much different from the kinds of techniques you use in a lecture course on, say, American history. You know you are going to be tested on the material, so you listen with great attention. Or do you? Have you ever found that you have taken 50 minutes worth of notes which, upon reading, you discover you have no memory of having written? Where was your concentration when you took those notes? You may have been thinking of what you planned to do that evening, or what you did the night before, or any of a thousand other remote subjects. In other words, you weren't listening at all: you were automatically writing down thoughts your ears were hearing, but that were not resonating in your present-tense mind. Why not? Well, maybe the subject did not interest you, or maybe you were already familiar with the topic, or maybe you knew, somewhere in your consciousness, that you could always go back and review the notes. You were not called upon, you see, to respond to the lecture in the immediate present.

All acting, of course, calls for an immediate response. You must listen to what is being said and allow your reactions to the dialogue to show, to be manifested in the face, the body, and—in subverbal responses, perhaps—in the voice. This means that your mind must be present. It must not be thinking of thoughts that pertain to the actor: your social life, what the next scene is, why you messed up a cue in the previous scene, what your next line is . . . any *thoughts pertaining to the actor should be relegated to a separate part of the brain with other performance control thoughts!* Listen to what is being said as if you were hearing it for the first time and respond to it as the character would.

Of course, hearing a line that you have heard a thousand times in rehearsal is difficult to listen and respond to as if you were hearing it for the first time. This spontaneity of response is a grave problem in the theater. We talk more about this (as well as those performance control thoughts just mentioned) when we deal with the problems actors face in actual performance; for now, let's just say that you must find a way to create a circle of concentration such as the ones we discussed earlier that allows all previous rehearsals and performances of the scene or play to exist in a closed-off corner of your mind to which the character has no access. You must face the dialogue as the character does: spontaneously and step by step in the order in which events are happening.

SCORING THE SCRIPT: CHARTING AND VISUALIZING THE SPINE

The next step in scoring your script with the graphic directional signals you need for effective study of the text involves an awareness of the dynamics of the scene or the play: the way in which the plot moves forward and what place your character has in the thrust of that movement. You must also take into account the balance of these forces as they develop in the ensemble, not just in your part.

As we noted in the section on making choices and their effect on your voice and body, decisions you make on your own may have to be adjusted when you encounter the decisions that others—the director and the rest of the cast—have made. These adjustments are, of course, part of the group process of creating the play. Toward the end of the working rehearsal, you should be increasingly aware of the way in which the scene or the play is developing in terms of the important emotional moments that need to be emphasized for the audience and how these important moments are distributed among the ensemble of characters throughout the play. It will be very helpful to find some way to chart or graph these moments as they develop and add these visualizations to the scoring in your script.

In order to do this, you will find signs, symbols, and words you can note in the margins of your script to help you visualize the growth or flow of an entire scene, not only for your character, but for all the other characters as you interact with them. Use different colored pens to do this, choosing the most vibrant color for your own character. Find a way to demonstrate in a graphic way what you see as the dynamics of tension and rest in the scene—or the play, scene by scene—as shared by you, the rest of the cast, and your director. Try arrows of various thicknesses and lengths that express fluidity of thought and language as well as degrees of importance and emphasis; curved lines—again of differing colors, lengths, and thicknesses—to indicate the rise and fall of emotions, indecision, lyricism, and the like; emphatic punctuation marks: big exclamation points, question marks, and full stops to help you visualize where (and how) thoughts end and the next one begins. Use any graphic symbols, in other words, that will help you give shape to thought and emotion. If you can visualize the thought process with some ease and definition, it will help you as you go on to another very important step in the internal process of your role: determining the spine of your role.

The spine is the direction in which your character develops, the pattern the character follows in its growth from the first scene to the last. It is composed of the individual motivation units that make up the characterizational subtext, which come together to make some kind of directional growth pattern, and includes the all-important fluctuations in rhythm and build. Ultimately, all the spines of all the characters in the play come together to support and accomplish the superobjective of the play in just the same way that your motivational units come together to form your character's spine.

In every scene of the play, your character will start at one level, develop through a series of builds and interactions with the ensemble, and finish the scene at another level, higher or lower in intensity. Movement from level to level results from the stimulus of the subtext and spines of the other characters, causing the person you are playing to react in a wide variety of emotional response patterns. This journey of your character, this spine, will be understood by you as you develop your motivational units and as you understand, with the director's help, the larger unit of the superobjective—the overall meaning—of the play. But while you may understand the spine as part of this process, it is also important for you to be able to visualize its progress through the play—and through the scene—and charting it as part of the scoring process is the most effective way to accomplish this visualization.

What are some of the ways in which you can visualize the various components of a scene and put them into your script in graphic form? You'll want to invent your own scoring markers to match your individual needs and the needs of the particular scene you're working on, but here are a few that almost everybody can use nearly all the time.

Arrows

Arrows of various size, thickness, and, perhaps, color, chart the build of the scene in a very general way. You might indicate an increasing emotional tension by putting one arrow, then two, then three (side by side) in the margin of the script. You might also make them bolder and/or thicker the higher the emotional content. In addition to this, you will probably want to indicate changes in emotion and in intensity by using different colored arrows. Remember, this process of making the spine graphic is a device to help you in visualizing what is essentially an intellectual and emotional process. There are no hard and fast rules: whatever helps you in seeing the various builds and emotional directions should be used. The direction of the arrows is also important, of course. Most of them naturally point forward, as the character progresses through the scene, but one or two may curve backward, perhaps indicating that the character is retrogressing emotionally to a previous state in which there is, maybe, more security, so the build retreats and lessens. Sometimes, too, the arrows might curve and seem to slither through the margins of the scene, indicating equivocation or indecision. The length of the arrows is also important, indicating approximately how long an emotional state endures.

Hash Marks (/)

Hash marks are pause indicators that augment both the motivational units and the stage directions. A single hash mark is usually interpreted as a caesura, which is mostly used in the metric line of a poem, but that I find helpful in speaking prose as well. A caesura is a pause just long enough to catch a breath, or to indicate a sharp, almost imperceptible pause used for abrupt changes of emotional direction, responses to unexpected events, and the like. Two hash marks (//) indicate a longer pause, three (///) even longer, and so on.

Metric Indications

These mark where vocal stress or emphasis is given in reading a line. Most of the scenes you'll be doing will be written in prose, of course, but you may want to borrow a technique used in deciding how to read a line of verse called *scansion,* or scanning a line. Various kinds of marks are used in determining the stress pattern, but we use the apostrophe (') for an unstressed word or syllable and a hyphen (-) for a stressed word or syllable. Be very careful in scanning a line of prose. While a line of metric verse can only be read in one way, at least regarding emphasis, a line of prose can be read and stressed in many different ways. Use the stressed/unstressed markings only as a kind of preliminary guide indicating the way you want to read the line, but don't get locked into a pattern that's too rigid. Remember that spontaneity is very important in speaking dialogue, and adhering to a predetermined emphasis pattern can lead to a stilted reading. Some of you, though, may tend to read lines with equal emphasis on all the words in the line. For you, at this point in your development, scoring the line and thereby determining the location of deemphasized words or syllables may be a very effective way of dealing with this problem.

The preceding techniques are just a few of the markings you might want to use as you score your script. Make up your own as you see fit (Fig. 6.3). Remember that scoring is a preliminary indication of builds, line readings, emphases, pauses, and the like. Don't let scoring force you into treating the process too mechanically or adhering too rigidly to previously made choices just because you've scored them into your script. They may look permanent, but the essence of any creative process is development and growth, and certainly all acting must appear to be spontaneous. Be ready to adjust. If a choice, scored or not, later turns out not to work, then change it. Be thorough, but be flexible.

● ● ●

EXERCISE 39

CHARTING AND VISUALIZING THE SPINE

Let's go back to the beginning of *Shopping Around.* We determined Lou's motivational units for his first 17 lines in Exercise 35, and we made some decisions about

Terry   *Jamie*

TERRY: Shut up!
JAMIE: Stop telling me to shut up!
TERRY: I'll keep telling you to shut up as long as you keep whining!
JAMIE: I don't whine stop telling me what to . . .

(*JAMIE is cut off as TERRY rises and slaps JAMIE hard on the face.*)

Oh!

(*JAMIE collapses, sobbing. There is a long pause.*)

dim.

TERRY: Everything's going to be all right We just have to keep calm keep .
we just have to keep . a tight hold on ourselves we just have to
keep . we just have to . . .

Dim

(*TERRY stops talking, sits, looking down, twisting a ring on one finger.
JAMIE'S sobs gradually diminish and there is silence. At last JAMIE looks up
at TERRY, who does not meet this gaze. JAMIE wipes tears away with the
back of a hand.*)

JAMIE: Terry

(*Voice still choked with tears.*)

TERRY: what?
JAMIE: I'm . . . thirsty.
TERRY: That's what they all said, Jamie. That's what they all said *Silence*
JAMIE: And now they're all . . . *Silence*

Figure 6.3 When a script has been completely "scored" it is a colorful road map of symbols which help the actor in visualizing the many tasks to be accomplished. Scoring is very personal; originate unique codes and symbols that are of most use to you personally.

how the subtext influenced the actor's choices regarding externals. We also know the director thinks the scene is about loneliness and how people deal with it by seeking contact with others. So we know the subtextual details, and we know the overall goal to which the scene aspires. Your question, as the actor playing Lou, is how your character goes from these details to the overall goals: what are the actual dynamics that the emotional path takes? We won't talk in any detail about how to build a scene until we get to the running rehearsal, but you can make some preliminary decisions about the general build of this scene now as you learn how to make the spine graphic. The dynamics of the spine of each character in the scene seem to show a clear through-line of rising energy and increasing uncertainty, even fear. These dual lines of development are the link between the motivational units and the superobjective: a visualization of your character's development in the scene. Think about using arrows to chart this development for your character. Also make use of hash marks to indicate your first decisions about where the pauses are. Find phrases where you know certain words are very important and need to be emphasized; make use of some kind of metric scoring to indicate that. Score the entire scene; then go over these scoring markings as you work on the scene, incorporating them into a real and spontaneous delivery of the lines.

Here are some questions to ask yourself as you score this scene: Why does Lou seem gradually to become afraid of Sal? How do you show that? Why doesn't Lou simply leave? Is there a way to chart this response? Does Sal have some kind of hold on Lou? Is Lou so weak that Sal is able to exert any kind of hold so quickly? Might pauses indicate any of this? How should they be scored?

● ● ●

Once again, let me raise a flag of caution. Scoring is a useful tool in early rehearsals, when you are making decisions about how to externalize the all-important internal choices you have decided on. Scoring is a way of visualizing those choices. Experiment with many ways to read lines, many ways to build scenes, many ways to demonstrate the underlying emotional decisions. Change the scoring if the line reading isn't working. Be flexible. Allow the rhythm and the dynamic of the scene to develop as you go through the working rehearsal period.

In summary, the working rehearsal is the actor's most important time in the rehearsal period. It is during the working rehearsal that all the many different choices are made which determine the validity of subtext and the external ways it is demonstrated. During this period you articulate and write down your motivational units—the smallest unit of subtextual change; you determine the transitional thoughts that take you from one unit of thought to another; you search your own life for the memories of emotions similar to those of your character and let them lend depth and reality to your performance; you learn to listen spontaneously and in the present tense to the rest of the cast. It's during the working rehearsal that you chart the spine and the developing energy of the performance and make it a part of the scoring in your script, marked in the most graphic way possible with signs and signals that are meaningful to you as you work on the externalization of the internal process.

Do you remember an analogy I used earlier? I likened the brain to a computer, and in that computer the actor is gathering bits of information about the performance. The working rehearsal is the period during which most of this information is gathered: the computer is programmed. Information is fed into it that determines why something is true and how it is expressed. In the next stage of rehearsals, the running rehearsal, a different kind of information is gathered, and the program begins, creakily at first, tentatively and jerkily, to run, or at least to flow more smoothly and with gathering speed.

CHAPTER 7

• • • •

THE RUNNING REHEARSAL

If the working rehearsal is the most important time for the actor—the time when essential decisions about subtext and the external manifestations which reflect it are made—then the next stage, the running rehearsal, or runthrough, is the time for the director and the actor to work together in shaping the rhythm of the scene or play.

During these runthrough rehearsals on a production of a complete play, the director is intent on finding the rhythmic pattern of the play, and actors are intent on maintaining the integrity of their subtextual and external choices as they shape the performance to the tempos that the director is imposing. It is far easier for the more objective director to see how all the individual scenes are flowing together to form a complete picture, and how all the rhythms of the actors and scenes are balanced to provide a varied, appropriate, and interesting pattern of sound for the audience. So you should make every attempt to follow the director's tempo suggestions. If, after dedicated attempts, the director's tempo suggestions are still in conflict with your choices, then discuss the problem with the director. This, of course, applies to any performance problems, but is especially apt at this point, when the director is trying to shape the cadences of the entire play. If you are working on a classroom scene without a director, then you must still devote the last series of your rehearsals to this process of determining builds and rhythms; the only difference is that you must try to discover and measure these aspects of the scene for yourselves.

Of course, with or without a director, the actor must continue to work on choices in running rehearsals: those small, essential, detailed building blocks made in workthroughs, refining them and fitting them into the overall ensemble. But the principal task of the running rehearsal is putting the scene (or play) together: discovering when to go fast, when to go slow, when to build to an emotional peak, when to let tension ebb away. The scene or play is gradually taking shape, and you must discover exactly what that shape is and how your character functions within it.

One of the things taking shape around you is the physical environment of the play or scene. If a full play, then you may now be working on the actual stage that will be used in the performance, and you may begin to see bits of the set—partial walls or furniture or platforms—appearing around you. If you are working on a classroom scene, you probably are not working in the space in which you will perform the scene, but you will have, by now, made some decisions about what rehearsal furniture or simple rehearsal props you will use in the scene. Either way, the runthrough is the time to familiarize yourself, as much as possible, with the environment of the piece.

SENSE MEMORY

Whether you are working on a fully produced play or on a scene, you will not have many (if any) of the actual props or set pieces during running rehearsals. You will be working with rehearsal props and costumes, items that approximate those you will have in performance. You should, however, treat these rehearsal props as if they were the real thing, and to do that you will need to work on sense memory. Just as emotion memory was the ability to recall a particular emotion as you have experienced it in your own life and apply it to the emotional situation of the character, sense memory is the ability to recall a particular sensory stimulus from your own experience in the real world and duplicate the sensory response when the actual sensual input is not present.

In running rehearsals for a play, for instance, you will need to know what it feels like to walk across a room (presuming that the play is set inside a building) and open a door or a window with as much authenticity as possible. While modern technology allows set designers to build doors, windows, and walls with a fair amount of solidity, they are never going to handle with quite the weight of heft of the real thing. Actors, then, have to remember, even in performance, what the real thing feels like: how much effort is required to turn the handle, lift the window, open the door, or slam the door without having the actual resistance or weight to work with. So the runthrough is a good time to get acquainted with the physical qualities of the set, and to what degree you will use sense memory.

For instance, back in the readthrough when the director showed the cast the ground plan (floor plan) of the set, it was then only a map. Now there are actual boundaries, real chairs and tables, perhaps some platforms that will eventually become mountains, or upper floors, or just varying levels in a nonrealistic set. In the blocking rehearsals you learned where these things were, and you planned, with your director, your movement around and on them. Now you must begin to treat them as if they actually were what they represent: mountain or upper floor or stairway. You must see how much extra time and effort are required to climb the mountain, run up the stairs, or fall off the cliff. All of these things, when treated with reality, are going to affect the rhythm of the scene. In runthroughs, never fail to treat all the physical qualities of the set as if they were real. As the scene or the play begins to come together, each of these physical actions will contribute something to the overall timing and flow of the piece.

Sense memory, of course, does not only have to do with doors and windows. Are you required to drink alcohol on stage? Play a game with a ball? Eat? Fight someone? Kill someone? None of these actions can be performed quite authentically. Some, particularly anything violent, won't even come close. They must all, to some degree, involve sense memory.

● ● ●

EXERCISE 40

WORKING ON SENSE MEMORY

This exercise works best in a group, but you can certainly do it with only one partner. You can even do some of these things by yourself. If you have a group, you might want to start off with some of the physical warm-up and relaxation exercises we have already worked on. Never start any kind of work or exercise without some kind of warm-up routine for the muscles—and the voice if you use it. Once you are ready to go, sit in a circle on the floor (if there are only two of you, then face each other) and begin to pass a ball about the size of a standard beach ball around the circle (or back and forth) from person to person. As the ball moves, each of you concentrates on establishing a size, weight, and texture for it and maintaining those dimensions and qualities. Is it 15 inches in diameter? 18 inches? 24 inches? 36 inches? You will find that your hands have a tendency to contract, making the ball too small, or expand, making it too large, in the rush of the game. Also, how much does it weigh? Test this by having someone announce at some point that the ball is now filled with cotton instead of air. How does that affect the way you handle the ball? What if it were filled with wet sand? Test your response to these changes in weight and the effort required to pass the ball around the circle. Also keep in mind the texture of the ball. Is it wet or dry? Is there sand on it? Are there irregularities on its otherwise smooth surface? Are there seams? Can you feel the tube that allows it to be blown up somewhere? Try turning the beach ball into a football . . . a tennis ball . . . a Ping-Pong ball . . . a bowling ball! Each of you needs to handle the object with as much authenticity as possible. Remember how it feels to handle such a ball in real life. Next have one person in that group (class teacher? director?) change the identity of the object unexpectedly as it is passed around the circle or back and forth. The leader might call out: "Feather!" or "Anvil!" or "Cat!" or "Angry Cat!" or "Bucket of water!" or "Bucket of water without the bucket!" or any number of difficult objects to test the responses of the participants in the circle. Next you might have two people sit at a table (or make the table imaginary as a further test!) and consume a full meal. The rest of the group checks them for maintaining appropriate consistency of size, weight, and resistance of all objects. Are the people chewing as if there was really food in their mouths? Do they swallow? Are their lips parted when they drink? Think up your own variations of these sense memory exercises.

● ● ●

If you have run into a specific problem in sense memory in a scene or play, of course, you must try to tailor the exercise to the problem. One of the most frequently occurring sense memory situations is that of physical violence.

It is appropriate at this moment to interject a general warning: *approach any kind of physical action in a play with great caution.* Even the simplest movements can be dangerous if you are not aware of exactly what you are doing and who and what is around you when you do it. One of the most enduring superstitions in the theater revolves around the play *Macbeth.* I wonder if Shakespeare knew what problems he was inflicting on actors when he put so many acts of magic and violence in his play. No wonder actors treat it with superstitious awe and reverence, when it is filled with trapdoors to fall in, flailing swords and plunging lances, sleepwalking scenes where one, perhaps, cannot be quite sure where one is walking, apparitions that descend and ascend, and all manner of dangerous activity. Most plays, in fact, contain levels and stairs and dangerous objects that frequently injure actors whose minds are concentrating with great intensity on the passions of the play. Get to know your physical environment and be careful!

Many plays today contain physical violence of one kind or another. It is very important for you to plan carefully any kind of physical contact with another actor. Certainly *any kind of violent confrontation needs to be choreographed by an expert!* Most schools and theaters today have specialists in stage combat. Consult them for any kind of personal violence called for by the script. Even the simplest slap can be dangerous: ears or eyes can be injured by the smallest miscalculation or misdirection.

Of course, these actions must have the feel of reality to the audience—this is perhaps the most frequent use of sense memory in the theater today—but they must never come even close to endangering an actor. When confronted with violence in a play, either consult an expert or don't do it!

Another situation is the problem of drinking alcohol on stage. Of course, real alcohol may never be consumed on stage. I tell my students to avoid taking *anything* that will interfere with the functioning of the brain and body. You need all the concentration and clear thinking you can muster, believe me. I avoid taking even so innocent a drug as aspirin when I have to go on stage, and I advise you to do the same. *Consult your doctor with this problem if you must take medication.* Don't ever think you can lend authenticity to a scene in which alcohol is consumed by drinking the real thing. It doesn't work!

A small part of this problem is one of sense memory: the burning sensation in the throat when straight alcohol is drunk, and the dizziness and other physical symptoms that result from alcohol in the body. Mainly, however, it is an emotion memory problem. One of the most distressing things for an acting teacher to see is a student pretending to be drunk. Usually there is a fair amount of stumbling and reeling, and a predictable and never believable slurring of speech. Of course, it should be obvious to you by now that a student doing this is doing something purely external with no internal thought process to produce it. So you know this is the wrong approach. What's the right approach then?

First of all, you do need to deal with the sense memory problem that makes up part of this challenge: what is the physical effect of alcohol on the brain and body? Yes, there is a lack of coordination that results in stumbling and slurred speech among other things. You need to find out exactly what these symptoms are, how tolerant your character would be to these physical effects, and then you need to work against them! Remember that someone who is inebriated is usually trying to give exactly the opposite impression. They are trying very hard to appear sober. Use emotion memory or observation to discover how your character would react in this situation.

Many times, the easiest way to produce real tears onstage is to try not to cry. So, too, in playing the inebriate. If you really have reproduced the physical symptoms of alcohol (or drug) intoxication and are thinking the correct thoughts in character, all these things will work together toward an authentic performance. Remember: sense memory and emotion memory work together to produce reality.

While you may be working on such problems as these in runthroughs, most of them will have been attended to in the working rehearsals. Still, dealing with them in the framework of the running rehearsal may produce some changes in the rhythm of the scene and certainly should be considered.

The most frequently occurring problems in runthroughs, however, are rate, pace, and build. All of these, once decisions about them are made, need to be indicated in the pattern of your script scoring.

SCORING THE SCRIPT
Rate

Rate is the speed with which an individual actor delivers her lines. Initial decisions about how rapidly or slowly an actor is speaking within her own lines is, of course, determined by her and her director in working rehearsals. But it is not until the rest of the scene is beginning to be run something like the way it will be run in eventual performance that the director and actor can see if these decisions are the correct ones.

It has been my observation that most young actors begin their class work by speaking too rapidly. The usual reason is that they are not thinking the character's thoughts. Mostly, when this problem is acute, they are just spouting forth the memorized lines as quickly as possible without thought. From what you have read so far, you know the importance of subtext and its effect on your external choices. If you are doing this correctly and your rate is still too fast, then your scoring must be more meticulous and your approach to slowing down needs to be, at least in part, very conscious.

Before we go any further, let me reiterate that any kind of work on voice and body which is in any way remedial or mechanical is not the kind of work that can be done in rehearsal. Such work must be done outside of rehearsal on the actor's own time and the results brought into rehearsal. Having said that, however, it may be that you have to spend at least some time in working rehearsals very consciously slowing yourself down.

Whatever your technique, by the time you arrive at the running rehearsal stage, you must be able to handle your individual speeches at the rate that best serves your character choices and the director's tempo decisions. In the running rehearsals, then, you and your director can determine if all the individual rates blend together to serve the entire scene or play.

What is the importance of rate? First of all, as I have said, rate is a direct result of your internal choices: if your character is thinking slowly and meditatively, then the rate is very likely to be slow; if the character is in an urgent, stressful situation, then rate will probably be fast. In the section on scoring the script for the character spine, we talked about marking your speeches for emphasis like metric lines of verse. In general, the emphasized syllable or word is spoken more slowly and the deemphasized more rapidly. You can, of course, score with hash marks to indicate caesuras or pauses that are going to slow rate down further. Let's look at a sample speech from the point of view of rate.

What more familiar lines could we pick than those beginning Hamlet's soliloquy in which he contemplates suicide? It also happens to include phrases that can be spoken with a wide variety of rates. Let's look at it:

> To be, or not to be, that is the question:
> Whether 'tis nobler in the mind to suffer
> The slings and arrows of outrageous fortune,
> Or to take arms against a sea of troubles,
> And by opposing end them. To die, to sleep—
> No more—and by a sleep to say we end
> The heartache and the thousand natural shocks
> The flesh is heir to. 'Tis a consummation
> Devoutly to be wish'd. To die, to sleep;
> To sleep, perchance to dream. Ay, there's the rub,
> For in that sleep of death what dreams may come
> When we have shuffled off this mortal coil
> Must give us pause. . . .

Go over this speech in a good edition until you are sure what all the words mean and have a good understanding of its overall meaning. Then do the exercise.

● ● ●

EXERCISE 41

DETERMINING AND SCORING RATE

First of all, note there are some specialized techniques in the reading of Shakespearean verse that we simply ignore at this point. We are merely using the Hamlet speech as a familiar, convenient, and appropriate vehicle for examining the question of rate.

Later, when you may be called on to play such a role, I hope you will have had some specialized training. For now, however, you should simply go through the speech and make motivational unit choices (rate, of course, depends on them) and then score the lines for emphasis. You will want to be more than usually sparing of emphasized words in a speech of Elizabethan verse, marking only two to three words per line to emphasize. Here are some suggestions for the first four and a half lines that will help you with determining rate:

Line 1

You'll probably want to put hash marks before the first word. Hamlet is in a *very* contemplative mood. When you are that deep in thought, you take more time before you speak. Also try another couple of hash marks before ". . . or not to be . . ." and before " . . . that is the question . . ." because of the meditative nature of this line. All these hash marks should indicate to you that the line is to be spoken slowly. At first try speaking the line with only the words *be, not,* and *that* (in that order) marked for emphasis. There are, of course, many other ways you can read these lines. Don't be content with my choices: make your own. And don't let the fact that there are only two or three emphasized words in this line speed up your rate.

Lines 2 and 3

Now Hamlet seems to have gotten on to a faster train of thought, so there are no hash marks until after ". . . outrageous fortune . . ." and that's because there's a new idea coming. Try reading these two lines smoothly and fairly rapidly as Hamlet develops the theme of his own troubles. Mark, at first, the words *nobler, slings,* and *arrows* as the only emphasized words in the two lines.

Line 4

With a hash mark at the beginning of this line to mark the new thought, try reading this line fairly slowly to contrast with the previous two and to indicate Hamlet's fascination with his new thought that he can fight his own problems. Try marking only *arms, sea,* and *troubles* for emphasis.

Line 5

We'll deal only with the first five words: ". . . and by opposing end them." There's a hash mark at the beginning of the line to show another new thought. Now, for contrast, mark all five words as emphasized, which will lead you to read them quite slowly indeed and deliberately. Watch putting too much emphasis on the pronoun *them,* as it is such an unimportant word it could sound stilted if emphasized too much. This slowness and emphasis shows that Hamlet realizes, perhaps, the futility of fighting his problems.

Go through the rest of the speech now, making subtextual decisions and reflecting them in the rate at which you speak the lines. Remember that one of the characteristics of effective rate is variety: contrast slow with fast wherever possible. Continue, of course, to score your scripts with these rate markings.

● ● ●

Rate is, more or less, an individual decision made by the actor for the speed of his speeches. *Pace* is much more a quality of the entire scene or play, and is usually mostly decided by the director.

Pace

Pace is the overall rhythm of the scene or the play, including the rate of individual actors and the length or brevity of their characters' speeches, the length and quality of pauses, and the manner in which cues are picked up by the responding actor. Just as good rate is characterized by contrasting slow with fast speech, the director will be working to see that the rhythm of the scene or play varies, and, of course, is in keeping with the emotional content of the subtext and with the meaning of the text.

We have just finished discussing the rate of the individual actor, and we have previously examined the role that pauses and their length play in developing the rhythm of the play. Now we need to talk about cues: how their treatment can be the most influential single element in pace.

In Chapter 6 we noted that lines ending in the ellipsis (. . .) are either lines the character allows to trail off from indecision or any number of other reasons or are lines that are interrupted by the succeeding line. Trail-offs, it can readily be seen, slow the pace of a scene down, as the character's indecisiveness will take more time than if the character finished the thought promptly. An interrupt, on the other hand, will obviously speed the scene up, as the impatience of the character who does the interrupting indicates that there is no pause of any duration at the end of the preceding line.

So a scene with a large number of trail-offs, of indecisive, vague endings to one or more of the character's lines tends to be slow, filled with the pauses that such uncertain line endings dictate. But if one of the characters is constantly interrupting the other's lines, then the scene will move much faster, and if two or more characters are busily interrupting each other, then the scene will be faster still. If two or more characters speak at the same time (and this sometimes happens, either shown in the text by the playwright or indicated by the director), then we have the fastest possible pace for a scene (Fig. 7.1).

A scene in which there are a large number of interrupted lines is said to be dovetailed, or telescoped. Be aware that not all dovetailed lines are indicated in the text by the ellipsis. The director will sometimes work with an actor to push the pace along a bit faster by having the actor begin to speak his line several words sooner than the end of the preceding line. Sometimes, as we mentioned, the director will even have the actors speak two or more lines simultaneously— although care must be exercised here by both actors and directors to see the audience doesn't feel it is missing important words. Dovetailed scenes are very interesting, and can often lend an air of immediacy and urgency to a scene.

There are several things to remember when you are working on a dovetailed scene. The first is that the actor whose speech is interrupted must continue to speak until the force of the interruption makes him stop talking. This means there will be at least a few words that will be spoken simultaneously. If the interrupted line ends in an ellipsis, then the interrupted actor must create the words which would have finished the sentence so that, if, by some chance, the interrupting actor fails to come in at the right time, the interrupted actor is not left hanging. Second, the interrupting actor must decide, usually in conjunction with the director, what the new cue will be. Obviously, the last word in the interrupted line is no longer the cue, and a new word must be designated as the cue for the interrupting actor to begin to speak. How far back into the interrupted speech the cue is moved will, naturally, determine how fast the pace will be in the scene. Let's look at an example.

CHARACTER A: . . . I'm tired. I think I'll . . .
CHARACTER B: What? You'll have to speak up.
CHARACTER A: If I don't get some sleep pretty soon I'm just going to drop. How can I go on? There's just no . . .
CHARACTER B: I can't make head or tail of what you're saying. Why do you talk like that? Are you sick?

Figure 7.1 Even the shortest exercise scene contains conflicts and choices that must be worked out, concentrated on, and gone through over and over again.

CHARACTER A: I give up. I just don't want to go on anymore. I'm just going to . . .
CHARACTER B: Oh, this is very frustrating. I don't understand you. Do what you
        want to do. I'm going to bed.

How many ways can this short exchange be played in terms of pace? If all
the ellipses are read as trail-offs, then, obviously, the scene will be quite slow.
It will also mean, incidentally, that neither character is communicating well with
the other, hardly listening at all, in fact. It could also be played with Character
B doing all the interrupting. This way the scene will be faster, but it places the
burden of aggression solely on Character B. If this works with the subtextual
choices the actor has made, that's fine. Finally, both characters could interrupt
each other. This is the fastest way to play the scene, of course, and it puts the
burden of aggression on both characters. The actor playing Character A, of
course, will have to decide what the rest of the interrupted lines should be, since
the playwright ends all the lines with the ellipsis. The actor playing Character B
will have to determine what her new cue is. She will have to back that cue far
enough back into the line to allow the interrupt to be effectively heard as such.
She might take the word *think* as her cue in Character A's first line, the word
There's in Character A's second line, and the word *anymore* in Character A's third
line. There are other choices for Character B's cues, of course, depending on
how fast you want the scene to go. Remember that the interrupted character
continues to speak (ellipsis or not) until the force of the interruption dictates that
the character would stop speaking. This kind of pace analysis can be very time
consuming, but it is essential if the scene is to sound spontaneous and alive.
Experiment! Don't be satisfied with your first choice.

● ● ●

EXERCISE 42

PACE VARIATIONS

Go back to one of the exercise scenes, *A Mountain Holiday* or *Shopping Around*,
and determine where pace needs to move rapidly or slowly. Find subtextual evidence to motivate your pace decisions. Score the script with hash marks, arrows,
and/or emphasis marks to indicate your pace decisions, if you haven't already done
that. Remember that in both of these scenes there is one character who seems to bear
the burden of aggression more than the other. Does this give you a direction to go
regarding interruptions? Always be certain that any external decisions you make are
firmly grounded in subtextual justification. Be sure to mark the new cues for interrupts. Change the spine markings for intensity and build or add new ones as you
work on the scene from this point of view.

● ● ●

You should see by now that pace and rate go hand in hand. Remember that
rate is more an individual actor's decision and tends to be determined in a
working rehearsal; pace tends to be set by a director in a running rehearsal.
Again, if you have no director, as is usually the case in the classroom scene, you

will have to make pace decisions yourself. This is good training, however, and helps you to be objective about your scene.

Don't forget the importance of subverbal responses as you work on pace. Most of the time a playwright will not actually write the words that suggest these responses into the script. The "uhs," "ahs," and "ums" and sighs, grunts, and groans that are a natural part of human communication will very often have to be put in by the actor. You will begin to think about these subverbals much earlier, of course, as you begin dealing with line reading choices; but, by now, they should be very much an important part of your pattern of responses.

Now we need to look at how both pace and rate work in conjunction to support and motivate the natural emotional build of a scene.

Build

Drama is based on conflict of one kind or another. From the life-or-death consequences of tragedy, to the suspense of cliff-hanging melodrama, to the mishaps and confusions of comedy, conflict changes the lives of the characters of a play, pushing them from one situation to another, accumulating energy, and carrying the audience along on a roller coaster of emotional accumulation. The ride ends, of course, with the resolution of the plot and the release of tension. Until that moment of release, however, the dynamics written into the text by the playwright must be guided by the director, if there is one, and controlled by the actor. The controlled release of this energy must be carefully planned and rehearsed both internally and externally by the actor, but must appear, in performance, to be happening spontaneously and naturally: this is *build*.

The key to the effective building of a scene is, first of all, the complete understanding of the text and subtext, and, second, variation of the emotional content so that no one level of energy is maintained for too long. Beat a bass drum loudly three times and you have my attention. Beat it ten times and you've begun to irritate me. Beat it for fifteen minutes and I've either left the immediate vicinity of the noise or have tuned it out.

Go back to the end of Chapter 6 and look at the work you did on *Shopping Around* when you began to score it for the spine of the scene. In making those decisions about the spine, you had to deal, to some degree, with the idea of building the scene. But you could not determine the final build pattern until now, until you had established the rhythm of the lines—the pace and rate—and experienced, in a runthrough, the kind of emotional feedback you would be getting from your partner and/or the rest of the ensemble. Now, with all of those pieces of the puzzle in place, you can begin to make some intelligent and concrete decisions about the build and release of emotional energy. You will need to decide three things in order to chart the build of the scene effectively:

1. what kind of emotion is being dealt with,
2. how much energy is involved, and
3. exactly when and to what degree the individual units of that emotion are released.

We dealt with the kind of emotion contained in the line when we established the motivational units. Go back and reexamine the subtextual units for *Shopping Around* as you established them for Exercise 35; be sure you remember what the character was thinking at any given moment in the scene.

To accomplish the second step, go back to Exercise 39 and review the scoring of the scene when you established your character's spine. Look at the direction of the arrows and be sure you remember what they meant. They were supposed, at that point, to give you a general idea of the emotional direction of the scene and how much energy was contained in each step in the development of your character.

Once these two steps are done (or reviewed), we are ready to go to the final step in establishing the build of the scene. The simplest way to determine the precise elements of build is to indicate, next to the arrows you used when you scored the scene, some kind of numerical equivalent of the amount of emotional energy that is being expended at any given time. Remember, you know in detail what kind of emotion you are dealing with—the motivational units tell you that. And you know the general direction of the emotional build—the arrows visualizing the character spine give you that. Now establish a scale of, say 1 to 10 that charts the emotion in terms of size or magnitude. Let's say the emotion is simple anger. The scale, with anger at the middle, might look like this:

1: mild annoyance;
2: growing irritation;
3: acute displeasure;
4: red-faced indignation;
5: full anger;
6: high wrath;
7: burst of red-hot temper;
8: explosion of outrage;
9: towering, shouting rage;
10: blind, violent, volcanic fury.

The first thing you will have to do is decide exactly what each of these degrees of anger means in terms of magnitude and what they sound and look like when put into practice.

● ● ●

EXERCISE 43

DEGREES OF EMOTION

With your partner, do some relaxation and centering exercises. Now face each other with one partner facing a blackboard where the scale of anger is written (or simply have that partner hold a piece of paper with the scale on it). The partner slowly reads the words that compose the scale, preceded by the number on the scale. At each level, the other partner repeats the word describing the emotion, but using an energy level that is appropriate to that point on the scale. Use voice and gestures, but don't move around the room. Find the energy for the emotion deep within you and let it come out only to the level indicated. When you have gone through the scale, discuss with your partner whether or not the energy was appropriate to the level. Did you peak too early? Did you never reach what should have been level 10? Did two or more levels seem to be exactly the same? Now swap and allow the reading partner to do the exercise. You can also experiment with other simple emotions: sorrow, joy, bewilderment. You can even do this exercise with something very basic such as simple laughter, increasing the degree of laughter as your partner says the numbers from 1 to 10. Use emotion memory to be sure that the emotion you are dealing with is fully motivated.

● ● ●

This exercise is useful if you need to loosen up and feel free in the display of emotion. Most of my students who are very new to acting think they are demonstrating considerable emotion, when what is actually coming out is fairly gray and passionless. If this exercise is done in class, try spotting this problem in others and, if possible, be able to demonstrate the full range of emotion when it is your turn.

Now go back to your scored script and examine the arrows you put in earlier to indicate the flow of emotion in your character spine. Compare the arrows to the motivational units on the other side of the page. At the top of the page list the simple form of whatever emotions are dealt with in that section of the scene: confusion, loneliness, boredom, irritation. For each of those emotions construct a 1 to 10 scale that further delineates the emotional state. Next to the arrows, write in the number corresponding to the graphic indication that the arrows make: number of arrows, their thickness, color, or any other device you have used to indicate increasing energy.

Another term connected to build is topping, which is simply the increase of emotional intensity from line to line until top emotional magnitude is reached. Topping is really only feasible if each character is speaking in very short lines. Then the topping is shared from actor to actor until the peak is reached.

At this point your script for this scene is fully scored. Go over the scene again, in runthrough, with your partner. Work the various builds until you are both (and your director, if you have one) satisfied with the overall build of the scene.

An element that might affect pace and rate, which should be mentioned before we leave this section, is what I call *searching for words*. This simply means that there are sometimes pauses—usually not written in by the playwright— which indicate that the character must think for a bit before finding the appropriate word to express what he's thinking. Remember that actors learn words; characters think of them spontaneously as they progress from stimulus to stimulus. Find the places where your character needs to search for just the right word, and take the thought pause that will allow you to do this. New actors usually have to be reminded to do this, and it does affect rate and pace. Experiment with searching for words with your director or partner and see how the rhythm is affected.

In this chapter, we have added the problems of rhythm and dynamics to all the material we have already worked on. Always remember that, though these aspects of the scene—rate, pace, and build—can seem very external and technical, they are always firmly based on the internal work that came first: the understanding of the text and subtext.

Before we move on to the all-important stage of the performance, let's review what we've done so far.

In the *readthrough* you gained a complete understanding of the text, its language and meaning. You also prepared your script for study and were working on learning your lines. The director, if you had one, showed you what the basic set would look like; if you had no director, you determined that for yourselves.

In the *blocking rehearsal* you were given the directions that showed you where you were on the set at any given time and you wrote them in your script. If you had no director you determined these physical movements for yourselves. You began to relate these moves to what your characters said in the dialogue.

In the *working rehearsals* you began to learn how to warm up your body and voice before rehearsals. You also began the very essential work of determining the motivational units that make up the subtext for your character's lines. You made choices about how these units would be externalized. You learned about listening, pauses, and transitions; you began to make decisions about the emotional direction your character takes within the play: the spine of your character. You scored your script with all this information.

In the *running rehearsals* or *runthroughs* you made much more detailed decisions about the emotional build of the scene or play and also determined its overall rhythm: its rate and pace.

If you have done thorough and detailed work at each of these stages, then you are now ready to take the final steps. Before we discuss some of the aspects of performance, however, let's take a brief look at the next step in rehearsing: technical and dress rehearsals.

CHAPTER 8
● ● ● ●

THE TECHNICAL AND DRESS REHEARSALS

If you are working through this book while you are preparing a classroom scene—as most of you probably are—then the material in this chapter will not be immediately applicable, but will be very useful later on. Scenes in a beginning acting class are, of course, not produced in any sense of the word: there's no attempt at costuming, makeup, scenery, lighting, or sound, and no props except for the most minimal kinds of rehearsal props.

In fact, I do not allow the students in any of my acting classes—beginning, intermediate, or advanced—to make use of these things except at the most basic level. I want the acting class student to try to avoid the pressures of the performance situation, and I encourage them to think of the classroom as a laboratory where they can experiment and take chances. I feel very strongly that the classroom is the students' workshop: a place where you are allowed to fail to accomplish your goals *if* that failure is the direct result of taking risks, of making courageous and committed choices. Soon enough you will find yourselves in front of an audience, and this public witness will tempt you to play it safe for fear of public failure. You will have a lot at stake in public performance, and you may fall victim to the stress of public exposure; perhaps you will not want to take the kinds of chances there that you can in the classroom. We deal with some of the problems inherent to the performance situation in the next chapter. Just remember, anything that introduces performance tensions to the classroom scene is to be avoided, including such physical enhancements as lights, props, and costumes.

In my classes, scenes are performed under standard fluorescent lighting, using only the barest of rehearsal furniture: classroom chairs, a rehearsal sofa and table, and a collection of black carpet-covered blocks that our scene shop constructed for this purpose. These blocks are very useful. They are cubes measuring 18 inches to a side and can be made into beds, tables, benches, platforms, mountains, or any kind of structure needed for a scene. The actors are told they may wear any kind of garment to which they have access that will allow them more easily to think or move as their character. Rehearsal props are allowed only to give actors physical objects to handle. In other words, costume and prop pieces are permitted if their presence will help the students with acting problems on which they are currently working, but not permitted if their sole function is visual enhancement for the audience. Scenes are not applauded in my classes: critiques, not applause, follow scenes.

But many of you will be going through a program of study in colleges and universities with active public production schedules in coordination with your classes, and a fair number of you will be participating in these productions, which will, of course, have technical and dress rehearsals. So let's spend some time talking about what goes on in these rehearsals—held just after the runthroughs and just before performances—even though this information doesn't apply to your classroom scene work. You'll need the skills discussed here someday.

THE TECHNICAL REHEARSAL

As we noted earlier, many productions tend to accumulate the physical environment of the set around them in the last stages of runthroughs—some even earlier—but sometimes, particularly in professional theater, the actors work in rehearsal spaces throughout this period and do not encounter any production aspects until the technical rehearsal. Certainly, this technical rehearsal is the first time actors find themselves working in the lighting that will be used for the production or using many of their actual props. The technical rehearsal, however, is not primarily for the benefit of the actors.

Technical rehearsals enable the director and the designers of a production to see how the set, lighting, sound, and props work together. Many times there will be a series of dry run, or pretech rehearsals before the tech, in which the director and the designers and crews involved in these production aspects spend long hours working without the cast. During the dry run, they set the cues and levels for light and sound, trying to determine how set pieces and props will work in the midst of the highly organized chaos of the backstage running of a production. In these dry runs they make as many decisions as possible in anticipation of the technical rehearsal. Eventually, however, the director, designers, and crews need the actors to be present to test these elements under actual performance conditions.

So one day toward the end of the runthroughs, you see on your rehearsal schedule that you have a call for a technical rehearsal on a certain day at a certain time. What can you expect? How should you prepare? What do you do when you get there?

Well, perhaps the first thing to say about the actors' part in technical rehearsal is stay quiet, stay available, and stay out of the way. Remember that, while the actors may be necessary at this point, this rehearsal is primarily for the director, designers, and crews to view the effect of these various design elements on the action: for this rehearsal, actors are surfaces off of which to reflect light, objects on which to focus light; hands to operate (or pretend to operate) light switches on the set or to carry props from one place to another; bodies to sit in chairs, open doors and windows, climb stairs; and ears to listen to and respond to sounds and music. These tasks frequently require multiple repetitions, depend on sometimes balky electronic apparatus, and require complicated communications among teams of people for their proper execution. Because of these elements, things frequently go wrong and thus tempers are apt to flare: don't add to the tension by not being where you are supposed to be at a certain time or by being in the way or, above all, by treating this rehearsal as a social occasion at which you are allowed to chatter with fellow cast members. It is true you are not required to work at performance-level energy, but you are still working. As always, do your job professionally: stay quiet, stay available, and stay out of the way.

There are several ways a technical rehearsal can be run, but perhaps the two most common techniques are the cue-to-cue technical rehearsal and the technical runthrough. The *technical runthrough* is only for a technically very simple play, in which the few sound and light cues can be worked out beforehand. Then, a simple runthrough with a few stops, perhaps, to set a cue will often suffice. It would be nice if all techs were that simple, but the unfortunate truth is they are not. Most shows are complicated enough to require the cue-to-cue rehearsal.

In a cue-to-cue rehearsal, the stage manager takes the company through only those sections of the text that have cues affecting lights, sound, set changes, and properties. If the play is a relatively simple one in which the lights come up at the beginning of a scene and the lights go down at the end of the scene, there are not too many sound cues, little or no set change, and the actors handle only a few objects on the set, then there is little to be done and the tech rehearsal should be fairly stress free. The stage manager and the light board operator run through the process of bringing the lights up and down on cue, establish sound cues with the actors, work through any set change, familiarize the cast with the few props and, if it all works properly, that's all there is to it. Of course, this is almost never the case. Inevitably, there are changes in lighting during the scene: the sun sets, lamps are switched on, the level and tonal quality of the light changes for the sheer theatricality of the scene; or a large number of complicated props are handled: books are read, cigarettes are lit, food is eaten, objects are broken; or music is played or telephones rung or thunder crashes are heard and frequently cue lines and action. Any of a thousand technical happenings will need to be worked on: cues set, levels set, actors worked with. In the midst of staying quiet, staying available, and staying out of the way, there is plenty of work for the actor to do.

The Actor and Lights

You should become aware of the way the stage is lit and your place in the pattern of light (Fig. 8.1). Some actors speak of finding their light, which simply means making sure, if you are meant to be the focus of an action and need to be seen clearly by the audience, you are centered in the pool of light cast by a particular lighting instrument or group of instruments. Some beginning actors may find this a little difficult at first, but after a while you will become accus-

Figure 8.1 Actors must be able to find the light that has so carefully been provided for them, but this must be accomplished as if it were the most natural of events in the real world.

tomed to the process and will be able to find and stay in the light with no difficulty. A warning: don't look directly up into the lenses of the lighting instruments to see where they are focused. First of all, this is not the most satisfactory way of finding your light, and second, it's harmful to the eyes: you'll find yourself having trouble seeing for a while, with the ghost images of filaments stamped on your retinas. If you should need to look up at the flies, beams, or light bridge (all possible locations of lights) to locate the actual lighting instrument itself, shade your eyes when you first look, then carefully examine the positions of the lights without looking directly into the lenses. You won't be able to find your light by standing in the middle of a pool of light on the floor, either. If your feet are in the middle of the pool, then because of the angle of the light, chances are your upper body isn't—your face might be in complete shadow.

The best way to find your light, I think, is to be sensitive to the amount of light on your face. Unless the instrument is very close to you (and it shouldn't be) you won't actually feel the warmth of the light—though some actors express it that way. What you're sensing is the reflection of the light off the skin of your face. Since the face is likely to be the part of your body on which the light is meant to focus, this is generally a good measure of having found your light. As you walk through the various light cues of the technical rehearsal, one of your jobs is to discover exactly the places you need to stand or sit in order to be most effectively lit and therefore seen. You can also hold a hand in front of your face to test the brightness of the reflection. Once you've found the light, orient yourself to furniture or set pieces so you can find it easily again. This process may require some minor adjustments to the previously learned blocking pattern. If it does, consult with the director to be sure the new position is all right. Don't be afraid to ask the director questions as you go along. He will be busy, so you need to be efficient and considerate in the asking, but if you need help finding your light or need to ask if you are a focus point in a scene where you don't feel adequately lit, then by all means do so. Even though the director is occupied with other things, the best time to ask questions like this is just after the particular cue seems to be set. Most directors will keep in touch with the cast during this process, making sure that all their questions are answered.

Another problem for actors during a technical rehearsal is turning lamps and other onstage lights on and off. Sometimes the lamp or other light source will be *practical*, which means that when the actor works the switch on the lamp or a light switch on the wall, the light comes on as a direct result of the actor's action. Much of the time, though, the actual turning on or off of the light is controlled from the light board, and the actor simply places her hand on the switch, not really operating it. In this latter case, it is very important to remember not to move your hand from the light switch until the light has come on or gone off. In real life we frequently turn lights on or off very quickly, just flicking the switch and walking away. Sometimes it takes a bit longer than this when the switching action is performed by an actor and the electrical current is turned on by the light board operator; sometimes there are mistakes, late cues, and you need to learn to deal with these. So when you are performing these actions, simply motivate a reason for leaving your hand on the switch until the light comes on or goes off. You'll work with these kinds of cues for the first time in a tech rehearsal, and you'll help everything to move along smoothly if you are ready for such problems.

One of the principal jobs of the tech rehearsal is the verifying of cues. Long before the actual rehearsal, the stage manager has written into her copy of the play all the cues that she must call over her intercom system to the light and sound operators, as well as any assistants she has on the stage to make set changes and so forth. The stage manager's copy of the text is usually called the *prompt script*, although the stage manager function of prompting an actor who has forgotten his line—*gone up* as it is sometimes referred to—is almost never needed these days. Although these cues are in the prompt script, they need to be checked with the actors *walking through* (performing actions at performance pace but not at performance-level vocal or physical energy) the action of the scene. If the cues work as written, well and good; if they do not, for any of a number of reasons, then they or the actor's action needs to be adjusted. Sometimes these cues are very important to the actor's performance and, sometimes, to his actual safety. Let's look at a number of ways in which this process of verifying cues affects the actor.

Let's say you are the first person on the stage at the beginning of a play, and your first entrance is down a flight of stairs; the cue for this action is also the cue for the lighting of the stage; and finally the cue is a sound cue: the end of the opening music. Fine. So you're waiting at the top of the flight of stairs to make your entrance and you hear the end of the music cue, the curtain rises . . . and there is no light. What do you do? You wait. Never perform an action that has the slightest chance of being dangerous, and walking down a flight of stairs in the dark certainly is. If you are in place and ready, you will not be blamed for not making your entrance in such circumstances. In a tech rehearsal, particularly, you can count on the stage manager calling a halt to the proceedings the minute she perceives there has been a foul-up. You might speak your line, if you have one, just to let the director know that you are there and know your cue, but don't go down the steps until the cue is adjusted (Fig. 8.2).

All right, suppose the lights come on the next time this is tried, but the music doesn't end? You perform your action: go down the stairs as blocked, since there is no safety hazard. Try waiting for the sound to stop to speak your line, but if it goes on too long, speak it anyway. Go on with lines and action, waiting for the stage manager to stop the rehearsal. Actors do not stop a tech rehearsal any more than film actors call "cut" on a movie set.

Let's say that by the time you reach the bottom of the stairs there is a second light cue that changes the lighting pattern on the stage; the second cue comes when you're halfway down the stairs, or doesn't come until you've finished coming down the stairs and doing something else, or doesn't come at all! What do you do? You go on, wait for the stage manager to stop the rehearsal, and see if the director wants to adjust your blocking or if the cue needs to be changed in some way. These kinds of adjustments continue throughout the tech rehearsal.

Figure 8.2 An actor waiting for a cue must be poised for action and fully concentrated on the job at hand. Remember that all the technical problems that set, props, lights, and costumes present in the tech rehearsal must be mastered *in addition* to all the tasks the actor has worked on for so long in previous rehearsals.

The Actor and Sound

Sound cues can cause other problems. Suppose the stage telephone rings and your action is to pick it up and start to speak. In our technologically advanced age, stage telephones may sometimes be wired in such a way that they stop ringing as soon as they're picked up, just as real ones do. But sometimes (particularly in university or community theater, where budgets may not quite extend to the more advanced sort of telephone), the bell is run separately from the sound booth. Under these conditions, sometimes, the actor picks up the phone, starts to speak—and the telephone rings again. What do you do? You go on speaking until the stage manager stops the rehearsal to fix the sound cue. To help avoid this situation, as with light switches, don't just pick up the phone as soon as you get to it. Find a motivation for delaying your cross so that you arrive at the phone just at the end of a ring. Then maybe you'll have to motivate holding your hand on the receiver for a moment or two until a ring stops and the sound operator has a clear view of your hand about to pick up the phone. Incidentally, if, in performance, there is a blatant error such as the phone ringing after you've started to speak, ignore it. The audience may laugh, but they'll quickly forget. We discuss such situations in more detail in the next chapter.

Talking on the phone requires you to "hear" the voice on the other end. The pace and the length of the pauses in your conversation may be slightly faster than in real life, but you've got to hear the other person and leave believable pauses for their replies. You should have worked this technique out in your working sessions, even though you probably did not have a real phone to use then.

You might not realize it, but push-button phones are a great boon to actors. Audiences notice very small mistakes and omissions, and will usually count the number of digits you enter on the phone pad. In the old days of dial phones, the dialing of seven numbers sometimes seemed to go on forever. Buttons can be pushed much faster and more easily.

Setting the level of sound is a very important function of the tech rehearsal. One of the few times in a tech when the director may ask you to work at performance level is if you are speaking at the same time as a sound cue. The director must hear your voice as the audience will hear it in order to know at what level the recorded sound must be set. Don't waste unneeded vocal energy at any other time, though. The same process would occur if the sound or music is performed live. The only difference would be that the orchestra conductor or the person (actor or crew member) performing a sound effect would be the one responsible for adjusting the level of the sound.

Sound can be tricky when it is the cue for you to speak or perform some action. You may need to adjust the pace of your performance when you hear the actual sound cue. Perhaps you will need to think about cueing your line in sooner, or wait until the cue is completely finished before you speak or perform your action. So you may discover in tech rehearsals that cues which have been long set may need to change or be adjusted. Be flexible and adapt to the new situation. Of course, any such adjustments should be made only in consultation with the director.

The Actor and the Set

The set itself can present many challenges to the actor at a technical rehearsal. Certainly, the rehearsal room where you have been working has had some approximation of the set; or, if you have recently been working on the stage itself, you may have had some of the more important actual set pieces to work with. But now everything is put together: you must work with the set while it is being lit and in conjunction with the sound.

Any variation in the level of a set can present particular problems: a staircase, platforms of varying heights on a nonrealistic or exterior set, trapdoors— anything that requires the actor to move vertically from one level to another can be tricky and, sometimes, dangerous. The technical rehearsal is the time to be sure you know how to deal with these levels; the next time you are confronted with them you will be thinking of other things, notably all the characterizational internals and externals you have put so much time and effort into during the preceding weeks of rehearsal. So be sure you use the tech rehearsal to gain a thorough knowledge of such irregularities in the set. And be sure you know what you're doing before you leave the problem. If it's a flight of stairs, go up and down them several times so that you familiarize yourself with the height of the steps, the surface of the treads, everything about them: program their peculiarities into your computer.

If there are levels requiring you to make vertical steps higher than 6 to 8 inches, you will have to pay special attention to how this is done. Climbing? See how long it takes and what effect it has on the rate or pace of your scene. Crawling through a window? How exactly is it done? Anything on the set that requires special physical effort to accomplish must be planned so that the action can be done without causing harm to the actor or to the performance. As grueling as technical rehearsals can be, it is better to spend the time on these matters as they are come to, rather than leaving them for later rehearsals, where other problems need to be addressed.

At a tech rehearsal you are probably working with the real furniture (presuming your play is set inside a room) for the first time. You need to familiarize yourself with the way the chairs, tables, sofas, beds, or rugs of this room relate to the actions you must perform in, on, and around them. Is the sofa softer than you expected and therefore difficult to get out of, making it impossible for you to maintain the pace the director wants from you? Try it a couple of times and see if it's just a matter of getting used to it. If it really is a problem, talk to the director about it and see if they can firm the cushions up. Do the rugs slip under your feet? Ask the stage manager to tape the rug down. Such things can be dangerous and the stage manager will want to make the set safe.

In a tech rehearsal, there is a very definite chain of command that must be followed if anything needs to be altered. Actors should always direct questions concerning performance modification to the director; requests for minor safety measures should be reported to the stage manager or his assistant. Actors usually do not communicate questions or comments to crew members: they have their own supervisors to whom to report and who are taking notes on anything that goes wrong. Follow the chain of command. That way everybody is informed of all the problems and the proper levels of authority are maintained. When you get to the professional level, you will find that there are very strict union rules in these matters that technical people as well as actors are bound to obey.

The Actor and Properties

Properties can be the most important part of a tech rehearsal to an actor. If the play you are in requires you to handle a good many props—if you must eat, or play cards, or get dressed, or make your face up, or cook, or any of a thousand other tasks involving properties—then the technical rehearsal is the time to become familiar with the props involved. Learn where they are going to be found (either on the set or offstage if you bring them on), where you return them (again, onstage or off if you take them off with you), and any special considerations that must be observed in the handling of props.

Before we go any further, let's examine the various categories of props. These distinctions can vary from theater to theater, but properties are generally divided into four groups.

1. *Stage props* are the objects that remain permanently on stage as part of the set. They include furniture items such as chairs, sofas, and tables, as well as books, pictures, and ornaments—sometimes called *set dressing*—which are not usually handled by the actors, or at least not removed from the set by them.

2. *Hand props* are stage props that are used by the actors but usually stay on the set. Hand props may include food and eating utensils, books and magazines, ashtrays, candles, and so forth.

3. *Personal props* are items that are brought onto and/or taken off the set by the actors. These props may include money, cigarettes, matches, watches, canes, umbrellas, and the like.

4. *Costume props* are accessories to the costume the actor wears, including jewelry, fans, handkerchiefs, medals, and ornaments of various kinds.

Stage props are usually a part of the design of the set and may remain there at all times; they are the responsibility of the prop crew and, if they are removed from the set each evening, this is done by them. You should familiarize yourself with them, but don't move them around or take them off the set unless it is part of your action.

Hand props and personal props are the responsibility of the properties crew and are set out each evening by them on *prop tables*. These prop tables are located offstage at a place convenient to actors making entrances onto the set. They are large tables—there's usually one on each side of the stage—organized to indicate clearly the nature of the prop and, usually, which actor or character uses it. These tables are often covered in brown paper with the silhouettes of the prop outlined on them in black marker for easy identification.

Costume props are maintained and set out by the costume crew. They are usually put into a drawstring bag that is hung with the actor's costumes. The actor must look as if handling the costume prop is easy, as if from long habit. Use the costume prop until you are very familiar with it, but always return it to the bag or to a costume crew member at the end of the rehearsal. These props will probably not be available until the dress rehearsals.

Actors have certain responsibilities for their props. Any personal prop you pick up from the prop table must be returned there by you after you have used it. The only exception is if you give the prop to another actor on stage, when it becomes *that* actor's responsibility to return it to its proper place on the prop table. If it is left onstage, then it is the prop crew's responsibility to return it. For instance, you may pick up some stage money from the prop table, take it onstage, and give it to another actor. That actor must return the stage money to the prop table and not simply place it in his pocket for the costume crew to discover (sometimes disastrously, after the costume has been removed from the washing machine!). Later, when you're dealing with costume props, don't wear such items as rings out of the theater; the costume crew must account for these props each evening and such thoughtlessness will cause trouble for them.

Each evening during the last dress rehearsals and always during the run of performances, the stage manager gives the actors an opportunity to *check their props*. Remember, even though it is the responsibility of various crews to set the props each night, you, the actor, are the one who will be inconvenienced (on-stage in front of the audience) if the prop is missing or not functioning correctly. So it behooves you to go onto the set each evening before the performance and personally see that each of your props is there and working as it should. Also check to see that all prop table items you use are there and functioning properly. Some time after the props are set by the crews and before the audience is permitted into the theater, the stage manager will indicate over the public address system that props are ready to be checked by the cast. There is usually not much time to do this—if it is an open set you must of course check stage and hand props before the audience is let in—but it is an important part of your duty as an actor and should be done carefully each performance.

Let me say, at this point, a particular word about a very special category of props: firearms. You know that all weapons should be handled with extreme caution. But familiarity and constant use sometimes make us careless. Knives, razors, and swords will be blunted and otherwise rendered harmless by the prop crew under the supervision of the fight master or the director, but they can still inflict damage if not treated with respect and care. Check with the fight master or the director for the proper precautions to use in dealing with them.

Guns and rifles, however, are in a class by themselves. Of course, the ammunition placed in stage firearms always contains a blank charge, which means that no projectile is emitted from them. Still, these blanks can be dangerous: very often there are sparks from gunpowder and packing, the noise of detonation can be very loud (deafening, in some cases), and the explosive charge, even in the absence of a projectile, can inflict serious harm. You may remember the tragic case of a young television actor several years ago, who discharged such a weapon, loaded with blanks, very close to his head and died as a result. *Always treat any firearms with respect and caution!* Never point such a gun directly at anyone. The audience will not be able to tell you are aiming a bit to one side of or above your supposed target, so point the weapon slightly away from the other actor. Never point the gun directly at the audience. Always be alert for sparks or bits of packing that might have ignited. Remember that stage sets are often very vulnerable to fire. The stage manager gives the cast and crew any information on safety in the event of fire or other emergency. Pay close attention to such talks: theater involves crowds of people, lots of electrical apparatus, and many other potentially dangerous devices. You should always know what to do in the event of an emergency, and a technical rehearsal is an excellent time to find out such things.

Tech rehearsals are very important times for the entire company. They are primarily for the director, stage manager, designers, and crews. But they are also essential for the cast. Utilize the time when lights are focused and cues are set to find your light; make sure of your sound cues during this time; use these rehearsals to familiarize yourself with the actual set on which you will be performing; and become as familiar as possible with the props you will be using, where they are obtained, where they are returned, and any problems they may present you in the performances.

Remember that tech rehearsals can be times of stress, tension, and anxiety—particularly for the director, stage manager, designers, and crew members. Actors are essential to the proper running of a technical rehearsal, but they are not the immediate focus, so be considerate and cooperative.

THE DRESS REHEARSAL

If the tech rehearsal is primarily for the designers and the director to integrate the various design elements into the show, the *dress rehearsal*—adding two other essential design elements, the costumes and makeup—is much more immediately concerned with the actor. For the actor, costumes and makeup are the most intimate technical aspects of the performance.

The Actor and Costumes

As noted earlier, you have been wearing rehearsal costumes that approximate the effect of any special costumes you might be wearing: footwear, wigs, large headdresses, voluminous cloaks, sword belts and scabbards, and so on, all require the body to move in certain ways, and you certainly should have been wearing something that produces the same effect. But here you are, finally, wearing the real costume on the real set using the real props. What are the problems that might arise here?

First of all, you have probably had a special rehearsal call a few days before the first dress rehearsal for a dress parade. The *dress parade* provides an opportunity for the director and the costume designer to see all the costumes on the actors and spot any difficulties. Dress parade is also an excellent time for the actor to report directly to the director and designer any last-minute problems with the costume. You have been fitted in the costume many times, of course, and any concerns should have been reported to the costume designer and his staff as you went along; but here are all the cast in all the costumes: everything can be seen together.

When the actual dress rehearsal arrives, the costumes should not present additional difficulties. Inevitably, however, they do (Fig. 8.3). Hats are too tall for doorways. Hoopskirts are too wide for chairs. Quick changes cannot be made in the time provided. Sleeves get in the way of teacups. All of these problems can be solved, of course, and the dress rehearsal is the time to do so.

Can an actor ask for a dress rehearsal to stop while costume problems are solved? Sometimes. If a quick change cannot be made fast enough, then the

Figure 8.3 Period clothing is often difficult and cumbersome to wear. Actors who have familiarized themselves with such problems by wearing appropriate rehearsal costumes are not shocked (and sometimes literally *thrown*) by the real thing at first dress rehearsal.

director will usually stop the rehearsal, but it is certainly within the province of the actor (or her dresser or the designer) to let the director or stage manager know there are problems and ask for time to solve them. If a costume item makes certain movements impossible, then the actor can ask for solutions. Usually, the director will observe these problems as they arise and stop the rehearsal; but if he doesn't, the actor should first try to keep the rehearsal going and solve the problem at the same time. If that is not possible, then stop and ask for time to work it out.

There will usually be a series of dress rehearsals, and, after the first one, the director will be anxious to begin to get the show back onto a performance level: stops, therefore, will be discouraged. But this first dress rehearsal is the time to work out these problems, and I believe the time should be taken by director, actors, and crews to do just that.

Remember to treat your costumes with respect. Every costume shop in every theater has different rules regarding what actors may or may not do in certain costumes, but in almost all of them there are rules against smoking or eating in costume. These are for good reason, of course, as cigarettes can burn holes in costumes and food can stain. Always obey these rules. Hang your costumes up neatly where they belong. Nothing infuriates a crew or a designer more than to see actors tossing costumes carelessly on the floor of the dressing room. The costumes have taken weeks of loving labor to construct and are very difficult to replace and expensive to clean. You want to look good on stage, so taking excellent care of your costume is to your advantage as well. It is also a sure sign of professionalism. But get used to wearing the clothes so you look as if you wear them regularly. Remember: you wear the costume; don't let it wear you.

The Actor and Makeup

Most of you will have a course in makeup as part of your undergraduate training. This is very important because stage actors, unlike film and television performers, are expected to do their own makeup. Sometimes, too, stage makeup can be as specialized and difficult as makeup for film and television, so it is well worth learning to do it well. In most theaters, too, you will be expected to buy and maintain your own supplies, so be ready for that.

Makeup is usually added to the rehearsal series after the first dress rehearsal. At this point, work will begin on hair treatment: wigs and the like. Perhaps the first thing to say to the beginning actor about makeup is to allow plenty of time to put it on. You do not want to have to rush this very important task, so be sure to arrive at the theater early enough. Remember, you still have to allow some time for warm-ups, which at this point may have to be boiled down into a short manageable routine that can be performed in costume and makeup without spoiling or unsettling either. You will also want to consult frequently with the makeup crew.

Regarding the design of makeup, many times you will be given a kind of chart indicating the sort of makeup you should apply. This has been designed by the costume designer or makeup designer and has always been approved by your director. Check with the makeup crew or with the designer if you have questions about this chart. The director will usually give you notes on your makeup after this first rehearsal in which makeup is used. Remember, makeup that looks all right to you (and even, sometimes, to the makeup designer) in the dressing room may not accomplish what is intended under the lights of the set, so be prepared to change and modify your makeup over the next few rehearsals. Stay flexible.

A final point about makeup: *never* leave the theater with your stage makeup still on. Nothing marks the beginner more easily than this sloppy affectation. Stage makeup belongs on the stage.

Costumes and makeup are very important tools that allow the actor to demonstrate to the fullest possible extent the characterization which has been worked on for so long. In a way, they are the final externalization of all the internal truth. Treat them as part of the characterization, not as some external layer that isn't really a part of you.

RELATING TO OTHER PEOPLE

By the time you have finished with this last sequence of rehearsals in which the final touches of costume and makeup have been accomplished, you are almost ready for the performances, the ultimate goal of this hard work all along. Before we consider the performance situation, however, let's talk about getting along with this large group of people who have been assembled.

Perhaps the first thing to say is that, although actors are the people of the company who are seen by the public, they are not accomplishing the work of this production alone. As you have seen during the technical and dress rehearsals, there is a veritable army of people backstage, without which the show would, literally, not go on. In our society, actors, particularly film and television actors, have become so popular, such icons and idols in the public eye, that a mystique, almost a cult, has arisen surrounding their rights and privileges. While there may be rights and privileges, I will leave you to discover them on your own. I like to adamantly discourage this cult of the actor and prefer to talk about the contributions of everyone who works on a production. I would rather concentrate on responsibilities of the actor, particularly to the people who are working so hard to see that his or her performance is properly and effectively presented. Treat these co-workers as you treat friends whose respect you want to keep. Above all, don't condescend to them as if they were servants.

The Stage Manager

Next to the director, the stage manager is the most important professional person in an actor's life. You have spent the last several weeks in an intimate working relationship with your director, working together to create your characterization and finding its impact and direction as it threads its way through the overall fabric of the play. As the rehearsal period ends and the run of performances begin, the stage manager takes the place of the director. He or she becomes the authority who makes all decisions regarding the artistic and technical life of the play.

Since the stage manager has been the director's first assistant during the rehearsal period, he has a complete understanding of the superobjective that was established and discussed during the readthrough, and has followed the progress of the actors as they worked with the director in bringing all the elements together to form the ensemble. The stage manager is now the director's surrogate, and it is to him that actors should bring all questions and problems that relate to the performances.

You may have established, during the rehearsals, a slightly more informal relationship with the stage manager than you have with the director. It is important for you to see, once the run has begun, that the stage manager, during working hours, is the final authority to whom you can go for assistance: the manager and controller of the production. Find a way, therefore, to separate the informality of any social relationship you might have developed with the stage manager from this professional situation. Once that is done, always take artistic decisions to the stage manager. Never make request for changes in, say, props or costumes directly to the crew head responsible for those areas: always go to the stage manager with such requests.

Be prepared for a good stage manager to make authoritative and disciplinary decisions if they are necessary. If this is a professional production in which you are involved, then Equity rules will demand that the stage manager do so: levying fines and reporting any unprofessional conduct to the management of the theater in which you are all working. Be aware that, in professional situations at least, the production itself is under the financial control of the management of the theater producing the play. The stage manager, in addition to having the authority of the director at this point, also represents management and acts as liaison between you and the theater throughout the run.

Incidentally, it is possible that the director may come back into the run of performances and call rehearsals if she feels that the play has gotten away from the rhythms and objectives that were established before opening night. Most directors will have gone on to new productions, but many, even so, make periodic inspection trips to be sure things are going as they should. If this happens, then, of course, the stage manager returns to the duties he held during the rehearsal period, resuming the position of authority when performances continue. Use these brushup rehearsals to prevent your performance from going stale with many repetitions and as good stimuli to the ongoing problem of maintaining spontaneity.

Designers

As an actor, you will probably not have a lot of contact with the various designers of the show. You may see the costume designer at the fittings for a costume, but, unless you are a very important actor, those will usually be conducted by the very efficient and capable costumer and his assistants. You may also meet the lighting, set, props, and other designers at readthroughs, or come in contact with them at the tech rehearsal (though, as we pointed out, those are usually occasions on which designers have other things on their minds), or you may meet and talk with other designers at various times during the rehearsal period. But, as a rule, the designer reports directly to the director, and director contact with actors is rare.

The principal thing to remember about any relationship with designers is that they are not going to be receptive to design suggestions from actors. Since their responsibility is toward the overall impact of the production and therefore their business is conducted through the overall production supervisor—the director—they would be derelict in their duty if they listened to, let alone acted upon, individual suggestions from actors.

The costume designer is particularly vulnerable to such suggestions. Every actor knows what he or she looks good in, which is important, but there are a few things to remember. First of all, be sure you *do* know what you look good in. Sometimes it is very difficult for us to be objective about how we look, and it very often proves true that the professional designer might have better ideas about how to present you or your character than you do. You would do well to listen carefully to what the good costume (and makeup) designer suggests for you. Second, remember that in the theater, where great artistic temperament abounds, it is very easy to develop a reputation for being hard to work with. Believe me, you want to avoid such a reputation at all costs. Jobs are difficult enough to get without dragging such negativity along with you. In short, do not make personal demands on the costume designer.

Which is not to say that you, the actor, have no input into such matters. As we mentioned earlier, the director will usually ask all the designers to present renderings of their designs at an early rehearsal, probably the readthrough, and if you have legitimate and valid suggestions to make on any of these designs, you should feel free to make them: to the director. Remember that the director is the overall authority in such matters, and a good one is going to listen to all opinions of the ensemble. Do not be surprised (and certainly not resentful) if your suggestion is not acted upon, however. You do not have the overall picture of the production, and may not see how it all fits together as the director does.

You also have the process of fittings to go through, and if you feel that, for whatever reason, there are problems with your costume, then by all means communicate these thoughts to your director, either directly to her or through the stage manager. You also have the dress parade, which is specifically designed to provide a forum for such suggestions.

Maintain good professional relationships with all the designers with whom you come in contact. In future productions, when you have expanded your reputation, you will perhaps have designers asking to work for you. The earlier you start to build on such a positive reputation, the better.

Crews

It may not be readily apparent at first, but the various crews of the production in which you are involved can be among the most important people in your professional life. I said before that there is an unfortunate tendency to think of the actor as the one indispensable element of a production. Of course, actors are indispensable. The show cannot go on without them. But the crews would prove their own indispensability if they once refused to show up and do their job. Obviously, these people are very important, and deserve all of your respect.

Not only do the production crews deserve your friendship, admiration, and respect, they provide a kind of professional insurance for the actor. If you have a good relationship with the crew, they are going to have a personal investment in seeing to it that the set, costumes, props, and other technical aspects of your performance function properly.

Perhaps it would be the easiest way to summarize this discussion by saying that it is important to treat the people with whom you work with courtesy and fairness. The theater, like all the arts, is home to many people who, perhaps because of their very creativity, may be apt to tread a thin line between equanimity and volatility. Actors, particularly, are said to be vulnerable in this regard.

I think it is important for the young actor, just starting out, to prove that is possible to be talented, creative, *and* easy to work with. Start your career by maintaining good professional work habits and by respecting all the people with whom you work.

Once you've gotten through the usually difficult and trying time of the technical and dress rehearsals, you find the goal to which everything has led looming before you: the performances. Is the actor's work largely done? Can you relax and have fun now? Well, it's true that performances will bring you much creative enjoyment and many artistic rewards if you have worked hard in the preceding weeks; but . . . no more work to be done? Let's talk about that.

CHAPTER 9

• • • •

PERFORMANCES

So here you are: rehearsals are over—you've read the text, discussed it, worked on it, run it; the arduous task of adding all the design and technical elements to the production is finished; even opening night—always a strained and unnatural session—is behind you. Ahead of you is the goal for which you have worked so hard: a run of performances. Nothing to do but get to the theater on time every night, press the right buttons, and let the performance run on automatic, right? No more hard work, right?

Wrong.

Remember our computer analogy? I said that the rehearsal period was the time to construct the program for the performance. A tremendously large and diverse amount of information was assembled and fed into the computer: who the character is, where the character is, who the character is with, what actions the character is performing, why the character is saying and doing these things, and what response the other characters make to all this. Now that all the information is in the computer, all the actor has to do is press a button and let the program run. That's true, but there are other factors that might interfere with the smooth running of the program.

Certainly you should be ready to trust all the hard work of the rehearsal period, to allow all the information that has been programmed into the computer to do its work when the program is run. But a good computer operator must watch the machine as the program runs, waiting for the unexpected: the malfunction, the power outage, the paper that gets stuck in the printer, the occasional bit of incorrect data. Just as this operator is watchful and alert as the program does its work, so, too, you must be alert and responsive as your character's life—the performance—unfolds in front of the audience. We talked in general about some of these actor control problems earlier. Let's look at some specifics.

What are some of these unexpected events that require this vigilance in the theater? Let's start at the beginning with a typical night of a performance. Keep in mind that, while we are drawing this picture of a performance of a real play in a real theater, all of these ideas and techniques can be easily applied to the performance of a scene in a beginning acting classroom. Leave out any information on costuming, makeup, and the other technical areas, and everything else applies. So how does this typical evening of performance begin?

PREPARATION: THE MOMENT BEFORE

A good deal of preparation leads up to the all-important moment before you step onto the stage. Let's see what some of the preparation might be.

If the performance begins at 8 o'clock in the evening, as it usually does, the rule is that all actors must arrive at the theater and be ready for work by 7:30. Of course, you will want to be at the theater considerably before 7:30, particularly if you are in the opening scenes. The stage manager will have posted a list of the cast with appropriate boxes by each of your names in which you write your initials, letting her know that you are in the theater; so let's say you arrive and sign in on this chart at 6 o'clock. Perhaps you stop by the green room to greet the rest of the cast and any crew members who are not busy setting up the show for the night. You might then go to your dressing room and begin setting out your various makeup items and checking your costume—if the costume crew has set it out—to be sure that everything is in order.

As you begin your basic makeup, you may be running lines—I make it a habit to go over every word I say on stage every day of a performance run—or you may have done that earlier in the day. It is also a good time to watch your character begin to emerge, observing your face disappear and the character's begin to show. This time of putting on makeup is an ideal time to begin, in various ways, to focus your concentration away from the distractions of your everyday life and onto the business at hand. You might, for instance, be summoning whatever emotion memory images that you will need for the night's performance; you might be going through the imagined life of your character, the events that the character would be living this hour and a half before the lights come up on the character's onstage life. Working on concentration during the essentially sedentary occupation of putting on makeup is an excellent use of the time.

Unless makeup is very complicated, you should be able to do any physical warming up with it on. There should be plenty of time between the time your makeup is done and the time when you put on your first costume to accomplish whatever performance routine you have established. Of course, you won't want to do any kind of routine that is too strenuous. Go over the exercises at the beginning of this book and see if any one of them can be adapted to this specialized situation. If there is some kind of group warm-up in this company, then there is also very likely an established time for doing it. If you are doing it on your own—or perhaps with a few other cast members—then you can set your own schedule. Doing your physical warm-up at this time is good, because you don't want to do it in costume.

It's probably about 7:15 or 7:30 by now. You have focused your concentration, warmed up the body and voice, and have your makeup on. As you begin to put on your costume, allow yourself the luxury of observing the character continue to emerge, to clothe herself in her clothing. If you take this process seriously, the moment of stepping onto the set will seem natural and inevitable: the character, having become fully visible, walks into her physical environment completely emerged and fully present.

While we're talking about stepping onto the stage, remember only actors make entrances; characters move from space to space. The actor is standing backstage about to step into an artificial environment; the character is in one space of the character's world, about to step into another space. See if you can bring some of that offstage character space on with you when you walk onto the set. Just before you move onto the set, think about where the character *is* . . . then move into the new space.

That moment before you move onto the new space is very, very important. All of the weeks of rehearsal, all of the meticulous preparation, all of the concentration and focus and energy and relaxation have brought you to this last moment. Just before you step onto the stage—just before you emerge into the character's world—find that mental formula (and it will be very individualized, tailored to your specific mental framework) that allows you to let go, to whatever degree is possible for you, of your own persona, grab at a last full breath, fully focus your energy, move into the new space, and start the performance.

This moment before is not, mind you, a particularly difficult or esoteric concept; it is not a kind of mystical formula by which a transformation is summoned; it is simply the moment before the trigger is pulled, the moment before the race begins, the moment before you dive off the high board: it is a last crucial gathering of all your mental and physical energies to concentrate and work together on the task that is about to be accomplished.

So you, the actor clothed in the character, take a deep breath, gather your wits, your focus, your concentration about you, and step onto the set: the world of the play for which you have worked so hard to prepare yourself. As you do, after all that preparation and even if this is the one hundredth performance, you step onto it for the first time.

SPONTANEITY

It is, remember, the first time for the audience. But more importantly, it is the first time for the character. No matter that the actor has done this some ninety-nine previous times. For the characters in this play and for the audience observing them, all the events of the next two hours have never happened before.

There is a play in London that has run for more than thirty years. There is a musical in Minneapolis in which a couple met, married, and had children over the years of its run. You have rehearsed this play for weeks and performed it for, maybe, months: how can you go through the movements, say the lines, as if it were the first time? How can it be spontaneous? Well, spontaneity is a matter of suspended disbelief. You, all of you in the play, are all asking the audience to forget they are sitting in a darkened room watching brilliantly lit people move and speak in what is a patently artificial environment. Just as you are asking for that suspension of disbelief from them—asking them to free themselves momentarily of their tendency to say, "This is not really happening"—you must yourself suspend your disbelief in the separation of the world of the play from your own life and from the memory that all of this has happened before . . . and before . . . and before.

Each person has a different level on which this suspension occurs. Some actors are able to forget themselves almost entirely; others say they are constantly aware of themselves as themselves and never, to any degree, lose that awareness. One of the recent legends of the British and world stages always claimed that he could do his laundry list while performing Hamlet. Well, maybe. It's certainly a different experience for different actors. Perhaps it boils down to a simple formula: whatever works. You may be able to submerge 90 percent of yourself in the character, or only 50 percent or even only 10 percent. Whatever degree that is accomplished may be sufficient for you to give the impression that these events that are taking place in front of the eyes of the audience are happening completely spontaneously. I, for one, do not believe the good actors who say they never lose any of themselves, and, as we have said before, some percentage of actor consciousness must be there: find the proportion that works for you.

You speak your first line. Yes, of course you know that you are saying it because you have heard (or seen or felt) your first cue. But you also know that you are saying it because it is the response the character feels to that first line (or sound or light cue). You worked hard enough in the working rehearsal to find out what the character thought: it is part of the program now. You erupt in anger, later in the scene or in the play, because you know it is the time in the play for your character to erupt in anger; yes, but you also know why the character does that, and you know the sequence of events, the spine, that has brought the character along that path to this moment, and you have allowed yourself to be carried along that path to this moment. You have suspended your own disbelief in the artificiality of the theatrical situation, this fictional, make-believe cardboard and tinsel world. And you have forgotten, to whatever degree this is possible, you own real life. You know the world of the character and the play is possible and you know the basis on which its possibility rests. You have learned that. Now you must allow yourself to respond, spontaneously, to its stimulus: not for the first time, but *as if* for the first time.

And you go through the rest of the first half that way. During the intermission, if you take my advice, you do not socialize, you do not let go of the concentration and the energy that you have worked so hard to obtain. You go, perhaps, to your dressing room, being polite, being cordial, being human; but, perhaps, letting it be known in a polite, cordial, human way, that you need this time to focus on the remainder of the play. Stay in character to whatever degree works for you, so that, when it begins, the second half is happening for the first time, too.

CONTROL

Very often, it is in the second half of the play that the most energy and concentration are required. The mounting dynamics of the play are bringing you rapidly to moments of crisis, conflict, and climax. As you go toward these moments, you will be able to allow yourself to move with these energies along this path of your character. And there are also, perhaps, an increasing number of things that the actor must control.

Perhaps, if it is that kind of play, there is an increase in the amount of laughter coming from the audience. If that is so, then you, the actor, must be in control to the extent that you know you must (remember?) motivate a pause until the laughter reaches its peak (Fig. 9.1). Then you repeat, in a new, spontaneous, motivated way, any line that may not have been heard. In other words, you, the actor, must hold for lines.

Or maybe there is a mistake on stage. Maybe the leading man's belt breaks and his pants fall down. Do you laugh? Well, does the character laugh? Certainly, the actor does not. The audience almost surely will. Very likely the character does, too, but as the character and in response to the immediate situation. Let the relationship between your character and the leading man's character dictate your response. React to any situation that happens within the world of the play as your character would, and exert enough actor control to be sure the audience does not see the actor react to events within the character's world.

What if you are playing Samson or Gregory in the scene from *Romeo and Juliet* that we worked on earlier? Shortly after the beginning of this scene, a major fight erupts involving many of the characters including yours. Believe me when I tell you that actor control is very important here. There are prob-

Figure 9.1 "Holding" for a laugh should always be fully motivated, but must be done for as long as it takes for the audience to hear the line.

ably going to be swords flashing among a lot of people. Yes, the swords are dulled; yes, the director and the fight master have carefully choreographed the scene for maximum safety; yes, you know your blocking perfectly well. But what if the actor playing Mercutio stumbles and falls? Suppose the actor choreographed to thrust at him with his sword instead thrusts at Lady Montague? Does the actor playing Lady Montague die? Of course not. We hope that everyone is exerting enough actor control *to be sure that no one is hurt* and to see to it that the audience, to whatever extent possible, is unaware that anything has gone wrong. It is one function of actor control to maintain the investment the audience has made in suspension of disbelief. It is a function of actor control, in other words, to support the illusion of reality and spontaneity for the audience. If it is necessary to break your own actor's suspension of disbelief in order to do that, so be it. The audience is, in effect, paying your salary. You owe it to them, and your concentration and preparation should be sufficient to exert such control and still, with relative ease, return to the world of the play.

The actor must deal with all mistakes that happen in the character's world. Remember the mistake we talked about in the tech rehearsal when the phone rang after you had picked it up? In the tech, you stopped and fixed the cue. In performance, you can't do that. Maybe you ignore it (as we suggested before) and the audience forgets about it very quickly. Or maybe you make an *ad lib*, a remark, which though *in character*, is, in effect, written by the actor. Ad libs are very difficult, and you must be very careful in using them. But, perhaps, in this situation, if it will help cover the moment, you might say something like, "There must be something wrong with the phone." Use your best judgment and deal with each mistake as it comes along by being alert and maintaining concentration.

As you progress as an actor, you will discover your own levels of actor control and character involvement. Find the combination that works best for you and develop the necessary concentration and energy skills to maintain them, whether the audience sees the performance on a Saturday night, in which the play goes perfectly and everyone is at peak energy, or on a Sunday matinee, at which many things go wrong and the company is tired and perhaps shows it. But every show is done to the best of your ability, at the peak of your concentration and control. Always give it your all. Remember that every audience deserves to see the show at its best.

CONSISTENCY

If you are preparing yourself correctly for every performance, if your energy and commitment levels are maintained, and if you are in control of both yourself and your character, then you should have no problem maintaining a consistent level of performance. Being human, however, there are going to be pressures on you in your everyday life that may influence any of these factors and so affect the performance.

Are you too tired to perform at peak energy? Are there problems in your personal life intruding themselves on the life of your character? Are there rivalries and jealousies among the company that detract from ensemble concentration? Do you have another job during the day? As a student actor, is your heavy school schedule intruding into your preparation time and your performance concentration? All of these factors, and many more, can be detrimental to the performance and sometimes cause a complete breakdown in consistency from show to show.

What is the answer? Well, it is going to sound too easy, but leave all these problems and distractions at the stage door. The old adage that the show must go on is true simply because of the nature of the theater. If you are reading a book and you are distracted, you put the book aside and resume reading it at a more convenient time. In these days of videotape, if you are watching a film on your VCR and the telephone rings, you put the tape on pause and answer the phone, going back to the movie when the conversation is finished. But the theater happens only in the uninterrupted present tense. Both actors and audience have invested energy and concentration in the onetime progression of these events. Actors are doing this job because they choose to, because they were lucky enough to be chosen to do so, and, in the case of the professional, because it is their job: they are being paid to do so. The audience cannot be put on hold; there is no pause button, so the actor must find a way to divorce all the distractions, pressures, and energy drainers from his professional life. The actor must perform the play as it has been rehearsed during the proscribed and unalterable hours dedicated to performance. There are no substitutes. Each of you must find the way to accomplish this, and ensure that each performance is of a consistent quality.

Work on ridding yourself of your everyday distractions in your concentration preparation time. Find a mental switch that can be turned on or off as you enter the stage door. Try to organize your time so that preparation time is not interfered with. Don't overcommit yourself. Try to anticipate the arrival at the theater each night with pleasure, even though you have done the play a hundred times and are tired of it. Try to imagine that every audience has an important family member or professional person in it, or critic, to whom it is important to you that a good performance be given. Whatever device you find works for you, just remember that, no matter how small or apparently unimportant an audience seems to be, no matter how bored you are with a long-running play, no matter how sick or tired or distracted you are—just remember that it's true: the show must go on!

So you can see there are techniques and disciplines that are as important to the performances as are those that are part of working or running rehearsals. You must find those techniques that work for you and be faithful to practicing them before each performance. If you do so, then your performances will be more consistent.

A LOOK BACK

We're nearly at the end of this book, so perhaps it would be a good idea to look back and review a little. What has happened so far?

You have read the play with your director and the rest of the cast. During that reading you have understood the text and your part in it.

You have worked through each of your scenes in detail and have understood the subtextual motivation for everything that is said and done onstage that affects your character.

You and your director and the rest of the cast have put the scenes together into a coherent and dynamic whole that works well in terms of pace, rate, and build.

You have worked with a team of designers, your director, the stage manager, and all the crews in clothing the production in all its technical aspects: scenery, lighting, costumes, props, sound, and music.

And you have found the correct balance between your own personality and the demands of your character so that you can control your performance, yet suspend your own disbelief to a level that will meet your audiences, allowing you to bring the play and your part in it spontaneously and consistently alive in performance after performance.

Remember, once again, that all the discussions in this book which seem to apply to full production of complete plays are just as applicable to your classroom scene work. The only difference is that your class scenes will not involve any of the technical aspects. Work with your class instructor as you would work with a stage manager or director in a full production.

Before this book is left to you as a workbook to be reviewed and consulted in your progress toward becoming a good actor, let's talk about one more subject that might be taken for granted, but certainly needs to be discussed.

Why, in the first place, do you want to spend all this time and energy being an actor? And, even if you can satisfactorily answer that question, how on earth do you get someone to let you do it?

CHAPTER 10
$$\bullet \quad \bullet \quad \bullet \quad \bullet$$

AN ACTOR'S LIFE

Most of you reading this book are doing so in conjunction with a class in beginning acting techniques, and some of you will already have made at least a tentative decision to pursue careers in professional acting. I hope the work that has been outlined so far has given you some idea of the rigors of such a career. I also hope my description of the hard work—not exaggerated, I assure you: minimized, if anything—has discouraged those of you who saw the life of an actor as an easy, glamorous one, filled with fans, romance, money, and adulation, and has, at the very least, sobered those of you with a more realistic vision and brought you to a beginning realization of the struggle ahead. Do you still think you want to be an actor? Fine. I wish you good luck. But first, let's take a good hard look at your motivations and then talk a little about what the future holds for you.

WHY BE AN ACTOR?

The life of an actor in the United States at the end of the twentieth century is a difficult one. Those who are very successful in films and television, like sports figures, are paid enormous sums of money and are the focus of a great deal of attention and adulation. No matter how realistic you may think your view is, chances are it is colored to at least some extent by the glamorization of these performers. Realize, however, that you are seeing these people after they have become successful. All of them have been in your position, and most of them had a long hard road to travel before they reached their present successes. If you could talk honestly to the most famous actor you can think of, your ideal, the one who is the model on which you would like to construct your career, you would, I think, be very surprised at some of the things he or she might tell you.

You might be surprised, for instance, to learn how long it took this actor to develop the skills now used with such apparent ease; you might be surprised to find what a large percentage of this actor's day is spent in thinking about career matters, and how exhausting and frustrating and long the daily hours of work are; you might be surprised to discover that it is difficult, even after success, to *maintain* that so admired position; you might be surprised to discover that film, television, and the stage are all harder on some categories of people than others: women, for instance, and racial minorities, and everyone, once they have gotten older; you might be surprised to discover how difficult it is to maintain personal relationships of any kind in the face of staggering career demands.

But since you very likely can't have this heart-to-heart talk with your idol, have it with yourself. Let's do one last exercise.

● ● ●

EXERCISE 44

AN HONEST LOOK

Sit yourself down in front of your mirror, look yourself squarely in the eye, and ask yourself this question: "Why, *exactly,* do I want to be an actor?" You are the only one who *really* knows whether or not you're being honest when you answer this question, so you must be ruthless with yourself. Be sure and look yourself straight in the eye. Be sure you are alone, so you don't have to play a role for anyone else or provide answers about yourself that you know aren't true but which you want other people to think about you (Fig. 10.1). This is just for you. Be honest! Go ahead. Ask the question: "Why, exactly, do I want to be an actor?" What was your reply? Well, here are some answers that might have popped out.

"I want to be rich."

"I want to be famous."

"I want everybody to like me."

"I want to live a glamorous life."

"I want to show everybody in my class that I *can* be beautiful (or handsome) and successful."

"I want to wear great clothes and travel and be somebody."

"I want to be a sex object."

"I want to do something to upset my parents."

Figure 10.1 Why be an actor? You must decide for yourself. Money and fame, however, are not very good reasons.

"I want to live a reckless and dissolute life."

"I want to get back at everybody who's given me such a hard time."

"I want to be on the cover of _____" (you fill in the name of the magazine).

Well? Did any of those answers come out? Are you sure? Are you certain you weren't thinking them? Somewhere? Deep inside? Go back and look at those answers again. Remember, you're alone; nobody else knows you're doing this. Are you sure one of those reasons doesn't lurk somewhere deep down in your soul? Well, if it does, then you're smart enough to realize they're *not good reasons for wanting to be an actor.*

This isn't a real exercise, of course. Not like the others in this book, at least. But take it seriously, and repeat it at various times and in various ways as you pursue the study of acting. Eventually, you will have to make a decision about whether or not to go on with these studies or to transfer your energies to something else. So keep asking yourself that question. I can't give you the right answer or tell you whether or not you should try to become an actor. I can, however, give you a sort of generalized answer that, while not a *right* answer, seems to hold a kernel of truth for many of the working actors I talk to. See if it applies to you.

I think people who want to go into acting should do so only because, after rigorous self-examination that eliminates all the wrong reasons, the decision is finally reached that *nothing else will satisfy them, either personally or artistically.* Note that I did not say ". . . nothing else will make them *happy."* When I talked to several of my friends who are successful actors, they all questioned the use of the word *happy.* Each of them said, vehemently, that acting did not make them happy. Not all the time. Not even part of the time. For some of them, not any time. But there is, they say, nothing else that gives them the feeling of personal accomplishment, perhaps fulfillment, that happens in this long, arduous, tough process of merging themselves with their characters; synthesizing the characterization with the work of other actors, directors, designers; and sharing the total work with an audience.

Is that too generalized an answer for you? Too fuzzy? Too philosophical? Maybe. Probably. I told you I did not have the right answer to the question. I don't know the right answer, but I do know some wrong answers. Some of them were just listed. All I ask is that you think about it—frequently, honestly, and in depth.

Why this persistent self-examination? Because a successful career in the performing arts is so difficult to obtain, for many, many reasons.

One of these reasons is that such a career is still primarily available in so few cities. We have seen in the last few years a major renaissance of regional theaters. There are many excellent theaters in such cities as San Diego, Seattle, Chicago, Hartford, Washington, Denver, Dallas, and many others, all producing superb seasons of new plays, classics, musicals, a wide variety of theater. But even with this exciting expansion, there are, really, only two cities in which a professional actor can live: New York and Los Angeles. The circumstances of casting and producing change very rapidly, and there are still myths and exaggerations about both cities. Every year, we hear that New York theater is dying. Certainly it has its problems; but the news of its demise has been heard for years and it's still there. It is a major casting center, if nothing else. We also hear that Los Angeles has no theater, that it is only for television and film that actors live there. Of course, the media dominate in Los Angeles; but there is theater there, in increasing amounts and of escalating quality.

But, you say, you know some working actors who don't live in either of those two cities. And, yes, it's true, in a way: many actors work the LORT (League of Regional Theaters) circuit. This simply means they have chosen to work almost exclusively in live theater, and therefore move from one major regional theater to another, from city to city. This kind of mobility appeals to many people; to others, its transiency is unpleasant. So most actors, those who want a more rooted life and are eager to earn the larger salaries of film and television, settle in Los Angeles or, though in decreasing numbers perhaps, in New York. If you don't want to live in either of those two cities and don't want the gypsy life of moving from place to place, then you need to reconsider your career goal or reconcile yourself to compromise in this decision.

So you make the decision to live in, say, Los Angeles. You go to your first "cattle call" (a general audition open to everyone), and you discover, upon walking into the room, that there are, first of all, hundreds of people there and dozens that look just like you (Fig. 10.2). Competition is fierce for the few available jobs. Maybe you're not a particularly aggressive person and the competitive nature of the profession causes you stress and anxiety.

And what about the fact that actors must be constantly aware of themselves: of selling themselves to producers, directors, casting agents, and the like? Will that cause you problems? The very difficulty of establishing and maintaining such a career is often very detrimental to the psyche. Before you leave the sheltered environment of the classroom, you will want to take a class that focuses on getting acting jobs. Many university drama departments have such

Figure 10.2 A "cattle call" audition can be a demoralizing experience, but it does bring the young actor in contact with the reality of competition in today's theater.

courses. Learn as much about this very difficult process as you can. Understand one thing: for the last few years, unemployment statistics in the various performers' unions have been roughly reverse the national figures. If unemployment at any given moment in the United States is, say, 10 percent, you might look at Equity's figures and discover that, at that same moment, perhaps 90 percent of the union's members are out of work—not a pretty picture.

A career in acting requires a very large part of your life, often asking great sacrifices in terms of family, personal relationships, any kind of permanence. Say you are successful. After totally dedicating ten years to your advancement as an actor, you start getting jobs on a fairly regular basis. First of all, the process for the past ten years has been so totally consuming that you have had little time to establish personal relationships. If you live with another performer, the chances are that you will both have jobs (if either of you does have a job) in different cities. This is typical not only of struggling actors, but of successful ones as well. Some people find this very difficult.

Well, all of these are factors to take into consideration as you think about choosing your career. I do not mean to be unduly negative. I have spent most of my own life working in the theater, but most of that effort has been directed toward the much less pressured life of university theater and teaching, and only peripherally to the professional centers. Although I am trying to be honest, I realize many of you will think I am exaggerating the debit side in order to discourage you from such a choice. I am not. The professional actors who have read this chapter agree I am not. We all concur that you, the beginning actor who is just starting out, must be aware of these difficulties and be very, very honest with yourself and know your own motivations extremely well.

Now, having said all of that, I will say this: if you are honest, if you are sure of your motivations, if they are good ones not related to a sense of false glamor, if you are willing to dedicate an inordinate amount of time, effort, and stress to the establishment of a career, if you are willing to sacrifice some areas of your life that people in other careers take for granted, and if you are cognizant of all that and are still willing to proceed . . . then I think you should.

More, if you work as hard as you need to (and that may be harder than you presently anticipate, but never mind) then I think you will succeed. You may not be a star. Being a star is not a matter of hard work alone. It is a matter of hard work, and luck, and who you know and . . . nobody knows what else. You must not set out to be a star. That you will not be able to control. Just set out to be a good actor. If you work hard and are lucky, then becoming a good actor will probably happen.

SOME NOTES ON AUDITIONING

As you walk this perilous Yellow Brick Road, you have to get your first jobs. In order to do this, you will have to audition, and auditioning successfully is an art unto itself.

Several years ago I introduced a three-credit course into the curriculum of my university called "Audition Techniques." I had a very difficult time convincing the university authorities that such a course was necessary, let alone worth three credits. "Why," they said, "do you need a course to teach people how to get a job? In business (or science or teaching or medicine), you simply go to an interview, résumé in hand, and apply for your job." Moreover, to these people this simple task is something that is done only two or three times in a lifetime. Well, actors audition for jobs countless times over a period of many years, until they are well known enough to be asked for, rather than auditioning. Not only is it an ongoing task, it is so specialized and complicated that it must be studied regularly by all actors, including some who are successful. I finally convinced the university committee the course was necessary. I still teach it, and the class is always full.

Some years ago, when the first *Godfather* film was being cast, Marlon Brando (certainly a star by any measure) made entertainment headlines by auditioning for the role. The director cast him, presumably, not because he was a star, but because the audition convinced him that Brando could play the part. The audition demonstrates what skills an actor possesses at various stages in that actor's development. The actor that is demonstrated in an audition at age 60 is a different actor than the one shown in an audition at age 20. Actors change as they grow older. Often they get better, but always they change.

Auditions are also specific to any individual actor. Everybody is going to give a different impression in an audition, so selecting and working on material is a very intimate, individual process. As the actor ages, the material must change: not just to reflect the maturing skill level, but to showcase accurately the maturing physical and emotional type.

Let's briefly discuss the art and craft of auditioning. You may not need it yet—except as you audition for university productions—but you should be thinking about it, developing a body of material for it, and training yourself to do well in this very complicated and personal discipline.

In most audition situations you need a photograph of yourself, called a head shot, and a résumé of your work. We do not discuss them here, although they each have very specific techniques and requirements. Before you arrive in Los Angeles (or New York or Chicago or San Diego) you will need to have them, and you will need to know how to get them done without spending a lot of money. There are many excellent books written on these subjects and your school may have a course, or part of a course, that teaches them. If neither book nor course is available, go to a teacher whose opinion you trust and ask about them. But you don't need them yet. You do, however, need an audition piece.

An audition piece is a short speech from a play that is suitable for you in terms of age and physical type; has a natural build, including a beginning, middle, and end; does not come from a play that is apt to be, in any given year, overused; and effectively demonstrates as many of your unique acting skills as possible.

Most notices that call actors to audition list some fairly specific requirements, often giving at least some information about the play or plays for which the producing organization is casting. Some calls ask for one piece of a specific type and length; others require the actors to bring two audition pieces of contrasting structure and content. Usually, if the audition is for a single specific play, only one piece is asked for. If the organization holding the auditions is a repertory company, they may ask for two or more. If the theater does many classics, they typically ask for one modern piece and one classical piece. You will need to keep a backlog of audition pieces (worked on and critiqued) of various types, lengths, and freshness so that you will have audition material available as these calls arise.

If you know the name of the play being cast, the first thing to do, of course, is to get a copy of the play, read it, and see if you can determine its basic superobjective, its flavor, and what you think this particular director will be doing with the play in this production. It always helps if you know the director and the kind of work she normally does. If you do not know the director, do some research and see what you can find out. When you have decided, generally, what kind of play this is, the next step is to determine which of the roles in the play you think you are right for.

It is always difficult to know what roles you can and cannot play. I believe that actors should take risks now and then, venturing outside of the type restrictions that can be so limiting. On the other hand, you, the actor just starting out, need to be realistic, seeing yourself, to whatever degree this is possible, as your director is apt to see you. It is an unfortunate fact that professional theater, with its extraordinary range of actors from which directors and producers can choose, too often casts too specifically to type. So you need to be very aware of this and very objective in choosing the roles you think you can play. Just don't be too restrictive in your judgments. Take a chance now and then.

I hope each of you understands that only very few people will be called on to play the so-called glamor roles in Hollywood. Quite honestly, I don't think they're often the most interesting roles anyway. You should be aware of the kinds of roles for which you are going to be considered, and be as good in them as you can; but don't try to fit yourself into a mold that is someone else's idea of who you are. Be yourself. You are better at that than anybody.

Having understood the play for which you are auditioning and chosen the roles you think you can play, the next step is to select the audition piece. You should have, in your repertoire of pieces, a selection that is suitable for this occasion. If you do not, and there is time to work on a new one, then you can shop around for a piece you think is just right for this audition. I think it is a mistake, however, to choose a new audition piece without a good amount of time to work on it, maybe finding someone to look at it and critique it for you, before you use it. As a general rule, use something that has been worked on rather than a new piece which may be a bit more suitable.

Find a piece the director will not have heard a dozen times that day. Look around at the most popular plays of the preceding year. Chances are that the piece you thought was such excellent material is going to be chosen by a lot of other actors simply because the play was popular and the material good. See if you can find something equally good from a less obviously popular play. There are sources other than plays for audition material if you're sure you know what you are doing. Plays are by far the best source, but I have had students do excellent auditions for me using material from novels, film scripts, and other sources. Poems do not make for good audition material. They are too structured and very often not meant to be immediate in their impact.

If you are auditioning for a repertory company and need to pick two pieces, they need to contrast in every possible way. One needs to be serious, the other comedy; one should involve as much movement as possible in order to show the director your movement skills, the other must demonstrate you can sit or stand quite still and still be effective; one, perhaps, needs to expend a good amount of energy, the other more quiet; perhaps one is reflective of real life, the other involves style of some kind. Since one of these pieces is usually classical, the style element will be built in.

Choosing the classical piece involves some special considerations. I think that Shakespeare is the best choice for this second piece, primarily because these plays are the most frequently done in the repertory theaters. But if, for some reason, you don't want to choose Shakespeare, there are other excellent sources of classical material: Restoration comedies, Jacobean tragedies, or the plays of Molière or Lope de Vega, for instance. Again, avoid the obvious choices: don't do Hamlet or Macbeth or Juliet. Go through the less familiar plays, such as *Troilus and Cressida* or *Measure for Measure* or the history and chronicle plays. There is an abundance of wonderful characters in these plays for you to work on. Be sure you thoroughly read and understand the plays, of course.

Select a classical piece written in verse, not prose. Most directors want to see that you can handle verse effectively, so choosing a prose piece does not adequately demonstrate your training. If you have any doubts about which pieces are in verse, check with one of your professors. You will, presumably, have had some courses in the speaking of verse at some point in your training.

Always observe the time limits that the audition call has established. The auditioners often see a very large number of actors in any given day, and many of them will cut you off at the time limit anyway. Time your piece accurately and be sure you're within the limits. Obeying all the instructions is the first thing directors notice about you: it indicates you are thoughtful, intelligent, and directable.

Introduce yourself properly. Say your name clearly and tell the director what piece or pieces you are doing for her. Your attitude is very important. You will be judged from the minute you walk into the room, so hit a balance between being too introverted and shy and too aggressive. Try to be professional, confident, and look like you are prepared and want to be there. If you look as if you are in pain and wishing you were elsewhere, who will want to try to penetrate that lack of confidence? They'll probably see to it that you *are* elsewhere. Don't be too cocky, either: nobody wants someone obnoxiously pushy around.

Students frequently ask me for advice on what to wear at auditions, and I am very unwilling to give it. What clothing you wear varies so much, depending on the individual audition situation, that it must be up to the actor to decide. But let me give you a few hints that apply to almost any situation: clothing must be easy to move in, allowing the actor complete freedom in which to work; clothing should make the actor look good—since everybody looks good in a different way, don't try to look like somebody else, but look your best; clothing may suggest, in a very limited way, the character or characters in the pieces you are using, but that should not be a primary consideration: don't wear a costume; clothing should not be distracting: colors, patterns, jewelry, or any part of the outfit that tends to draw attention away from you is not good. Use common sense and think professionally rather than fashionably and you should be all right.

Always end your audition with a simple "Thank you" and wait for the interview that usually follows. Answer all the questions truthfully and directly; remember, most directors are hiring the whole actor, not just the actor's skills. Be yourself. Be relaxed. Be professional.

The artistic director of one of our best regional theaters, coming out of several days of cattle call auditions in which he had heard, literally, hundreds of actors, said to me: "I would never hire an actor who looked like he needed the job." All this really means is that you should give the impression you want to work, that you can do the work, that you are willing to work, but you are not desperate. I think it is good advice.

If you become a professional actor, you will be auditioning very frequently for many years. Keep your selection of pieces fresh, up to date, and carefully worked on; audition as often as you can; be realistic: don't leave any audition trying to predict what impact you made. If you are called back for further auditioning or interviews or if you are eventually hired, good! But don't waste time and energy worrying about it. Walk out of one audition confident you have done your best; then forget it and walk into the next one. Maintain a good professional attitude.

Remember that an audition is a chance to demonstrate all the skills you've worked so hard to develop, a chance to enjoy the difficult and rewarding profession you've chosen. An audition is a chance to act, which is, presumably, what you want to do.

ENDING AT THE BEGINNING

Now that you are at the end of this book, what is next for you? You probably have a few years yet before you need make a final decision about whether or not to pursue a career in acting. So, what next?

Well, you may go on to a scene study class where you will continue to build experience, learning to make many choices based on a wide variety of characterizations in scene after scene. Or you may go on beyond that to classes in historical and classical styles, where you can study problems in language, voice, and movement as actors from other times have perceived and practiced them. You may find yourself auditioning for parts in educational or community theater productions.

Whatever comes next, try to remember that what this book has given you is only the first step in what will turn out to be quite a long walk. You have learned, for instance, that thought produces action; but only after some time in those scene study classes, doing scene after scene, will you find yourself able to allow thought to produce action with some ease and confidence. You have learned some basic exercises in movement and voice and thought that will help you train your body and your mind to communicate to an audience the physical, vocal, and mental impact of your characters; but only after much rigorous daily use of these exercises will your body and mind be able to respond as you wish them to when you wish them to. You have worked on exercise scenes designed to introduce you to the complicated maze of truthful characterization; but only after you have clothed yourself with person after person in play after play will these garments become comfortable and effective.

What happens next for you is experience. This book is just the beginning.

APPENDIX A

• • • •

FIVE MORE EXERCISE SCENES FOR ADDITIONAL WORK

The following scenes are here for you to use as an extension of the laboratory scenes found in the main body of the book. Remember that all these scenes set purposeful problems in subtext and external choices. In fact, they are deliberately subtextually indefinite, so that you have more room to make choices. Be very thorough in your examination of them and realize that you must supply most of the thought that motivates the text.

Each of these scenes is preceded by an introduction that will guide you to some of the problems and questions inherent in the individual scene. Like all the scenes in this book, the characters can be played by either men or women.

Supplementary Exercise Scene 1

This scene sets up several levels of characterizational reality for you to explore. Find your way through all the levels. Be sure you know when the characters are acting and when they are being actors. What differences are there in both internals and externals on each of those levels? What are the differences in the way the two characters react to each other on both these levels? Find emotion and sense memories that will help you make choices in this scene.

Working Through

(*The living room of an apartment in Los Angeles. The occupants are obviously young and very interested in parties: there are bottles and fast-food packages scattered everywhere. The shades are drawn, so the room is dark. SIDNEY is asleep on the sofa. The front door opens, sending a shaft of light into the room. DANA stands in the open door.*)

DANA: Oh, no! (*SIDNEY stirs on the sofa, groans.*) What are you . . . wake up! Wake up! (*No response. DANA crosses to the sofa, feet stomping the floor, and shakes SIDNEY.*) I said WAKE UP! (*SIDNEY groans again, louder, but still does not wake up.*) Sidney! Wake up! NOW! (*DANA shakes the sodden body so hard that SIDNEY falls on the floor with a bang and a shout.*)

SIDNEY: OW! Hey! What's . . . (*With a different kind of noise: a groan more than a yell, SIDNEY collapses on the floor.*) Ooooooooh . . .

DANA: Yeah, go on. Groan. Head hurts, huh?

SIDNEY: Yeah. What . . .

DANA: Eleven o'clock.

SIDNEY: . . . day is it?

DANA: Oh, for heaven's sake. You're not that hung over are you?

SIDNEY: Uh . . . yes.

DANA: (*Collapsing into a chair.*) Well, you deserve it. (*SIDNEY groans again.*) What time did you go to sleep?

SIDNEY: I have no idea.

DANA: Who was here last night?

SIDNEY: I have no idea.

DANA: How *many* were here last night?

SIDNEY: I have no . . .

DANA: Oh, shut up. (*Rises, crosses to the bedroom door.*) Well, I told you what would happen if you did this again. I warned you.

SIDNEY: Oh, please . . .

DANA: I warned you. That's it.

SIDNEY: Please don't. I promise . . .

DANA: (*Whirling in the doorway to face SIDNEY.*) No! I've heard promises before and I'm not listening anymore. You knew what would happen if you started drinking again. You knew what would happen, and you did it anyway.

SIDNEY: I won't . . .

DANA: Yes, you will. I know that, now. I think I knew it a long time ago, but I told myself to be patient. To give you a break. But no more. I can't do it. (*Turns again to the door.*)

SIDNEY: Please don't go.

DANA: I have to.

SIDNEY: Please don't. Give me another chance.

DANA: I can't. I can't work a night shift at the hospital and come home to this. I just can't do it.

SIDNEY: I won't . . .

DANA: You will! You know you will!

SIDNEY: I won't!

DANA: You will. You're weak. You know you are.

SIDNEY: All right! All right, I'm weak! I'm nothing! I'll do it again! So, go on! Leave!

DANA: I'm going to. (*DANA goes into the bedroom. SIDNEY waits a moment, then weakly crawls to a sitting position on the sofa, then stands up, walks to the window, raises the shade, winces. SIDNEY then walks uncertainly around the room, picking up a bottle here, a can there, then collapses on the sofa again, dropping the litter back onto the floor.*)

SIDNEY: . . . this is my apartment, too. (*This mumble was not meant to be heard by anyone but SIDNEY, but it must've sounded like a good idea, so it's repeated, much more loudly.*) This is my apartment, too!

DANA: (*From inside the bedroom.*) It's all yours now.

SIDNEY: Fine! (*Pause.*) . . . I'm sorry. (*No response.*) I said I'm sorry. (*No response.*) I said I'm sorry!

DANA: I heard you.

SIDNEY: Please give me another chance.

DANA: (*From the bedroom door.*) Why should I?

SIDNEY: Because . . . because if you don't . . . I'll . . .

DANA: Wait a full week before you give another party?

SIDNEY: No! If you leave, I'll die!

DANA: You're going to die, anyway. You're going to drink yourself to death. I don't want to watch.

SIDNEY: Please don't leave.

DANA: Sorry. I can't do this anymore. (*Goes back into the bedroom.*)

SIDNEY: I know . . . I know I've said this before, but this time I really mean it. You're right. I know I . . . that I've got a problem. And I'll fix it. I will. I'll go back into therapy . . . I'll . . . go back to AA. But . . . you've got to stay. I can't do it without you. I can't. I'll . . .

DANA: (*Coming out of the bedroom, carrying a small bag.*) I'll come back for the rest of my stuff tomorrow.

SIDNEY: No! Where are you . . . where are you going?

DANA: To a motel. I've got to get some sleep.

SIDNEY: Stay!

DANA: No.

SIDNEY: Please!

DANA: No. (*DANA opens the door, exits. The door closes with a firm click.*)

SIDNEY: (*With a howl.*) Dana! Come back! Please! (*Silence. SIDNEY, face in hands, sits silently for a moment, then looks up, stares for a moment, rises, walks into the bedroom, comes back out holding a razor blade.*) All right. Fine. Leave. Go on and leave. (*SIDNEY sits on the floor in the center of the room.*) But you're the last person who's going to leave me. I'll tell you that much. The last one. (*SIDNEY holds the razor blade tightly against the wrist arteries that will spurt blood the most fiercely.*) The last one . . . (*The front door opens and DANA enters, turns on the lights.*)

DANA: That was pretty good.

SIDNEY: What are you doing here? Go back out! You came in too soon.

DANA: Haven't you finished yet?

SIDNEY: No! You're too soon! Get out so I can . . .

DANA: No, come on, you had plenty of time. You can't take forever.

SIDNEY: I need that time! A person doesn't decide to kill themselves in three seconds.

DANA: Your character would. Don't be stupid.

SIDNEY: Don't tell me what to do! This is as much my scene as it is yours!

DANA: It's both of ours. And it goes up in acting class tomorrow, so if you take forever on the last bit, we're never going to finish rehearsing it.

SIDNEY: I'll take as long as I need!

DANA: Oh, yeah?

SIDNEY: Yeah!

DANA: Then find another scene partner.

SIDNEY: You know I can't! It's too late. We'd flunk.

DANA: So, speed up the suicide.

SIDNEY: . . . okay, okay. Let's do it again.

DANA: Fine. Just remember to pick up the pace generally.

SIDNEY: Yeah, yeah . . . (*SIDNEY lies down on the sofa. DANA turns off the lights and shuts the door. There is a pause, then the door opens and DANA stands in the light from the hallway.*)

DANA: Oh, no!

BLACKOUT

Supplementary Exercise Scene 2

It will be apparent to you right away that this scene has pace and rate challenges. A good deal of the dialogue is interrupted by one character or the other, though some of them can be trail-offs. Find out which is which, of course, and work on balancing the dynamics of the scene. Try to find ways, too, where the character of Stacey is not completely submissive to the near dominance of Jan's aggression. Are they not balanced at the end? How do you arrive at that balance? Be sure each of you knows what the other's spine is, and plan the build of the scene around them. It is very important for both of you to establish where these people are: hospital? hotel? prison? The location, of course, will be your primary key to who these people are and, therefore, to what exactly they are doing here.

Neighbors

(*A public park on a summer evening, just before sunset. JAN sits on a bench doing nothing.*)

STACEY: Excuse me. Can you tell me where . . .

JAN: What? What did you say?

STACEY: . . . Oh, well, I was just going to ask you if . . .

JAN: I can't believe you. Do you do this often?

STACEY: Do I . . . do I do what?

JAN: Come on, don't give me that. You know what.

STACEY: No, I . . .

JAN: You must be nuts. Trying to pick up strange people like this.

STACEY: I wasn't . . .

JAN: Of course you were! What, do you think I'm stupid?

STACEY: No . . . but I wasn't . . .

JAN: Not that I blame you. I mean, I know how attractive I am.

STACEY: . . . you do.

JAN: Of course. What am I? A dummy? Blind? I know.

STACEY: I see.

JAN: I know all right. I know.

STACEY: Yes.

JAN: But you got to be careful these days. Somebody like you, well, somebody like you could wind up . . . could wind up . . .

STACEY: Dead?

JAN: Right!

STACEY: Or worse!

JAN: Uh . . .

STACEY: Much worse.

JAN: Much, much worse.

STACEY: . . . what could be worse than . . .

JAN: Wow!

STACEY: . . . being dead?

JAN: Look at that!

STACEY: . . . what?

JAN: Never mind. What do you mean?

STACEY: . . . what?

JAN: What do you mean, what could be worse than being dead?

STACEY: Well, just that, actually.

JAN: Just that.

STACEY: Yes. Exactly.

JAN: You are really a piece of work, aren't you?

STACEY: I mean, dead is dead. What could be worse?

JAN: Amazing.

STACEY: I guess being buried alive is worse, of course.

JAN: Ah.

STACEY: Or being permanently paralyzed from the hairline down.

JAN: You trying to be funny?

STACEY: No. Are you?

JAN: I look like I'm trying to be funny to you?

STACEY: Yes, actually. Now.

JAN: Right. I'm confusing you, right?

STACEY: Not anymore, no.

JAN: Not like at first.

STACEY: No. Not like at first.

JAN: You've undergone some kind of change.

STACEY: I guess. I . . .

JAN: A character transformation.

STACEY: Well . . .

JAN: I did that.

STACEY: . . . you did.

JAN: Sure.

STACEY: Okay. How?

JAN: Tune in on the neurometric wavelength, wiggled around a little bit with some . . . oh, call them subliminal screwdrivers, and there you are.

STACEY: I'm here, certainly. I just don't . . . I don't know if I've made any kind of radical change. I . . .

JAN: How do you know?

STACEY: Well, I've been conscious the last few minutes and I don't . . .

JAN: How do you know?

STACEY: How do I . . . oh. That I've been conscious the last few minutes?

JAN: Bingo.

STACEY: Because . . . because I can look at my watch and see that only a very few minutes passed since I started to talk to you and . . .

JAN: Dangerously.

STACEY: . . . since I . . . dangerously started to talk to you and I've been . . .

JAN: Foolishly.

STACEY: . . . I've been aware of every word I've said, our entire conversation, so . . .

JAN: With excessive foolhardiness.

STACEY: . . . so I think that proves . . .

JAN: Right. So that proves you're conscious. Right.

STACEY: I think so.

JAN: Yes, a real piece of work.

STACEY: You're very unique yourself.

JAN: You think so?

STACEY: Yes.

JAN: And very attractive. (*Pause.*) Right?

STACEY: Well, actually . . .

JAN: Yes?

STACEY: Yes. You are.

JAN: Right. I told you.

STACEY: So.

JAN: Very.

STACEY: Yes. Okay. Very.

JAN: So. That settles that.

STACEY: Yes. I guess it does. (*Long pause.*) So, can you tell me where . . .

JAN: Not again!

STACEY: . . . your room is?

JAN: . . . oh. (*Pause.*) Wing Four.

STACEY: Me, too!

JAN: Third Floor.

STACEY: Me, *too!*

JAN: Corridor Five.

STACEY: I'm Corridor Six!

JAN: Room 305.

STACEY: I can't believe this.

JAN: What?

STACEY: I'm in Room 316.

JAN: Ah. (*Pause.*) Well. (*Pause.*) That's pretty close.

STACEY: Very close.

JAN: Dangerously close.

STACEY: Dangerously?

JAN: For you.

STACEY: Yes. But then . . .

JAN: Very, very . . .

STACEY: . . . like you said . . .

JAN: Dangerous.

STACEY: I'm foolhardy.

JAN: Yes. You are.

STACEY: Right. (*Pause.*) And?

JAN: Very, very attractive . . .

THE LIGHTS FADE TO BLACK

Supplementary Exercise Scene 3

This is a fairly straightforward scene, in which the two characters are related in an unknown way. Part of your job, of course, is to determine that relationship. What holds them together? Why do they stay where they are? Where, in fact, *are* they? Another interesting factor is the age of the characters. Sometimes they seem very young indeed, even call each other children. But do children do that? And at other times they seem very mature. Be very specific, then, in your character choices.

Stuck

(Interior of an ordinary dining room. TIP and BEANIE sit at the dining table. BEANIE works at a large jigsaw puzzle. TIP is putting together a model airplane. TIP looks around for the scissors.)

TIP: Hand me the scissors, please.

BEANIE: Get them yourself. Who do you think you are?

TIP: Oh, will you cut it out?

BEANIE: No!

TIP: I'm so sick of this . . .

BEANIE: *You're* sick of it?

TIP: Yes. You're driving me crazy.

BEANIE: *I'm* . . . what about *you?*

TIP: What about me?

BEANIE: You're impossible to get along with. You're thoughtless, you're weird . . .

TIP: *I'm* weird?

BEANIE: You bet you're weird.

TIP: You're sitting there with your feet in a bucket of lemonade, and you're calling *me* weird.

BEANIE: It's not lemonade.

TIP: It certainly is.

BEANIE: It's lemons and water.

TIP: Right. Lemonade.

BEANIE: And it's good for the feet.

TIP: Right.

BEANIE: It *is.*

TIP: Could you hand me the scissors, please.

BEANIE: No. Get them yourself. *(Pause. TIP seems to consider, then reaches across the table, purposely scattering BEANIE's puzzle pieces on the floor.)* Hey!

TIP: That'll teach you to be obnoxious.

BEANIE: Pick them up.

TIP: Certainly not.

BEANIE: Pick them *up!*

TIP: *No!*

BEANIE: Pick them up *now!*

TIP: No! I *won't!*

BEANIE: *Fine! (BEANIE reaches across the table and slams a fist down on TIP's model airplane, crushing part of it. TIP screams, then becomes very quiet, staring at BEANIE ominously.)*

TIP: Why did you do that?

BEANIE: *(Picking up the puzzle pieces.)* Because you messed up my puzzle.

TIP: You are very childish.

BEANIE: So are you.

TIP: I'm not. You are.

BEANIE: You.

TIP: You.

BEANIE: Oh, just shut up.

TIP: You shut up.

BEANIE: You.

TIP: You.

BEANIE: Leave me alone!

TIP: Fine. (*Starts to put the airplane back together. Silence.*) This is ruined.

BEANIE: Good.

TIP: I hope you're missing some pieces. (*Banging scissors on table.*)

BEANIE: Well, I'm not! So there!

TIP: Oh, I've had enough of this! (*Rising abruptly from the table and crossing to the window. Pause.*) I've got to get out of here.

BEANIE: So, go.

TIP: You know I can't.

BEANIE: . . . yes. I do.

TIP: And neither can you.

BEANIE: No. (*Pause.*) I'm not . . . I don't think I want to.

TIP: What?

BEANIE: I don't think I want to leave.

TIP: You *don't?*

BEANIE: No. I don't.

TIP: You're *happy?*

BEANIE: Well . . . no, but . . .

TIP: You want to *stay* here?

BEANIE: Where would I go?

TIP: Anywhere else.

BEANIE: You're not . . . you really want to go?

TIP: Yes.

BEANIE: I see. (*Pause.*) Where would *you* go?

TIP: To . . .

BEANIE: Yes?

TIP: . . . to Los Angeles.

BEANIE: Oh, sure. Right.

TIP: I would.

BEANIE: Sure.

TIP: You wait and see.

BEANIE: I will.

TIP: That's where I'll go. Los Angeles.

BEANIE: Hollywood.

TIP: Right.

BEANIE: And be a movie star.

TIP: Maybe.

BEANIE: Sure.

TIP: Why not?

BEANIE: You really want to know?

TIP: Anybody can do anything they want to if they really want to do it.

BEANIE: And that's what you really want to do, huh? Suddenly? Be a movie star?

TIP: Sure! I . . . (*Suddenly flopping down in a chair.*) Oh, I don't know. Leave me alone.

BEANIE: Gladly. Whatever Your Majesty wants.

TIP: You're such a jerk. (*Long pause.*)

BEANIE: Actually, I agree with you.

TIP: What? That you're a jerk? Good. About time you realized it.

BEANIE: No. That anybody can do anything if they really want to.

TIP: You do? You agree with that?

BEANIE: Yes. I do.

TIP: Well, then, why don't we both go to Hollywood? Why don't we both . . .

BEANIE: Because that's not what I want to do.

TIP: New York, then. We could . . .

BEANIE: I don't want to go anywhere. I want to stay right here. I . . . like it here. (*Pause.*)

TIP: I can't believe you said that.

BEANIE: It's true.

TIP: Why on earth . . .

BEANIE: Because . . . because it's . . . home.

TIP: Because you're scared!

BEANIE: Maybe.

TIP: You're a chicken!

BEANIE: So what?

TIP: Well, I'm not. I'm . . . (*Stands. Doesn't move.*) I'm . . .

BEANIE: What? You're what?

TIP: I'm . . . (*Suddenly sits down.*)

BEANIE: *What?*

TIP: . . . I'm going to fix my airplane.

BEANIE: Right.

TIP: Then I'm going to . . . (*Pause. They look at each other.*) . . . I'm going to . . . (*A hopeless pause.*)

BEANIE: . . . yes.

TIP: Yes . . .

BEANIE: You want the scissors? (*Picking up the scissors and holding them out.*)

THE LIGHTS FADE OUT

Supplementary Exercise Scene 4

This is a fairly straightforward, low-key scene. It will give you a chance to work on two characters who are not doing much, just sitting and drinking and talking. Their history, however, will give you an opportunity to construct a fairly elaborate characterizational subtext. Something is apparently bothering both of them, and has been for a while. What? Is the end hopeful or catastrophic? Find good motivations for everything that happens. Use this scene to write a long character analysis.

Looking and Looking

(A dark, smoky, and not very attractive bar. J. P. and BUZZ sit on two stools, drinking.)

J. P.: What a drag.

BUZZ: Yeah.

J. P.: Just when I was getting good at that job they fire me.

BUZZ: Hard to believe.

J. P.: What a lousy day.

BUZZ: What a lousy week.

J. P.: How was your day?

BUZZ: Lousy. *(They look at each other and laugh.)*

J. P.: No luck, huh?

BUZZ: Nope. Nobody wants to hire somebody like me.

J. P.: What do you mean, somebody like you? You're okay. You don't have two heads or anything.

BUZZ: Right. I don't have any skills, either.

J. P.: Sure you do.

BUZZ: Name one.

J. P.: Well, there's . . . you can . . . you . . . *(Plainly at a loss, J. P. mumbles something and turns away.)*

BUZZ: See what I mean?

J. P.: Not fair.

BUZZ: Who said it was?

J. P.: My mother.

BUZZ: Yeah, well, she was wrong.

J. P.: How dare you? My mom was never wrong. She was . . .

BUZZ: Yes?

J. P.: . . . just never right. *(They laugh again.)*

BUZZ: Mothers.

J. P.: Yeah.

BUZZ: Bless 'em.

J. P.: You can say that again. *(Quickly as BUZZ's mouth opens.)* But don't.

BUZZ: Whatever you say. *(Pause.)* How long we known each other?

J. P.: Oh . . . nearly twelve years now.

BUZZ: That long?

J. P.: That's what they tell me.

BUZZ: Who?

J. P.: What?

BUZZ: Who tells you?

J. P.: Joke, Buzz. Just a joke.

BUZZ: Oh. I thought you meant . . .

J. P.: No. Don't worry.

BUZZ: Well, I wasn't worried. Not really. It's just . . .

J. P.: I know. Gets to you.

BUZZ: It does. After a while.

J. P.: Gets to all of us.

BUZZ: You do okay.

J. P.: I get by.

BUZZ: Me, though, I don't know. I just seem to be . . .

J. P.: You're fine.

BUZZ: Thanks, but . . . not quite.

J. P.: You're *fine*, I'm telling you.

BUZZ: Actually, I'm not.

J. P.: You are.

BUZZ: Actually, I'm falling apart.

J. P.: Don't say that.

BUZZ: I thought somebody followed me home last night. I must have stopped six times on the way home. Kept looking behind me. Checked every closet when I got home.

J. P.: Nothing wrong with that.

BUZZ: No way to live.

J. P.: No, I agree with you there.

BUZZ: Will it ever be over?

J. P.: Someday.

BUZZ: Maybe. (*Pause.*) Also, I'm turning into a drunk.

J. P.: Nothing wrong with a drink now and then.

BUZZ: No. Too many drinks. I'm a drunk. We both are. We both . . . look at us.

J. P.: Rather not.

BUZZ: We're . . .

J. P.: Want another?

BUZZ: No, I . . . sure. Why not? (*Pause. They drink.*)

J. P.: You worry too much, you know? I mean, if they were going to do any more, they would have done it by now. Long ago.

BUZZ: You think?

J. P.: Sure. Long ago. That's the way they are. They're thorough, say that much for them. No, they're through with us. Long ago.

BUZZ: I hope so.

J. P.: They are.

BUZZ: I hope you're right.

J. P.: I am. I'm always right. (*J. P. laughs, BUZZ doesn't.*)

BUZZ: I . . . hope so. Because . . .

J. P.: It's going to be okay. We'll get jobs soon, and everything will be fine. You'll see.

BUZZ: Because . . . I can't go on like this.

J. P.: You can.

BUZZ: No. I can't.

J. P.: You can and you will. I'll see to that. I'll . . .

BUZZ: Look.

J. P.: What?

BUZZ: Look who just came in the door.

J. P.: Where? Who is . . . oh, no!

BUZZ: Yes. Oh, yes.

J. P.: No!
BUZZ: Well . . . at least we don't have to worry anymore.

BLACKOUT

Supplementary Exercise Scene 5

This scene is almost ostentatiously simple. There is very little indication in the text as to the characters' histories or what they plan to do when they get wherever they're going. Like many plays, the subtext must be constructed on very little evidence and the interest and energy of the scene lies almost exclusively in the thoughts of the characters and the dynamic of its expression. Keep the scene moving, but find the reasons for the pauses and give them full value. The scene also allows you to work on sense memory: the rhythms of the bus and the passing scenery.

From Santa Fe On

(SANDY and JESSE sit side by side on a bus.)

SANDY: Where are we?
JESSE: Uh . . . Santa Fe.
SANDY: New Mexico?
JESSE: No. Massachusetts.
SANDY: Okay, okay. Give me a break. I've been asleep.
JESSE: You certainly have.
SANDY: How long?
JESSE: Couple of hours.
SANDY: Yeah?
JESSE: Yep.
SANDY: You'd think I'd feel better.
JESSE: You don't?
SANDY: Nope.
JESSE: No. Me neither. (*Pause.*) Tired.
SANDY: What?
JESSE: I'm tired.
SANDY: Me, too.
JESSE: You just woke up.
SANDY: Still tired, though.
JESSE: We've been on this thing for days.
SANDY: Weeks.
JESSE: How long before we're there?
SANDY: Tomorrow.
JESSE: At last.
SANDY: Yeah.
JESSE: Will they be there to meet us?
SANDY: Said they would.

JESSE: I certainly hope so.

SANDY: Well, even if they aren't, we'll be okay. We can get a cab.

JESSE: Expensive.

SANDY: I got a few bucks.

JESSE: Exactly. A *few*.

SANDY: Enough. (*Pause.*) Think we'll like it there?

JESSE: No idea.

SANDY: What's it like?

JESSE: Hot.

SANDY: Good.

JESSE: Sunny.

SANDY: *Very* good.

JESSE: Surfers, tourists, sailors.

SANDY: Not so good.

JESSE: Harmless.

SANDY: Maybe.

JESSE: A place is what you make it.

SANDY: Who said that, your first-grade teacher?

JESSE: Second-grade.

SANDY: Which is why she never left Vermont, right?

JESSE: I guess.

SANDY: I can't even remember who my second-grade teacher was.

JESSE: Stop this bus, I'm getting off.

SANDY: Huh?

JESSE: I'm not riding with anybody who can't remember who their second-grade teacher was.

SANDY: Very funny.

JESSE: I'm a very funny person.

SANDY: Only problem is, I'm not in the mood for very funny.

JESSE: Why not?

SANDY: I'm worried.

JESSE: About?

SANDY: New job. New school. New friends.

JESSE: What's to worry?

SANDY: I'm not good at any of that.

JESSE: We'll be fine.

SANDY: Didn't I say that last time?

JESSE: I think so.

SANDY: Well, we can take turns being upbeat.

JESSE: Okay. Whose turn is it now?

SANDY: Mine, I think.

JESSE: Go for it.

SANDY: Not now, I'm depressed.

JESSE: I thought you were worried.

SANDY: Worried and depressed.

JESSE: Go back to sleep.

SANDY: No. I wake up in a bad mood.

JESSE: Worried and depressed.

SANDY: Yes.

JESSE: You are doomed to sleeplessness.

SANDY: On this bus, yes.

JESSE: Long night ahead.

SANDY: I'll be okay.

JESSE: Ah. It is your turn.

SANDY: I guess it must be.

JESSE: When's the next rest stop?

SANDY: I don't know. When did we stop last?

JESSE: Santa Fe.

SANDY: Oh, yeah. I was asleep.

JESSE: Yeah. Here. I bought some candy.

SANDY: I'm thirsty.

JESSE: Bingo. (*Passes out candy and two cans of soda.*)

SANDY: Wow. A magician.

JESSE: I do my best.

SANDY: It's warm.

JESSE: So's Santa Fe.

SANDY: So's this bus.

JESSE: So's where we're going.

SANDY: And sunny.

JESSE: And surfers.

SANDY: And tourists.

JESSE: And sailors.

SANDY: And us.

JESSE: Yeah. (*Pause.*)

SANDY: I'm worried.

JESSE: That mean it's my turn again?

SANDY: Yes.

JESSE: Uh, let's see . . .

SANDY: Quick.

JESSE: We'll be fine.

SANDY: More.

JESSE: We'll be *very* fine.

SANDY: Okay. Good. I'm fine. We'll be fine. (*Pause.*)

JESSE: Will we?

LIGHTS FADE

APPENDIX B

• • • •

STRUCTURE OF A TYPICAL WRITTEN CHARACTER ANALYSIS

Several times during the book the term *character analysis* was mentioned. Teachers of acting vary so greatly in the kinds and quality of paperwork they require that you will want to check with your teacher or director to be sure exactly what, if any, he or she will ask for in this regard. A written character analysis is valuable to the beginning actor whether or not an instructor or director requires it. This sample is the kind of analysis I require from my students: adapt it as you like. I think a good character analysis has three areas:

1. a birth-to-death biography of the character;
2. the answers to some specific questions about the character;
3. a section that lists the problems you are having in developing this character.

The birth-to-death character biography involves a very thorough analysis of your character. You can write this biography in first person (I tend to prefer that:

it's more immediate) or in the third person. You will almost never find a play in which the character is born at the beginning, so you will have to use your imagination and extrapolate from the information given in the play a sequence of events that led the character from birth to the age at which we see him or her in the play. Do the same thing for the time that follows the last moment of the character's life in the play to his or her death. Very often we find characters dying within the confines of the chronological framework of the play, so you may not need to think this up yourself. But if the character is still alive at final curtain, decide (again, based on what the playwright has given you) what happens to the character after the play ends. Use your imagination!

This birth-to-death biography will give you a very complete picture of the person you are playing. Make it as detailed as you can. Some of my students put it in the form of a diary (not giving me every day, of course), and that seems to work. Don't let your fantasy, however, wander outside the realm of possibilities that have been set up within the play.

The list of questions that I have my students answer about their characters are these:

1. How old is the character at the beginning of the scene?
2. What is the character's state of mind at the beginning of the scene? Use active verbs and adjectives.
3. Where, precisely, is the character geographically, and what is the character's attitude toward the environment?
4. What sort of clothes, if fully costumed, would the character wear in this scene?
5. What has the character had to eat and/or drink in the last six hours? Does the character feel good or not so good as a result?
6. What is the character's primary objective? What exactly does he or she want to obtain in this scene?
7. What are the ten adjectives that best apply to the character during the scene's progress?
8. What is the highest emotional peak for the character during the scene? The lowest? Describe these emotions.
9. Have you, the actor, ever experienced any of these emotions? If yes, how did you apply your own experience to the scene? If no, what methods did you use to relate to these emotions?
10. How do the following physical qualities of the character differ from your own?
    a. Walk
    b. Usual way of sitting
    c. Voice
    d. Basic body gesture
    e. Nervous mannerisms, if any.

These questions, of course, apply to classroom scene work. If you make up a character analysis for a role in a production, adapt these questions as needed. You may think of other questions, of course.

The section in which you list and discuss any problems you have had with this characterization is the most personal part of the analysis. It can include anything. Many of my students keep performance diaries or journals, and include the appropriate sections of those in this section. Remember, nobody but you and your director or instructor reads this, so you can include your reactions to people and other personal circumstances. You can discuss the difficulty of relating to a character who is very dissimilar to you. Or you may find problems playing a character who is too much like you. You can include technical problems and progress in solving them (or not): voice, body, and mental. Anything causing you problems in working on the scene should be written down in this section.

If you do keep a journal, be as flexible as you can in the kinds of things you include in it. The journal can be a very valuable tool for charting your progress over a period of months or years. An excellent example of such a journal that was published as a book is British actor Anthony Sher's *The Year of the King*, which records his experiences playing Richard III.

GLOSSARY

The following terms are found in *The Stages of Acting*. The definitions are those which are generally accepted by actors and directors in contemporary theater in the United States.

acting edition Version of a play put out by a well-known publishing house usually after a successful commercial run of performances. These editions often include the blocking and other stage directions of that run.

action Mental, physical, or emotional activity motivated by a textual or subtextual source that moves the character along the emotional and rhythmic build toward the objective of the scene.

actor control that part of the actor which remains in control of the performance, dealing with differing audience response, emergencies, and other inconsistencies from performance to performance. Actor control should be present as little as possible, but is necessary to some small extent.

actor's journal Any diary kept on a regular basis by actors in which they record their progress through a role they are performing or in which any notes regarding character observation, sense memory, emotion memory, or any other helpful material can be found.

articulation   Formation of the sounds of speech using the lips, tongue, teeth, lower jaw, and soft palate.

audition piece   Selection from a play or other source material used by actors when they are auditioning for roles. A good audience piece is suitable to the actor's commercially castable type and demonstrates as many of the actor's strong points as possible in a limited amount of time.

autonomic level   Level of memory that is as close as possible to one on which reflexive action takes place. Lines, the blocking, and any other memorized material in a performance should be at this level.

black box   Generic term for a theater structure that uses nonproscenium staging methods. Such a theater, where experimental works are often performed, may also be referred to as a theater-in-the-round, an arena theater, or the like.

body gesture   Use of the hands and arms as they directly relate to the rest of the body. The body gesture may express action, but is most often used when the body is at rest: folded arms, hands on hips, hands in the pockets, and so on.

body stance   Way in which the body relates to the surface where it is standing, sitting, or lying. Generally speaking, a relaxed, connected, centered stance is the basis for all effective gesture and movement (*see* **stance**).

build   Increasing emotional and rhythmic intensity of a scene.

caesura   Very short rhythmic break, most usually for sense rather than breath, in the speaking of a line or phrase.

cattle call   Common slang term for an audition for a play or film that is openly announced to the general public and to which large numbers of aspiring actors respond.

centering   Internal point of concentration that focuses mental energy and from which all effective balance and movement derive.

center line   Imaginary line drawn on the upstage-downstage axis of a proscenium stage that provides point of reference for the center of focus on such a stage.

character analysis   Written statement of the life and goals of the character as perceived by the actor. Based on textual material and subtextual choices, this analysis often includes a biography, psychological profile, physical description, and individual motivations that aid the actor in making choices. Directors often collaborate with the actor on ideas relating to the character analysis.

character biography   Written statement of the life of the character as perceived by the actor. Character biographies are drawn from the text, but may be expanded to include the character's life before the play begins (sometimes from birth) and after the play ends to the character's death. In such cases, the actor's projections of the origin and destiny of the character must be based on extrapolations from valid textual sources.

characterization   Incarnation of the textual persona in the mind and body of the actor.

choices   Decisions the actor makes on how a subtextual thought or emotion is expressed externally.

circles of concentration   Selected circles of awareness into which actors focus their attention. These circles include a *personal* circle that expresses the focus area when the character is alone or in deep thought; a *shared* circle that includes the entire acting area and any other actors in it; and an *infinite* circle in which the character projects the focus of thought into memory or extended physical space.

cold reading   Part of the audition process in which the actor demonstrates skill level and understanding of the material by reading from the script, either with a staff assistant or another actor, without having had an opportunity to study the script or prepare characterization.

commenting   Performing external actions without internal motivation, usually in order to elicit a specific response from the audience (*see* **indicating**).

conflict   Opposing textual forces in which the character is caught.

consistency   Ability to deliver a characterization from performance to performance with essentially the same truth, honesty, energy, and rhythm.

cues   Words, physical circumstances, or technical units that indicate to an actor when it is time to speak or perform an action. Usually, a cue is the end of the preceding line of dialogue, but often might be a variety of stimuli such as sound, lighting effects, other physical actions, or even an individual internal process.

cue-to-cue   Technique of going from one technical cue to another in a rehearsal specifically for that purpose.

dialogue   Spoken words of the characters in a play.

diaphragmatic breathing   Process of allowing natural breathing to originate from and be controlled by the diaphragm. This process must become automatic in order for the actor to possess good vocal quality.

diction   Clear, proper pronunciation of the sounds that make up the spoken words of American English.

director's concept   Overall vision of a director of a specific play indicating how all the various components of a production (designs, acting style, rhythm, music, and so forth) will form a unified whole that will effectively deliver the intent of the play as the director sees it.

dovetailing   Beginning to speak before the preceding speech is completed, often in fast-paced situations (*see* **telescoping**).

downstage   Area on a proscenium stage closest to the audience.

dress parade   Special rehearsal call for the cast of a production to appear before the costume designer and the director in the costumes they will wear. This is an opportunity for all concerned to discuss possible problems with the costumes.

dress rehearsal   One of several rehearsals just prior to the opening of a production when costumes are added to the other technical aspects.

dry run   Technical rehearsal that is held without the presence of actors. It is during such a rehearsal (often called a *pretech*) that the director, stage manager, and light and sound designers set cues for lights and sound.

ellipsis   Three dots (. . .) that most frequently occur at the end of a phrase or sentence (sometimes within a line) indicating a pause or incomplete or interrupted thought.

emotion memory   Ability of the actor to recall a specific emotional response from his or her own life and apply it to the emotional circumstances of the character. Sometimes called *affective memory*.

ensemble acting   Listening and responding to the other actors in the cast to such a degree that the entire unit appears to be reacting to each other in a spontaneous and unified way.

environment   Physical surroundings of the scene. Often more than a room, the environment may include exterior phenomena such as weather, differences in terrain, noise, and so forth.

externals   External manifestation of the acting process: voice, gesture, and movement, all of which exist as a result of the internal thoughts and emotions (*see also* **internals**).

facial gesture   Use of the face as a gesture plane.

filled pause   Pause said to be filled when the internal thought process is completely gone through so that the length of both thought and pause are the same.

finding your light   Ability of actors to know when they are standing in the pool of light provided by the lighting design. Accomplished by a combination of peripheral vision and reflection.

floor plan   Blueprint of the set as seen from above (see *ground plan*).

frontal visibility   Maintaining the body so that the face is visible to the audience without seeming unnatural.

grounding   Maintaining a relaxed, secure physical stance, firmly resting on the floor or other surface.

ground plan   *See* **floor plan**.

hand/arm gesture   Use of the hands and/or arms away from the body in order to describe or emphasize objects, events, or conditions.

hash marks   Two slanted lines (//) inserted in the script during the scoring process to indicate a caesura or pause.

head shot   Photograph of the actor brought, along with a résumé, to auditions or sent to agents, directors, and others as reminders that the actor is still looking for a job.

holding for laughs   Waiting for an audience response to die down before preceding with the dialogue so as to be heard. The actor waits until the laugh has reached a peak, then repeats any words that may not have been heard before going on.

improvisation   Acting without a prepared script. Often used as a useful exercise to find appropriate emotional responses or line readings in classroom work or early rehearsals. Improvisational comedy is, of course, a technique unto itself.

in character   Term used to indicate that the actor is thinking and reacting as the character in the play would.

indicating   *See* **commenting**.

internals   Thoughts and emotions the actor must go through in order to motivate the physical expression of the character (see also *externals*).

interrupt   Specific kind of dovetailing in which, out of peremptory emotion, a character begins to speak before the preceding line has ended.

isolation in public   Ability of actors to react naturally even when being observed.

learning lines   Process by which the dialogue is committed to memory on the autonomic level.

line reading   Rhythms and stresses, based on subtextual choices, that the actor gives to the dialogue when delivering it.

listening   Part of the present-tense acting process in which the actor listens in character as if hearing the lines for the first time.

LORT   League of Regional Theaters.

method acting   Name given to a version of the approach to acting pioneered by Russian director Constantin Stanislavski toward the end of the nineteenth century. In the United States, method acting came to suggest paying complete attention to the internal process at the expense of the external manifestation, toward which little or no importance seemed to be attached.

moment before   Brief but very important moment just before going onto the stage, during which all the actor's forces of energy and concentration are gathered to focus on the many individual tasks of the performance.

motivation   Reason for any speech or action in a performance. The actor must determine the character's motivation by thoroughly examining the subtext that underlies the text and discovering these basic reasons for speech and action.

motivational unit   Smallest unit into which the subtext can be divided. The demarcation of the subtext into these small transitional units or sections allows the actor to move smoothly and effectively from one thought to another and begins the process that builds the scene's overall intent, rhythm, and build.

movement   Stage movement may be divided into several broad areas: movement on and around the general stage environment that is usually planned by the director in the blocking rehearsals; actor stance, whether sitting, standing, lying, or in any position the character takes him; body gesture, which is the hands and arms moving in relation to the rest of the body; hand/arm gesture, which is the hands and arms functioning as vehicles of description and emphasis; and facial gesture, which is using the face as a plane for gesture.

mugging   Facial gesture that is unsupported by subtextual motivation, often exaggerated, and always done for external effect alone.

objective   Purpose the character is trying to achieve at any time in the development of the scene.

obstacle   Event or emotional development that works at cross purposes to the character's obtaining of the objective. Often the primary creators of conflict, obstacles are valuable aids in the building of characterization.

pace   Overall rhythm of a scene, primarily dependent on the length of pauses between textual divisions.

peak   Moment of greatest emotional intensity in a scene.

phrasing   Division of dialogue into discrete yet cohesive units as dictated by intellectual and emotional sense. Close examination of the phrasing of the longer speech is particularly important to the actor.

point of concentration   In doing relaxation or loosening exercises, the point of focus on which the acting student concentrates in order to discipline the mind and maintain balance.

present-tense acting   Process in which the actor's thought and response occurs at the same time as the character's. In present-tense acting, actors do not refer to a split level of thought or concentration in which they think of past or future events (whether inside or outside the play). They do not try consciously to recall the next line or lines, evaluate the performance, or attempt to bring about a specific audience response.

present-tense listening   Present-tense acting when the actor is not speaking. Defined separately from present-tense acting because acting students so often overlook it.

production concept   *See* **director's concept.**

projection   Psychological and physical focusing and placement of the voice in order to be clearly and easily heard and understood.

prompt script   Copy of the script held by the production's stage manager that has all cuts and blocking as well as light and sound cues and other technical data.

properties   Any of the small objects used and handled by characters on stage. These are usually divided into *set props*, which are part of the set, usually functioning only as set dressing; *hand props*, which are props that usually remain onstage but are used by the actors; *personal props*, which are brought onto or off the stage by actors; and *costume props*, which are part of the clothes worn by the actors and handled by the costume crew.

proscenium stage   Kind of theater in which the performance area is separated from the audience by an arch that functions like a picture frame. These theaters are usually quite large.

published edition   Version of the play as it was originally written by the playwright, before cuts and other production detail is added. The published edition can sometimes shed detailed light on characterization.

rate   Speed with which actors speak the words of their individual speeches.

readthrough   Rehearsal in which the entire cast reads the play aloud in order to understand the text intellectually and to begin to adapt to the director's concept. The readthrough is usually the first rehearsal.

realistic characterization   Building of a character in a play that is recognizable as having a possible existence in the everyday world inhabited by the actor and the audience when they are outside the theater.

reality level   Concept of realistic characterization as applied to the entire production.

relaxation   As applied to actor training, process by which the actor consciously releases as much tension from the body as possible in order to apply character muscular involvement to the body without being in conflict with actor muscular habit.

research   Any work the actor does outside the script itself to build an effective characterization.

rhythm   Dynamic of a scene's progression as it relates to pace, rate, and build.

running rehearsals   Rehearsals toward the end of the rehearsal period when the entire scene or play is run without stopping in order to work on the rhythm of the play.

scoring   marking the script with a series of graphic indicators that assist the actor in matters of interpretation and rhythm. Scoring graphics can be compared to the marks a composer inserts into a musical score to assist the performing musician in interpreting the music.

sense memory   Ability to recall a physical sensation and apply it to a theatrical situation in which the stimulus that produced the sensation is absent.

sharing   Physically and emotionally sharing focus with another actor or actors.

sight-reading   *See* **cold reading**.

spine   Through-line of a character's objective progress. Spine includes such matters as the subtextual motivation of actions in pursuit of the objective, the dynamic of rhythm (pace, rate), and the fluctuation of energy in the scene.

spontaneity   Ability to perform a scene as if for the first time.

stage combat   Any aggressive physical action in a play. All stage combat must be carefully planned and choreographed to appear realistic but be absolutely safe.

stage directions   Words (usually in parentheses or italics) in the text that indicate movement or interpretation. Stage directions might be written by the author (in a published version) or come from the director of a famous production (in an acting edition). Actors must not feel bound to stage directions (particularly those in an acting edition), but should thoroughly analyze them, then utilize them in combination with those they and the director construct.

stage environment   Entire physical structure of the production of a scene or play.

stage left   Left side of the sage as the actor perceives it when facing the audience.

stage manager   Production staff member who is second in command to the director. The stage manager writes all blocking and technical information into the prompt script, calls the light and sound cues, supervises all technical crews during a production, and functions as the director when that person is absent (typically after the opening night performance).

stage right   Right side of the stage as the actor perceives it when facing the audience.

stance   *See* **body stance**.

subtext   Psychological and emotional meanings and motivations that are the basis of the text. Why and in what context a character speaks and acts.

subverbal   Vocal sound that is not framed in words, for example, moans, cries, screams, sighs, grunts, and stammers. These subverbals are frequently not a part of the written text and can add to the effectiveness and reality level of the actor's vocal delivery if used judiciously.

superobjective   Statement of the overall goal or meaning of a play or scene. The superobjective in capsule form provides the through-line of motivation for the director's concept as well as the basic motivation for individual as well as group action.

technical rehearsal   Rehearsal usually just before the first dress rehearsal in which the lights, sound, and any other essential technical component are run through and timed with actors present.

telescoping   *See* **dovetailing**.

text   Entire written script of the play, including dialogue, stage directions, introductory essays, and any other conceptual material.

thinking the thought   Active component of present-tense acting and spontaneity. The actor must actually think the specific character thought that motivates speech or action in and at the same time the character does.

through-line of action   Linking of objectives in individual scenes to provide a motivational and objective guide for the sense and build of the scene or play.

thrust stage   Theater in which the performance space protrudes into the audience seating, often in a wedgelike shape, so as to provide more intimacy and immediacy for the performance. The audience, in such an arrangement, is then on three sides of the action.

topping   Geometric increase of vocal intensity and energy between two or more characters in a scene.

trail-off   Incomplete ending of a speech in which the character is unable or unwilling, for various reasons, to finish the thought.

transitions   Thought patterns that take a character from one motivational unit to another.

upstage   Area of the performance space farthest from the audience.

upstaging   Taking of focus from another actor by standing upstage, thus forcing him or her to face away from the audience. This is never done unless it is intentional, either for comic or unusual focus reasons.

vocal color   Speaking words as a reflection of their emotional content. Vocal color is one of the primary tools of vocal characterization.

vocal energy   Application of various levels of emotional intensity to the spoken word. Vocal energy is a primary tool of vocal characterization and, like vocal color, is never mere loudness. Vocal energy is also a primary tool of individual and group build.

vocal placement   Use of any of several natural resonating areas in the body which, if used in the producing of vocal sound, enhance vocal tone and give variety to the pattern of speech.

vomitorium   Passageway on the downstage side of a thrust stage that allows actors to make (often quick) exits in areas other than those upstage.

warm-up exercises   Regimen of physical, mental, and vocal exercises that prepare and relax the actor's mind and body for the performance situation.

working rehearsals   Rehearsals, usually immediately after the blocking sessions, in which actors work with their directors on motivation, subtext, and other mental and physical choices that will eventually motivate the external manifestation.

Contemporary Architectural Drawings

DONATIONS TO THE AVERY LIBRARY

CENTENNIAL DRAWINGS ARCHIVE

Contemporary Architectural Drawings

DONATIONS TO THE AVERY LIBRARY

CENTENNIAL DRAWINGS ARCHIVE

Janet Parks, Editor

Avery Architectural and Fine Arts Library

Columbia University

Pomegranate Artbooks ▪ San Francisco

Published by Pomegranate Artbooks,
Box 808022, Petaluma, California 94975
© 1991 Avery Architectural and Fine Arts Library,
Columbia University

Library of Congress Cataloging-in-Publication Data

Avery Library.
  Contemporary architectural drawings : donations to the Avery
Library centennial drawings archive / Janet Parks, editor. — 1st ed.
   p. cm.
  Catalog of an exhibition of drawings by American and
international architects that was on display at Columbia
University Apr. 3–May 4, 1991.
  ISBN 0-87654-767-6 : $35.00. — ISBN 0-87654-766-8 : $24.95
  1. Architectural drawing—20th century—Exhibitions.
2. Avery Library—Exhibitions. I. Parks, Janet. II. Title.
NA2695.U6A86 1991
720′.22′2—dc20   91-4216
                   CIP

Designed by Bonnie Smetts with John Malmquist
Printed in Korea
FIRST EDITION

CONTRIBUTING ARCHITECTS

A & G

ACE ARCHITECTS

TAKEFUMI AIDA

ROBERT EVANS ALEXANDER

STANLEY ALLEN

EMILIO AMBASZ

AMY ANDERSON

ROSS ANDERSON, OF ANDERSON / SCHWARTZ
    ARCHITECTS

JOHN ANDREWS

NADER ARDALAN

ARQUITECTONICA

TAKAMITSU AZUMA

DAVID BAKER

DIANA BALMORI

JACQUES BARSAC

PIETRO BELLUSCHI

GUNNAR BIRKERTS

KENT BLOOMER

RICARDO BOFILL

FRANCOISE BOLLACK

KEVIN BONE

MARIO BOTTA

JEFFERY BUCHOLTZ

LUIS BURILLO

BUTTRICK, WHITE & BURTIS ARCHITECTS / PLANNERS

COLIN CATHCART, OF KISS AND CATHCART, ANDERS

LO-YI CHAN, OF PRENTICE & CHAN, OHLHAUSEN
    ARCHITECTS AND PLANNERS

ALAN CHIMACOFF, OF THE HILLIER GROUP

LUIS CLOTET

DAVIS, BRODY & ASSOCIATES ARCHITECTS

PEGGY DEAMER, OF DEAMER PHILLIPS

NATALIE GRIFFIN DE BLOIS

PETER EISENMAN

ELLERBE BECKET, ARCHITECTS AND ENGINEERS

WENDY EVANS, OF PEI COBB FREED & PARTNERS
    ARCHITECTS

JAMES FAVARO, OF JOHNSON / FAVARO

CARLOS FERRATER LAMBARRI

vi

PREFACE

THE SECOND HALF OF THE TWENTIETH CENTURY SAW A RENEWED INTEREST IN architectural drawing, not just as a notation system for the art of architecture but as an art form in itself. This catalog and the exhibition it accompanies are ample proof of the richness and variety of that art.

The notion of forming a collection of contemporary architectural drawings in conjunction with Avery's centennial took many forms as we tossed around ideas for a suitable celebration. The idea galvanized in its present form when the opportunity arose to have an exhibition in the Wallach Gallery of the Department of Art History and Archaeology. Bernard Tschumi, dean of the Graduate School of Architecture, Planning and Preservation, then invited us to extend the exhibit to the Arthur Ross Gallery he had recently inaugurated in Buell Hall.

The magnitude of the response to our appeal for donations from architects throughout the world has been a heartwarming recognition of the widespread distinction achieved by the name of Avery during its first century of existence. Thanks to the generosity of the architects, we can today have a proud celebration of the art of architectural drawing with the first exhibition that joins the two new dynamic galleries on campus and positions Avery once more at the nexus between the historians and the practitioners of architecture.

It takes the efforts of many and multiple contributions to organize an undertaking of this sort. The visible part is no more than the proverbial tenth of a floating iceberg. Janet Parks, Avery's curator of drawings, has thrown herself body and soul behind the enterprise, and it could not have happened but for her enthusiasm and hard work. Edward Wendt has been a capable and fully engaged collaborator; Barry Bergdoll, as faculty adviser, has provided invaluable counsel.

The long list of thanks has to be headed by the Avery family, whose foresight created a library with the well-rounded mission of collecting all the documentation necessary for the study and practice of architecture. We wish to thank Miriam and Ira D. Wallach for the judicious support of the gallery that bears their name, a support that made it feasible for us to start planning this exhibition. The steady hand of Sarah Elliston Weiner and the support of her staff, Toni Simon and Larry Soucy, were essential in giving us the confidence to proceed. To Bernard Tschumi, Arthur Ross and Terence Riley, our thanks for facilitating the resources of the Arthur Ross Gallery. To Ted Gachot, assistant to the curator of drawings, and to John Farmer, Tatiana Ginsberg and Christopher Hatchell, who ably assisted him, a profound debt of gratitude for matting and framing the works in this exhibition. To our eagle-eye photography staff, Dwight Primiano, Denise Evarts and David Ortiz, our appreciation for the beautiful reproductions of the works illustrated in this catalog.

In addition to thanking the architects represented here for their generosity in donating the drawings exhibited, as well as the others that will form part of the permanent "Avery Centennial Archive," we wish to extend our thanks to those people in architectural offices without whose assistance the collection might have been less rich: Ginne Aamodt, Janet Adams Strong, Alisa Aronson, Sheila Bannon, Judith Blankman, Susan Brozes, Paul Davis, Melode Ferguson, Sarah Francis, Lisa Green, Jennifer Gridley, Claire Grossman, Meg Inglima, Sheryl Jacobs, Manjit Kingra, Laura Latermann, Greg Lynn, Patricia Moore, Jim Nichols, Miry Park, Rick Rosson, Jane Sager, Chris Siefert, Susan Strauss and Marie Wildman.

We are grateful to the Graham Foundation for its support and also to John Deermount of the Blueprint Company. And last but not least our thanks to Thomas Burke and the staff of Pomegranate Artbooks for supporting the production of this catalog. Their dedication and cooperation made this catalog a reality.

Angela Giral
Avery Librarian

INTRODUCTION

THE DRAWINGS COLLECTION AT THE AVERY LIBRARY IS AS OLD AS THE LIBRARY itself. Founded in 1890 as a memorial to the architect Henry Ogden Avery, the original gift by the Avery family consisted of Henry's professional library and the drawings of his brief but prosperous career. From this initial bequest, the Avery Library has grown to include more than 250,000 volumes, 1,100 serials titles, 10,000 rare books and over 400,000 architectural drawings and other architectural records.

The strength of the Avery Drawings Collection lies in the depth and richness of its holdings in American architecture of the nineteenth and twentieth centuries. Many of the collections document the careers of architects who were based in New York but built buildings throughout the United States and the world. Of particular importance are the collections of drawings and documents by Louis Sullivan, Frank Lloyd Wright, Hugh Ferriss, Alexander Jackson Davis, Richard and Richard Michell Upjohn, McKim, Mead and White, Warren and Wetmore, Greene and Greene, Walter Burley Griffin, Carrère and Hastings, Delano and Aldrich, Harrison and Abramovitz, Philip Johnson, Serge Chermayeff and Ely Jacques Kahn, among many others.

The drawings illustrated in this catalog were donated by the architects in celebration of the centennial of the founding of the Avery Library. The drawings arrived in response to an invitation extended in the spring of 1990. We hoped for a large enough response to guarantee a catalog and an exhibition, and we were not disappointed. The total archive numbers more than 320 drawings from 120 different architects. At least one drawing from each contributor was included in the exhibition; nearly all of the exhibited drawings are featured in this catalog.

The letter requesting a contribution enticed the architects with the promise of joining the distinguished company listed above as well as participating in the exhibition and catalog. No restrictions, or even suggestions, were made regarding the content of the donations, leaving the contributors free to donate a drawing that best represented their work. (We did make some suggestions regarding the size of the drawing.) With such freedom of choice also came the great dilemma of what to choose, and we spent many hours on the telephone in conference with the architects, discussing options. As the drawings started to arrive, the early donations became points of reference for architects calling for advice; it became possible to give something that was like or different from something already received. All means of persuasion and enthusiasm were used in order to assure donors that their contributions were welcome.

We hoped for a great diversity of drawings and in the end that is what we got. The archive as it stands reveals a great deal about the issues important to the architectural profession today and in that sense is a very fitting beginning to the second century of collecting architectural drawings for the Avery Library.

Janet Parks
Curator of Drawings

FOREWORD

An exhibit like this could be viewed as no more than a convenient excuse to satisfy, in the words of one donor, mere "curatorial greed." That may in fact be true, but nonetheless the Avery Library centennial has given us the opportunity to document, as broadly as possible, the architectural productions of a lively—some might say contentious—artistic period. Anyone who scans the following pages will likely come away with the impression that contemporary architects are far removed from a consensus of any sort. We could have chosen from the beginning to downplay that fact by limiting the range of architects invited to participate, but that would have undermined our given archival task. Instead we swung the doors wide open, and the results, rather than providing a tidy historical narrative, seem to suggest that architects today follow no comprehensive agenda, be it aesthetic, theoretical or otherwise.

This state of affairs is reflected in the very structure of our collection—the drawings cut across many different categorical boundaries. In addition to numerous drawings for private houses, there are others for urban redevelopment schemes, cultural institutions, office towers, monuments, decorative elements and, in one case, a garbage recycling plant. Most of these are plans, elevations or perspectives, but sections, axonometrics and aerial perspectives, among others, are included here as well. Not all of the drawings depict a proposed or existing structure; sometimes the subject of study is purely theoretical.

While many of the drawings reflect the creative struggle of working through a seminal idea, others appear to have been made at a more advanced stage in the design process—some at the very final stage (note the inclusion here of working drawings). Others, it seems, were conceived with the art gallery very much in mind. In fact, a few drawings arrived with appraisal sheets attached, something that might not have occurred had this show been held ten years ago, before architectural drawings became a fashionable target for collectors. One transmittal, however, quite frankly stated "no commercial value."

Regardless of their intended audience, the architects who contributed to this collection seemed willing to consult any number of artistic media in communicating their ideas. Scanning the examples of text that identify each plate, you will see pencil, ink and wash, watercolor, acrylic, gouache, pastel, Pantone, metallic paint... on Mylar, tracing paper, sepia print, Japanese paper, board and even electrostatic film. One label reads, "Collage: balsa wood and marbleized paper on xerox of FAX of computer drawing." Another collage is graced with the proverbial "ink sketch on napkin," made no doubt at the restaurant table, the architect drawing his client into an even more substantial mortgage.

I could continue in this exercise, but it should by now be clear that these drawings form a quite disparate whole, pregnant with any number of conflicting points of view. Sorting out the many arguments that result is by itself a complicated task. Fitting them into a coherent discussion is next to impossible. On the gallery wall we can juxtapose drawings that may operate together by means of subject matter, composition or representational techniques, but in a catalog arranged alphabetically those relationships are submerged. Thus I will attempt to duplicate here a partial walk through our exhibit, extracting segments that may suggest a strategy for unraveling this collection.

The most comprehensive group consists of drawings for domestic projects, which span a period of three decades. By comparing the earliest and the most recent examples, we can observe a fundamental shift in thought among architects that occurred during the intervening years. Pierre Koenig's Case Study House #22 of 1959–60 was one of a series of projects by various architects attempting to formulate a housing type for Los Angeles based on the use of modern materials and methods of construction. The steel and glass structure rested on a reinforced-concrete foundation that was cantilevered over the edge of a precarious hilltop site. Thirty years later Keenen and Riley likewise explored the properties of steel and glass in their design for a rural "casino," but they erected their structure on the ruined stone walls of an eighteenth-century millhouse.

Unlike Koenig's design, which could have occupied any number of sites around Los Angeles, Keenen and Riley's building related to a specific historical context. Whereas Koenig tested the physical limits of modern materials—simultaneously expressing exterior form and interior space—Keenen and Riley attempted to mediate between a transparent skeletal structure and one that was opaque and immobile. While Koenig was enamored of technology in and of itself, the latter could not allow it to override historical constraints—twenty-five years of post-modern theory have effectively suppressed the architect's faith in technology, reinvesting the act of construction with multiple layers of meaning.

The Case Study House by Koenig was built during the period in which the freeway had just begun to dictate the whole structure of life in Los Angeles, a mobile suburban culture celebrated in the very walls of his design—a transparent envelope that kept the sprawling city below in constant view day and night. By 1986, when Kevin Bone submitted his "Botanical Freeway" to the competition for redeveloping Pershing Square—the only contained public space in downtown Los Angeles that could qualify as a traditional urban center—the city was viewed by many to be approaching its limits of growth. Here the freeway is presented as a historical artifact replete with the trappings of decay. Has this fragmented emblem of metropolitan sprawl been set into the confines of a dense urban fabric, or did the latter grow up around it?

The implicit challenge of such a proposal is to reconcile contemporary urban forms with those of the preindustrial city we continue to inhabit in memory if not in fact. This is precisely the issue addressed by Machado and Silvetti in their scheme for a site at the edge of Palermo, a site that encompassed the peripheral freeway with views back to the "historic" center of the city. We could expand our discussion to include Richard Plunz's sketches of the ancient Roman theater at Ephesus, an elemental civic form present as well in Bone's scheme for Pershing Square. We may also want to cite Paul Rudolph's proposed housing for a "new town" near Washington, D.C. Here the buildings, landscape and automobiles coexist as a late manifestation of Le Corbusier's urban ideal, not yet challenged by the demand of the subsequent decade that society reinhabit the traditional "human-scale" city.

While these drawings point to a body of theoretical issues via subject matter, others do so in compositional and figurative terms as well. The entry by Peggy Deamer, for example, explores the multiple formal "games" evident within a single dwelling, the Wittgenstein House of 1926–28 in Vienna. Her analysis, as she states, proposes a relationship between Wittgenstein's philosophical writings and his design for this house. Deamer composed the parts of her analysis, which have a completely mechanical graphic quality, as though they were characters on a page of text. Wendy Evans, on the other hand, extracted the elemental forms of a single building type, the Roman palazzo. Evans's graphic technique conveys the compositional centrality of the palazzo type, and her choice of watercolor as a medium expresses its formal solidity. Both of these characteristics are directly opposed to the shifting, ambiguous nature of Deamer's subject.

The drawing of a nineteenth-century Islamic garden by Nader Ardalan and that of the Public Library of Mexico by Abraham Zabludovsky are more graphically compatible. The library, originally a factory built during the eighteenth century, is organized around a series of internal courtyards bordered by arcades. Both this complex and the Islamic garden are based on the orthogonal subdivision of a rectangular whole, the walls and arcades of the former loosely corresponding to the *allées* of the latter. Presented with a similar problem, the two architects chose similar graphic techniques: both drawings are frontal isometrics showing plan and elevation at once. While these two projects are introverted schemes that can be isolated from their respective contexts, the site plans by James Favaro, Carlos Ferrater Lambarri, Kolatan/MacDonald and Thom Mayne all suggest a visual expansion beyond the borders of the page. Each project deals with the measuring and cultivation of the landscape, which is conveyed to varying degrees of abstraction. The graphic similarities among these examples may be derived ultimately from the aerial photograph (or fuzzy satellite image) and the surveyor's map, both of which are fragments of a larger image.

One series of drawings operates purely by means of representational devices. The elevations by Alexander Kouzmanoff, Abraham Zabludovsky (housing), Richard Meier, John Miller and Takefumi Aida progress respectively from a distant position in the picture plane to one that fills it entirely. This last example brings the successive degree of abstraction within the series to its absolute limit by threatening to dematerialize. Look again at Kouzmanoff's contextual and material depiction. Viewed together these drawings underscore the dual nature of architectural drawing as a representational and conceptual exercise. All refer to actual designs, but the representational characteristics of the drawing by Aida are almost completely suppressed in his attempt to convey theoretical issues.

Other drawings, such as those by Frederick Fisher, Paola Iacucci and John Hejduk more vigorously challenge the representational assumptions of the viewer. Although the watercolor by Fisher, as he explains, is "an image of the disassembled parts" of his design for an apartment complex, it is impossible to form a mental picture of the actual building from the visual information provided. Only after reading Fisher's statement that the apartments are composed of "distinct units of shape and material" can one begin to see that the drawing has a representational function. Iacucci makes no claims of representation whatsoever for her drawing, which she likens to a hallucination. As she states, it is "not a project but an ephemeral vision of the possible reality of a space that from this idea can be born." If we can make a very loose connection between Iacucci's image and a "real" space, any relationship between Hejduk's lithograph and the act of building remains squarely within the bounds of semiotics.

Does the architectural drawing cease to function as such when all traces of spatial and formal representation are expunged from the image? Is its representational effectiveness undermined by a dependence on outside text? At which point is the boundary between architectural and art practice crossed? These are the questions that architects should keep in mind as they adopt the media and methods of artists. By definition the architectural drawing, regardless of its degree of autonomy from any real or possible space, can never completely escape a reference to external conditions. The artist during this century has not always faced the same restriction.

If architects often seem to follow the lead of artists in adopting certain media, one area in which they may be experimenting more actively is in the use of digital technology—note the inclusion here of drawings made in whole or in part using computers. Although computer-aided design systems may initially have been adopted by architectural firms as a way to save time and money, they have since proved useful for tasks far beyond the efficient production of working drawings. We did receive two examples of that sort—by Lo-Yi Chan and by Venturi, Rauch and Scott Brown —but most could be termed presentation drawings—those by Colin Cathcart and Gregory Kiss; Davis, Brody; Ellerbe Becket; Frederic Schwartz; and Workshop. One may be surprised to recognize that each of these examples has a distinct graphic character achieved by adopting techniques of traditional representational media. This fact should dispel any preconceived notion that computer-aided design systems will invalidate the architect's hand.

Compare the entry by Workshop, which was made entirely with computers except for the red, air-brushed areas, to that by Hanrahan and Meyers, a product of the drafting board. Although these drawings share dynamic qualities that one may associate with computer graphics, they could also have been inspired by the drawings of Soviet visionary architects from the 1920s. The visual qualities of both drawings, however, may be ultimately derived from the mechanical, highly abstracted illustrations to Auguste Choisy's *Histoire d'Architecture* of 1899. The give and take between graphic effects made possible by the computer and those that result from the use of more traditional tools is not as clear as one might assume.

While some architects using computers may adopt techniques from the drafting board, others employ the methods of artists. The near-photographic-quality image by Cathcart and Kiss, for example, has a curious affinity with the watercolor by Richard Haas. If we could enlarge a segment of the former example, we might discover techniques quite similar to those employed by Haas in his large-scale architectural murals, or, more likely, to those used by Richard Estes in his photo-realist paintings. The Cathcart and Kiss drawing was made by scanning an actual photograph and superimposing it onto the constructed, or artificial, digital image. The whole was then rendered on the computer. This suggests that architects, as they begin to use computers more frequently, should verse themselves in the techniques of photography.

The applications of this technology in architecture are not limited to the use of photographic imagery. In his film *Le Corbusier,* Jacques Barsac showed the Plan Voisin of 1923—which every student of modern architecture should know from Le Corbusier's drawings—rising up from its intended site in the center of Paris. Barsac and his collaborators used computer graphic technology to create a cinematic image of Le Corbusier's design, which they then superimposed on actual footage of Paris. Here the static architectural representation becomes an experiential simulation that points to an entirely new field of exploration for architects (and architectural historians). The integration of the cinematic image into the design process may prove to be a vital creative impetus in the years ahead.

The problem now faced by architects is developing an effective theoretical framework through which to implement these new representational techniques. Although the reevaluation of modernism has greatly expanded the architect's formal and theoretical arena, the essential link between the modernist aesthetic agenda and principles of industrial production—which was its real source of strength—has largely been ignored by theorists in their determination to prove that architects must address issues far beyond the positivistic aspects of technology. If the system of production in developed countries continues on its present course toward one based on computer-guided robotic technology—a highly flexible and variable system —the architect may be presented with a much wider range of building components and means of fabrication than those available under the standardized, assembly line system of this century. The expanded formal archive that has grown out of post-modern theory, and likewise the expanded means of representation promised by digital technology, may be matched in the years ahead by an expanded means of realization in the act of building. In that scenario the computer as a representational tool gains a sound theoretical justification.

As architects enter a decade in which they are faced with a decreasing flow of commissions, they will certainly devote more time to theoretical concerns and to the art of drawing. Perhaps this will allow them to properly explore the advanced technology now at their disposal. Still, regardless of how sophisticated their tools of representation may become, or how elevated a position their drawings may achieve as art objects, architects will never forego the seminal creative act recorded by the slip of a pencil, which in the end may lead to a building of great complexity. In fact, one of the donors to this collection expressed a conviction that the "real stuff" of architectural drawing was the freehand sketch made well beyond the confines of his office. Another was more indifferent. His secretary, we were told, had fished his drawings from a trash can several years back, musing perhaps that *some*day they might be hanging on a gallery wall. We are certainly grateful for such presence of mind.

Edward Wendt

Contemporary Architectural Drawings

DONATIONS TO THE AVERY LIBRARY

CENTENNIAL DRAWINGS ARCHIVE

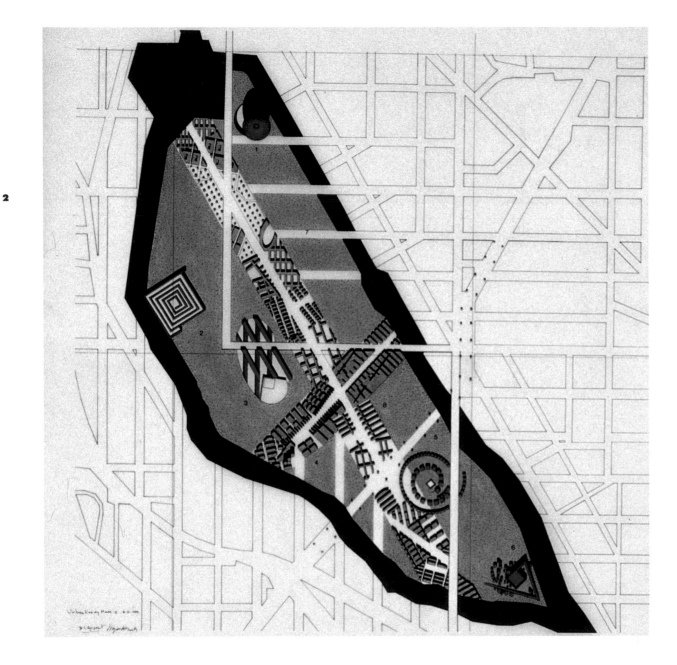

A & G

New York (Diana Agrest, b. 1944, and
Mario Gandelsonas, b. 1938)

Urban Ready-Made I and II, Goose Island, Chicago,
August 31, 1989
Black ink and colored pencil on paper.
Each 18⅞ × 16¹⁵⁄₁₆ in.

THE CITY IS THE PLACE FROM WHICH ARCHITECTURE
can be understood at this point in history: the city as
the unconscious of architecture, the city as an open
text to be read and rewritten, transcending questions
of style, which debase the architectural discourse to a
reductionist, noncritical level.

In reading the city, fragments of urban structures are
found and recombined in a different organizational
form, thus producing a different type of space. These
pieces are the product of an anonymous space, collec-
tive author, pieces of nondesigned fragments of the
city. These urban fragments, the ready-mades, come
from urban configurations not readily apparent. These
ready-mades are born from the forms that the city
itself has generated through its history and not from

imitation or the picturesque nature of our modern urban culture, perception and use of the city.

In these urban ready-mades, fabric is incorporated as object instead of placing the object building on a green field. Some objects, monuments and other architecture as such are situated on a neutral plane.

Pieces of fabric are either selected from various readings of American cities or from typologies developed by us, a work of exploration of the relationship between object and fabric. Streets and places are rehabilitated in this fragmentary urban organization. While the fabric is mostly residential buildings, the objects are institutional.

A bar of fabric is created from a typical Chicago block configuration as a real condition and as ideal. Encroaching on it are fragments of fabric conditions. These are cultural and social programs: an athletic complex, a museum of architecture, a museum of industrial archaeology and an observatory.

[architects' statement]

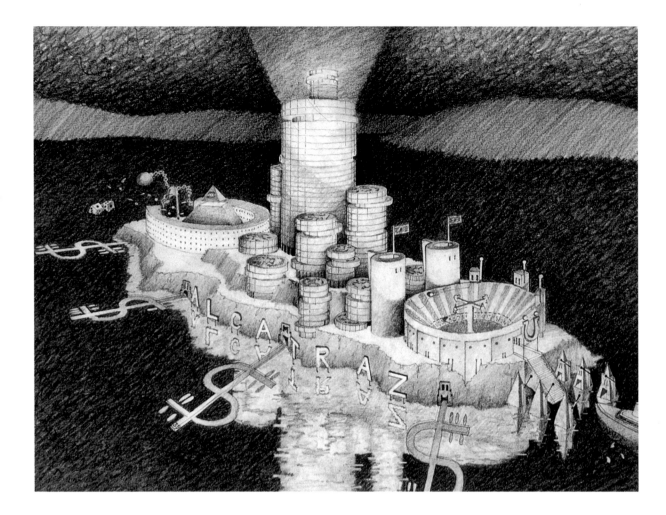

ACE ARCHITECTS

San Francisco (Lucia Howard, b. 1950, and
David Weingarten, b. 1951, principals;
Keith Rivera, delineator)

Proposal for a Casino, Alcatraz Island,
San Francisco Bay, San Francisco, 1988
Pencil on paper. 18 × 23⅞₁₆ in.

THE PROPOSAL DEPICTS A GREAT CASINO. GAMBLERS
would arrive by boat at an entrance flanked by
obelisks and framed by a great upturned horseshoe.
Through the horseshoe, across a wide wheel-shaped
chimneys arena and through twin muzzle-shaped
chimneys are the glittering multiple towers of the
casino. Between sessions at the tables, players may
stroll out onto the several curvilinear piers. Separated
from their money, gamblers retreat through a horse-
shoe-shaped piazza with a pyramid at its center and
exit the Rock's aft end.

[We] have selected this drawing because it exempli-
fies our philosophy of Literalism. We believe that
architecture should be accessible and enjoyable. It was
drawn by Keith Rivera, a former employee.

[architects' statement]

TAKEFUMI AIDA

Tokyo (b. 1937)

Conceptual Elevation, Yuragi 2, 1987
Pencil on Japanese paper. 25¼ × 38⅛ in.

IF I HAD TO USE ONE WORD TO DESCRIBE THE CONCEPT behind my present works, it would be *yuragi* (fluctuation)—"a disturbance that nearly overturns the prevailing order but falls just short of doing so" or "a condition in which the existing order is transcended and a new system of a different dimension is created."

Architecture is basically three-dimensional, and that, reasonably enough, is the premise of architectural design. Nevertheless, it occurred to me to reduce space to two dimensions.

The intention is to heighten the effect of space by reducing the degree to which it is determined.

[From *Takefumi Aida Buildings and Projects*. New York: Princeton Architectural Press, 1990, pp. 76–77.]

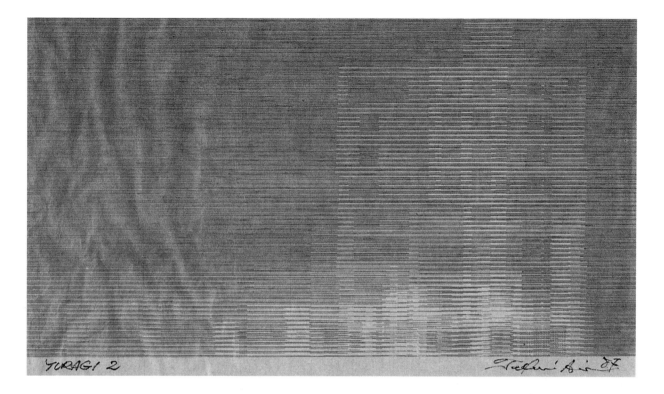

YURAGI 2

MONASTARY AT SILOS, SPAIN 1930 A
Robert Evans Alexander

ROBERT EVANS ALEXANDER

Berkeley, California (b. 1907)

Monastery at Silos, Spain, 1930
Pencil on paper. 7⁵⁄₁₆ × 10¾ in.

IMMEDIATELY FOLLOWING MY ARCHITECTURAL STUDIES at Cornell, I went to Europe and toured France, Spain and Italy in a Model A Ford for three months in the summer of 1930. *Monastery at Silos* and *Guadalajara, Spain* are two sketches I made at that time.

[architect's statement]

STANLEY ALLEN

New York (b. 1956)

Piranesi's Campo Marzio: An Experimental Design, 1989
a. Black ink and photocopy on Mylar. 24 1/16 × 17 15/16 in.
b. Black ink and photocopy on Mylar. 25 5/16 × 18 7/8 in.

THIS PROJECT INTENDS AN EXCAVATION—THROUGH DRAWING AND WRITING—OF THE "negative utopia" drawn by Piranesi for the *Campo Marzio* of Rome. I have conceived of Piranesi's large plan (the *grande pianta*) as a site to be colonized, covered over and modified, as when a building is erected on ruins. My attempt is to uncover and articulate the surplus residue of meaning that confirms the inexhaustibility of a work of architecture. This process of rereading establishes a relationship parallel to that which Piranesi maintained toward his own (archaeological) sources: dreamlike, inventive and improvisational.

[Stanley Allen, "Piranesi's Campo Marzio: An Experimental Design." In *Assemblage 10.* Cambridge, Mass.: MIT Press, 1989, p. 72.]

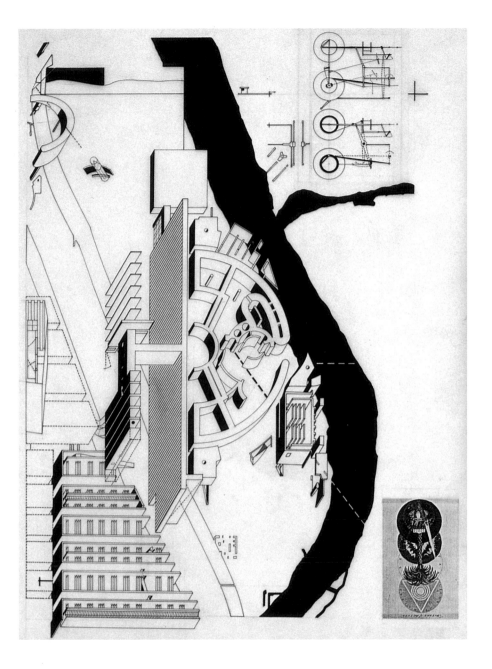

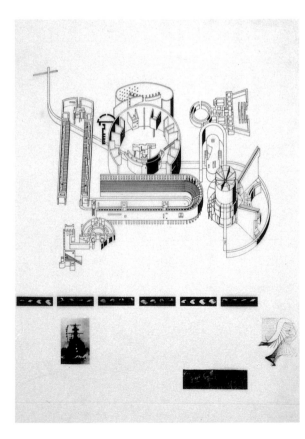

EMILIO AMBASZ
New York (b. 1943)

San Antonio Botanical Gardens, San Antonio,
Texas, 1977
Black ink on paper. 8⁷⁄₁₆ × 10⁷⁄₈ in.

AMY ANDERSON
New York

Competition Entry, Acropolis Museum, Athens,
February 1990
Silkscreen on paper. 8¹³⁄₁₆ × 13⅛ in.

THE PRESENT ACROPOLIS MUSEUM TO THE SOUTHEAST of the Parthenon is a simple stone structure without any external architectural ornamentation and is thus in no way incongruous with the archaeological site. The original building was erected between 1865 and 1874, to plans of the architect Panagis Kalkos, but soon proved inadequate to house the wealth of finds

from the Acropolis, especially after the excavations of 1885–1890. The first extension dates from 1888, but large-scale modifications and additions were made after the Second World War to plans of the architect Patroklos Karantinos.

Judged by present conceptions of how monuments should be preserved and displayed, the museum, built as it is next to classical monuments and despite its modest proportions, could well be considered as a bold intervention, indeed an obstacle to the completion of excavation work. The main problem, however, is that the exhibition areas, totaling 1,460 square meters inclusive of workshops and storerooms, are no

longer sufficient for the numerous exhibits. . . . Furthermore, the envisaged return of the Parthenon pediment marbles (the so-called Elgin Marbles) necessitates the creation of corresponding areas for their display. Finally, works now found in the storerooms and thus inaccessible to the public should be provided with space to be exhibited together with those items which are still displayed out of doors. The cramped nature of the museum is intensified by the increasing number of visitors.

[excerpt from competition guidelines]

ROSS ANDERSON
of Anderson / Schwartz Architects, New York (b. 1951)

Project, House, and Studio
for Sculptor John Newman, 1988
Charcoal, pencil, colored pencil and pastel on paper.
24 × 36⅛ in.

THE WORK IS ROOTED BOTH IN THE IMAGES OF THE vernacular and in concepts of abstraction. I try to be inclusive as well as reductive, communicating function and program as well as allowing randomness and conflict to coexist. By forcing early sketches into three dimensions, volumes and forms mutate and blur. The early diagram is amplified. As modern people we are disoriented and our form making lacks power. As an architect, I focus on the relationship between mundane rituals, architecture and site. Layered randomness and being neither too neat nor too conclusive are a partial antidote to our own unconnectedness and amnesia.

[architect's statement, from *Manhattan,* no. 4, Summer 1989]

JOHN ANDREWS

Sydney, Australia (b. 1933)

Invitational Competition Entry for Park Place Development, Los Angeles; Parkhill Partners, client, 1988
Gouache on board. 40 × 29¹⁵⁄₁₆ in.

THE [COMPETITION GUIDELINES] CALLED FOR AN AMBITIOUS MIX OF TWO MILLION square feet of office space, a shopping center, a hotel and an apartment complex to be built in stages on a site of nearly five acres west of the Harbour Freeway, bounded by 8th, 9th and Francisco Streets. The size and location of the project had the potential to create a Los Angeles landmark [that would] lend its burgeoning skyline some needed identity and verve and give the streetscape some interest to link downtown with South Park and an expanded convention center.

Twin groupings of 8- to 36-floor-high office module towers flanked a central retail plaza defined at the end of a ceremonial avenue from Figueroa Street by a crescent-shaped 500-bedroom luxury hotel. A high-medium rise apartment precinct was also incorporated with a 3,600-space carpark and a proposed subway station.

[architect's statement]

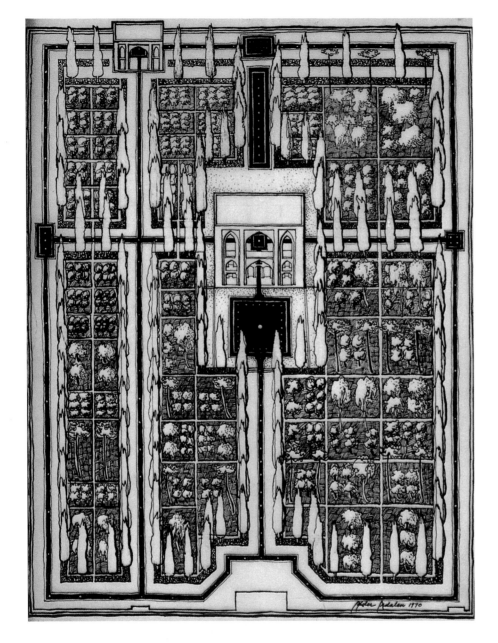

NADER ARDALAN

Boston, Massachusetts (b. 1939)

Travel Sketch of a Nineteenth-century "Paradise" Garden Known as the "Bagh-i-Fin,"
Kashan, Iran, 1970
Black ink on paper. 11⁵⁄₁₆ × 8½ in.

COMPLEMENTING THE HARSH, DRY DESERT ENVIRONMENT, THE LEGENDARY COOL AND
lush paradise gardens of Persia came into being more than 2,500 years ago.

Here at the Bagh-i-Fin, hidden behind high mud walls, an order is traced in the earth
by the structural waterways that flow from the highest to the lowest point, distributing
the life-generating waters to the verdant, geometric compartments of the garden.

The garden is viewed archetypically as a recapitulation of paradise. Perpetuating
this view, the mirrorlike pools cause the heavens to be reflected in their shimmering
surfaces, thus uniting the high with the low, the *Alam-i-Mithal* (imaginal world)
with phenomenal reality, in a profound symbolism central to the Persian view of
existence.

[architect's statement]

TAKAMITSU AZUMA

Tokyo (b. 1933)

The Biblical Church, Tokada-no-Baba, Tokyo, 1982
Black ink, pencil and colored pencil on paper. 46¹¹/₁₆ × 33 in.

THE BIBLICAL CHURCH, ERECTED ALONG THE KANDA RIVER IN TOKYO, IS THE EMBODI-ment of "polyphonic architectural composition" recently advocated by Azuma. It is, he explains, a method which, instead of synthesizing all elements under a single compositional principle, allows different elements to coexist as such and permits people to visually enjoy the choice and combination of elements, thereby effecting a meaningful encounter between people and architecture.

[From Suzuki, Hiroyuki, et al., *Contemporary Architecture of Japan: 1958–1984*. New York: Rizzoli, 1985, p. 113]

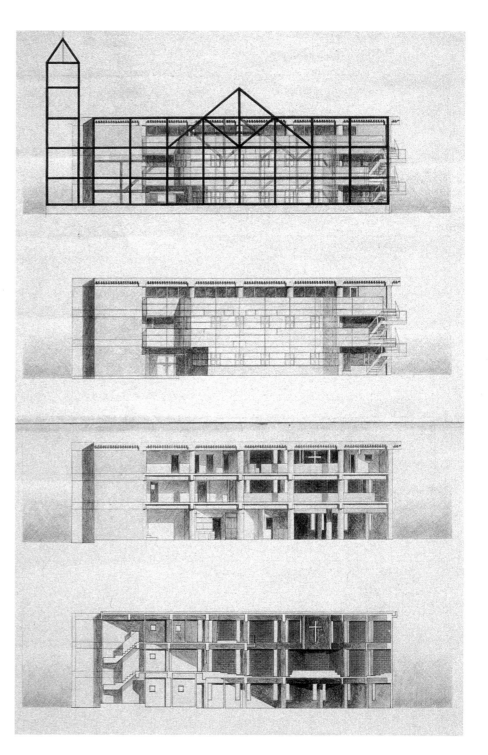

13

14

A R Q U I T E C T O N I C A
Coral Gables, Florida
(Bernardo Fort-Brescia, b. 1951, and
Laurinda Spear, b. 1950)

Walner House, Glencoe, Illinois, 1987
Black ink, colored wash and colored pencil
on paper.
a. 22¾ × 39⅜ in. (sight)
b. 23¹¹⁄₁₆ × 37³⁄₁₆ in. (sight)

THE CLIENT'S CRITERIA FOR DESIGN OF THIS 7,800-square-foot house were threefold: that it be single story, that it take full advantage of the spectacular site and that it provide space for the wife's art collection. The heavily wooded site rises 65 feet from Lake Michigan to a large grassy plateau scattered with stately oaks.

The pink granite house is an irregular Z-shape, responding to the unusual site that is frontal in at least three directions. Marble and granite planes intersect the volume unexpectedly. The roof lifts and tilts, making the rooms less uniform. A glass prism encloses the swimming pool. The exercise room, made of boulders, breaks through the glass.

The house is a study of controlled chaos. Things are planned to seem as relaxed and happenstance as possible. We wanted comfort and delight but not balance or symmetry—the random window, the interrupted cadence, naturalism.

With the exception of the window mullions, which are stained a gray blue, the house is made entirely of natural materials and natural colors—but nature at its outer limit of blue granite, brilliant green marble.

We also wanted a house that would at first glance blend into its environment but would become more and more unfathomable with each passing minute.

[architects' statement, from *G.A. Houses,* November 1987, no. 2, p. 40]

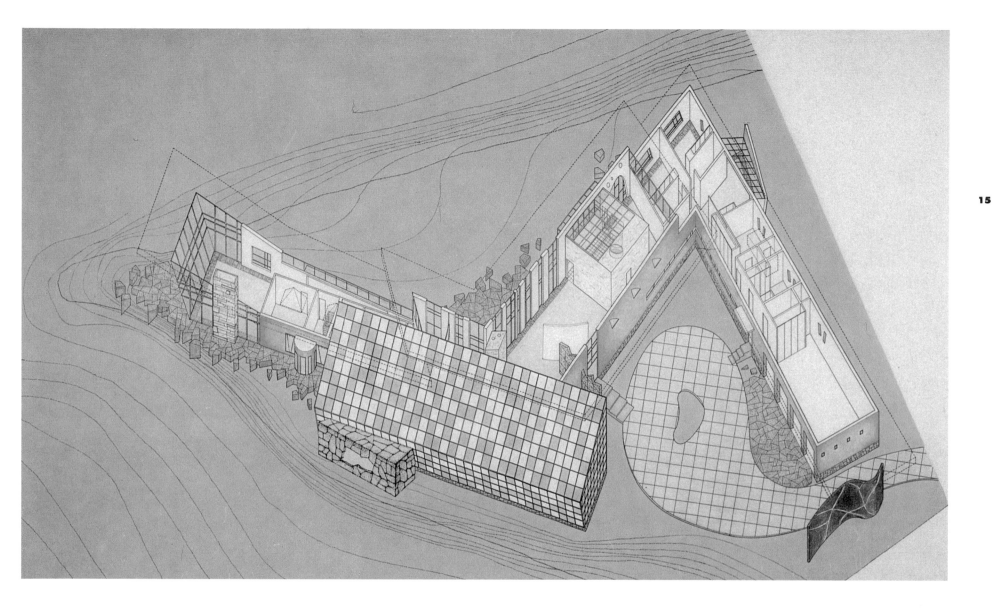

DAVID BAKER

San Francisco (b. 1949)

Cafe Milano, Berkeley, California;
Sandy Boyd, client, 1986
Mixed media collage. 14 × 17 in.

THE PRIMARY FOCUS OF OUR FIRM IS DESIGN AS A RESULT of the interaction between formal concept, program, client desire, construction technique, codes and budget. The office comprises nine professionals committed to high design standards, construction integrity and artistic expression.

Our office emphasizes the integration of quality design and efficient project management. To facilitate such standards we have integrated graphic computers into our practice for design in two and three dimensions, presentation, working drawing production and budget and time analysis.

Our practice is experienced in diverse project types: recreational facilities, affordable multifamily housing, live/work housing, custom residences, commercial office and retail buildings, restaurants, retail and commercial interiors and medical offices.

We have successfully completed new construction, renovation, and interior tenant improvement projects. Our goal is the realization of high-quality projects within the parameters of the client's budget and requirements.

[architect's statement]

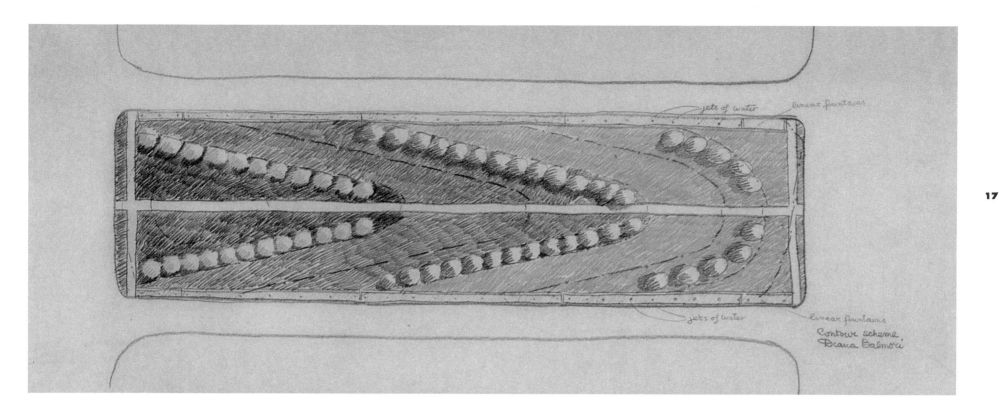

D I A N A   B A L M O R I

New Haven, Connecticut (b. 1936)

Cleveland Clinic Green, Cleveland, Ohio; Cleveland Clinic Foundation, client, 1984
Pencil and colored pencil on tracing paper. 13⅞ × 33¼ in.

LOCATED AS A FRONT LAWN OF A NEW FOURTEEN-STORY CLINIC BUILDING, THE GREEN serves as the unifying core of the entire campus, around which future additions will take place.

A very important function of the green is that it is the view from the clinic's waiting rooms, which are all centered on the building's main facade. Because of this the green has been designed as an "axial perspective" scheme—a view from the clinic building shows telescoping lines of trees at designated points on the green. The result is that the green looks longer than it actually is.

At the far end, an oval of trees has been planted to end the perspective. Seen from the highest floors of the clinic, the oval becomes a perfect circle. At ground level, it serves as a small enclosed landscape within the overall linear pattern and is suitable for small gatherings.

The plant material is appropriate for a campus. *Quercus alba* (white oak) will become sculptural giants to anchor and frame the whole landscape fifty years hence; *Liquidambar styraciflua* (sweet gum) offer fall color; *Thuja occidentalis 'techny'* (techny arborvitae) provide green in the winter; and *Malus "snowdrift"* and *M. "American Beauty"* (crab apples) supply both spring flowers and fall color. These materials were also chosen for salt tolerance (since Cleveland streets are heavily salted in winter). Two paths, paved with granite and lined with teak benches, travel the full length of the green. They have proved to be a very popular space for the medical staff at lunch time and at the end of the day. Patients use the green around the clock.

The green's landscape is a "time" landscape. As trees grow and fill in, some will be removed and a different landscape will emerge. Landscape has usually been drawn and presented as if it had one fixed moment in time. This is a misinterpretation taken from the fixed sizes of buildings in architecture. This landscape was presented to the client as changing over time and was shown at twenty, fifty and a hundred years to transmit the sense of constant change which it goes through.

[architect's statement]

J A C Q U E S   B A R S A C

with Thomson Digital Image

Reconstruction of the Plan Voisin from the Film "Le Corbusier"
(produced by Cine Service Technique), 1987
Video stills

LE CORBUSIER RELATES HIS LIFE [AND] HIS STRUGGLES, EXPLAINS HIS APPROACH, AND gives the keys to his work as an architect, planner, painter, sculptor and writer. The film is made from recorded interviews and films of each period, few ever made public. A film of the whole life and work of the greatest architect of the twentieth century. [This is] a film which shows projects and buildings.

Historical archives, taken from government newsreels and the National Audiovisual Institute, are used to show [Le Corbusier's] work in context, in relation to living conditions and to tendencies in the arts and techniques in the twentieth century. Over forty films and recordings were used to achieve this continuity.

The film contains twelve minutes of computer-generated perspectives [from which these film stills were produced] made by Thomson Digital Image, which give the spectator the realistic illusion of strolling through projects Le Corbusier was not able to build; the "City of Three Million Inhabitants," the "Plan Voisin de Paris," and the "Durand Building of Algiers" are thus brought to life. This work required probably the biggest data bank ever set up in Europe for the treatment of architectural projects.

Thanks to the computer, the Voisin plan of Paris of 1925 seems to exist on its actual site, and the Firminy church, for a second, is completed. These visualizations make it perfectly possible to judge the possible impact of the projects.

[This] is also the first documentary film in the world post-produced in digital video image.

[filmmaker's statement]

PIETRO BELLUSCHI

S.M.P. Architects, St. Louis;
associated architects, Portland, Oregon

United Hebrew Congregation Synagogue,
St. Louis, Missouri, February 5, 1988
Pencil and colored pencil on mylar. 17$\frac{15}{16}$ × 24 in.

GUNNAR BIRKERTS

Birmingham, Michigan (b. 1925)

Sketch of plan, Museum of Glass, Corning,
New York, 1976
Colored pencil on yellow trace. 23¾ × 20½ in.

THE BUILDING WAS DESIGNED PRIMARILY TO DISPLAY
the history of artistic glassmaking. A library and
research center for scholars occupies the center portion, with offices and preservation and restoration
areas on the lower level. The museum level itself is
lifted above the ground plane as a positive requirement
to protect the contents from potential flooding. The
adjoining Glass Center displays the more scientific
aspects of glassmaking.

The museum was conceived as a flowing extension of
the existing Glass Center building. The most expressive analogy is to glass itself, which is amorphous in
the molten state and acquires highly structured crys-
talline properties in the solidified state.

[architect's statement]

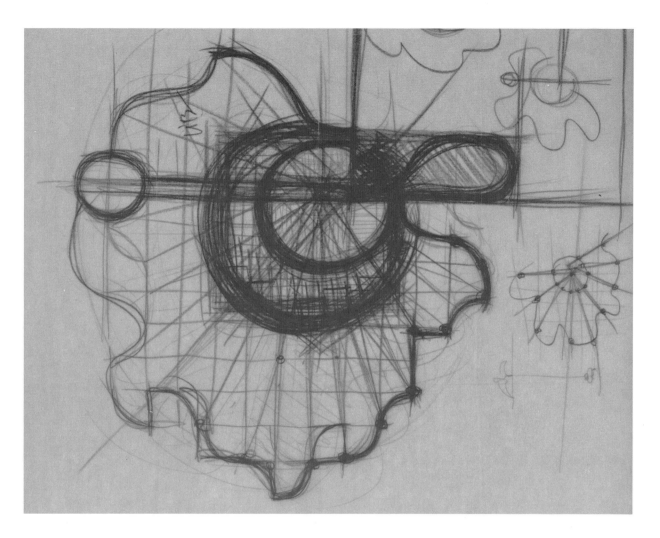

KENT BLOOMER

New Haven, Connecticut (b. 1935)

Curtain Wall Ornament, Harold P. Washington Library,
Chicago; Thomas Beeby, architect, July 1990
Pencil on paper, mounted on board. 17⅛ × 29½ in.

THE ORNAMENT CENTERED UPON THE CURTAIN WALL is one of seven antefix and acroterion to be placed on the roof of the Harold P. Washington Library in Chicago designed by Thomas Beeby. The building is presently under construction and scheduled for completion in 1991.

The ornament, which is an endwall antefix, is approximately 35 feet high and 70 feet wide and will be fabricated out of aluminum. The basic form is descended from the Greek palmette-and-scroll motif and proclaims classicality as an appropriate symbol for a major collection of books. A seedpod producing a Y-shaped efflorescence respects the work of Louis Sullivan. The spears and shields in the curtain wall recall a motif rendered by Frederick Schinkel, who influenced Mies van der Rohe.

[architect's statement]

RICARDO BOFILL

Barcelona and Paris (b. 1939)

Alice Pratt Brown Music Hall, Shepherd School of
Music, Rice University, Houston, 1987
Black marker on tracing paper. 24 × 37¹³⁄₁₆ in.

[THE MUSIC HALL] CONSISTS OF A SCHOOL OF MUSIC
and a performing arts center. The building is carefully
sited so as to reconfirm the existing Beaux Arts campus
that was compromised by the constructions built over
the last twenty years. The building resembles a town
in its layout. The public spaces are intentionally austere,
with white painted sheetrock walls and dark gray car-
peted floors in contrast to the main concert hall, which
will seat a thousand spectators in a monumental interior. The performance spaces will be furnished in terra
cotta hues, using mahogany wall surfacing with rich
red carpeting and seating. Brass handrails and velvet
curtains will help to complete this symphony of interior visual delight.

[architect's statement]

F R A N C O I S E   B O L L A C K

with Thomas Killian, New York (b. 1944)

Competition Entry, Monument for Melbourne,
Australia, 1974–75
Blue pencil on paper. $23^{15}/_{16} \times 35^{7}/_{8}$ in.

MARIO BOTTA

Lugano, Switzerland (b. 1943)

Sketch of Elevation, Gotthard Bank, Lugano,
Switzerland, September 1985
Pencil on tracing paper. 12¼ × 30⁹⁄₁₆ in.

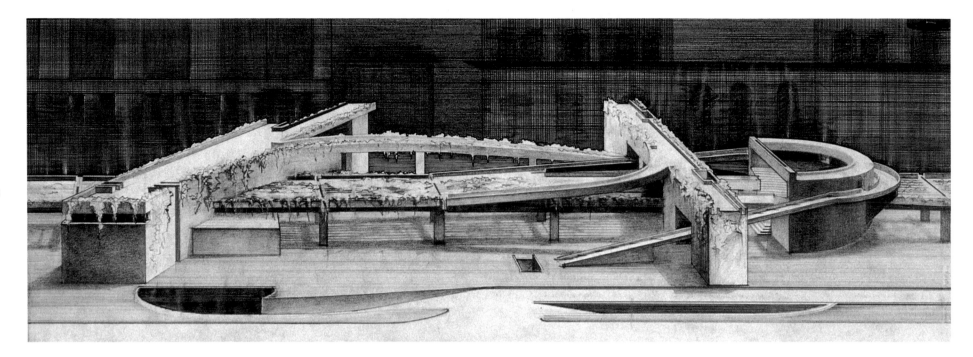

K E V I N   B O N E
New York (b. 1955)

Competition Entry, Pershing Square Redevelopment, Los Angeles, 1986
a. Perspective
   Pencil on tracing vellum. 7⅜ × 19¾ in.
b. Plan
   Black ink on Mylar. 24⁷⁄₁₆ × 33⅛ in.

[T]HE FREEWAY HAS SYMBOLIZED A TENSION LONG PRESENT IN AMERICAN CULTURE: THE pastoral versus the technological, the conflict of the machine in the garden. . . . There is no metaphor more apt to evoke the contours of the Machine Age than the freeway, yet it is also of the organic. . . . The forms of the curvilinear elements that have grown from movement could well have been taken from the organs of a man or from the stems and roots of the plant kingdom. It is a beauty we have resisted but perhaps silently admired.

[Excerpt from competition statement by Kevin Bone; quoted in: Scott Harris, "Visions of Pershing Square Redesign Narrowed to Five." *Los Angeles Times,* June 24, 1986, 2:3.]

JEFFERY BUCHOLTZ
San Francisco (1957–1990)

Student Project for a Youth Hostel in the Berkshire
Mountains, Massachusetts, 1982
Black ink on Mylar. 15¼ × 33⁹⁄₁₆ in.

BUTTRICK, WHITE & BURTIS ARCHITECTS / PLANNERS

New York; H. Herbert Kashian, delineator

Restaurant and Discovery Center at Harlem Meer,
Central Park, New York, July 1989
Pencil on tracing vellum. 22¹¹⁄₁₆ × 35⅛ in.

THE NEW DISCOVERY CENTER AND RESTAURANT AT the Harlem Meer is the centerpiece of a sixteen-million dollar rejuvenation of the north end of New York's Central Park. Buttrick, White & Burtis, together with a team of public and nonprofit agencies and private developers, has designed a series of landscape and architectural improvements to surround the eleven-acre lake near Fifth Avenue and 110th Street.

The site features two new buildings; a complement of terraces, walls, paths and gardens; and an island wildlife sanctuary. The buildings frame a central plaza to create a public gathering place and a gateway to the park. Changes in level and articulation of the buildings separate outdoor spaces and circulation into public, private and service zones. Indoors, the restaurant program calls for three types of dining—a 50-seat cafeteria, a 180-seat restaurant, and a 140-seat catering hall, each with opportunities for outdoor dining.

The Charles A. Dana Discovery Center accommodates the Central Park Conservancy's public education program, visitors' information and public restrooms. School children will meet in the Discovery Room to learn about the ecology of the Meer and to see exhibits of park history. The classroom on the second floor will permit simultaneous use of the building by different groups.

The design of the two structures uses traditional massing, materials and details to enclose modern structural, mechanical and electrical systems. Slate roofs, painted wood windows and detailed brick shapes enliven the facades and connect the buildings to the nineteenth-century architectural traditions of the historic park.   [architects' statement]

29

LUIS BURILLO
Madrid (b. 1949) and
JAIME LORENZO
(b. 1951)

Restoration of Goya's House, Fuendetodos
(near Zaragoza), Spain, April 1982
Pencil and colored pencil on Mylar. 16⁹⁄₁₆ × 23⅜ in.

AROUND THE 1920S, THE SPANISH PAINTER IGNACIO DE Zuloaga bought at Fuendetodos, a village near Zaragoza, the small peasant house where Francisco de Goya had been born in 1746. He had it repaired and furnished with a few items of eighteenth-century rural furniture and then opened it to visitors freely, as an homage to the great painter.

When in 1981 the house was declared a national monument, and we were commissioned to undertake the restoration, time and visitors had seriously damaged it (Zuloaga died in 1945), but it kept receiving an increasing number of visitors.

The job had a simple, technical aspect, that of strengthening the structure (from foundations to roofs) to prevent ruin, while mimetically restoring the house to keep the mythified atmosphere of Goya's childhood years.

But there was also a more important problem. We felt the house not only should be a snapshot of rural life in the eighteenth century but also should provide some hints about Goya himself. So we designed this piece, on the staircase side wall, a limestone facing engraved with quotes from the painter's own letters, where visitors could review his life as they ascended from the ground floor to the upper level. The wall was to be crowned with a bronze relief by one of the leading Spanish contemporary sculptors, but for the project drawing we borrowed one of Goya's most superb etchings, *The Sleep of Reason Produces Monsters.*

[architects' statement]

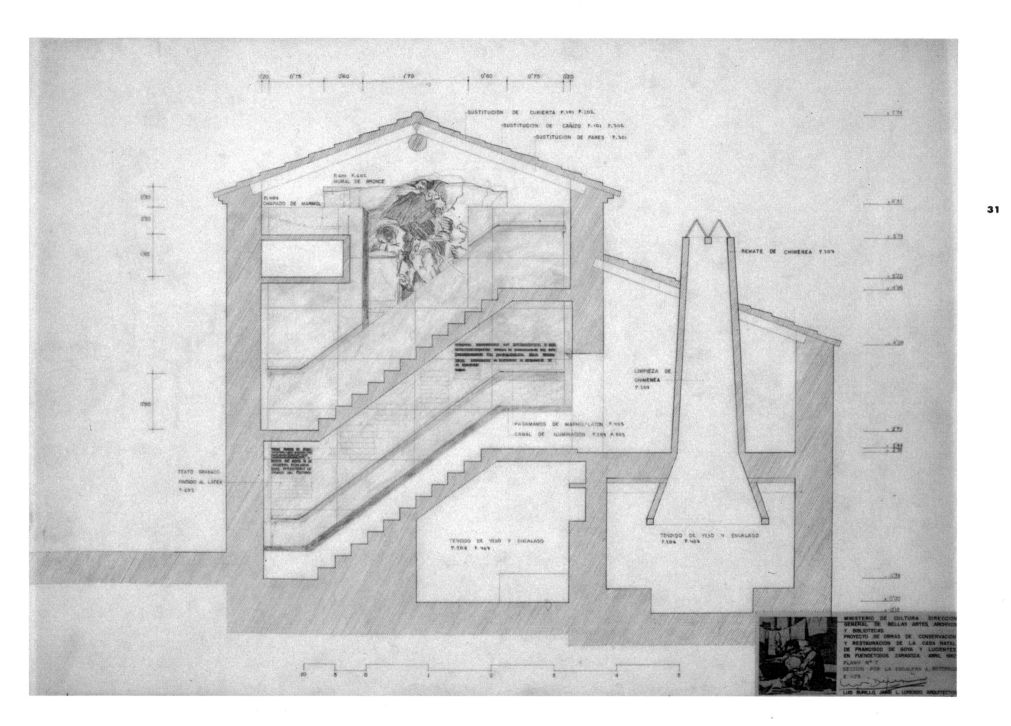

COLIN CATHCART
designer (b. 1955) and
GREGORY KISS
renderer, of Kiss and Cathcart, Anders,
New York (b. 1957)

Chess King Prototype Store, New York:
Nocturnal View, 1990
Colored ink on photographic paper (computer-aided
drawing). Size varies according to print-out.

LO-YI CHAN

of Prentice & Chan, Ohlhausen Architects and
Planners, New York (b. 1932); Perry Hall, delineator

Arthur M. Sackler Museum of Art and Archaeology,
Beijing University, Beijing, February 26, 1989
Colored ink on paper (computer-aided drawing).
25⅝₁₆ × 37¼ in.

THE BUILDING SHOWN IS THE ARTHUR M. SACKLER
Museum of Art and Archaeology at Beijing University, Beijing, PRC. The campus is laid out with traditional Qing period structures forming open spaces on
several axes. The two-story wing of this museum
completes an exterior court, and the one-story extensions create an interior court. The first floor of the
museum thus follows a traditional courtyard plan.
The upper floors house academic offices. The exterior
shown on the drawing is polychromed paint on wood
and masonry. The structure is reinforced concrete.
Prentice & Chan, Ohlhausen are the architects, associated with Beijing University's Office of Architectural Design.

[architect's statement]

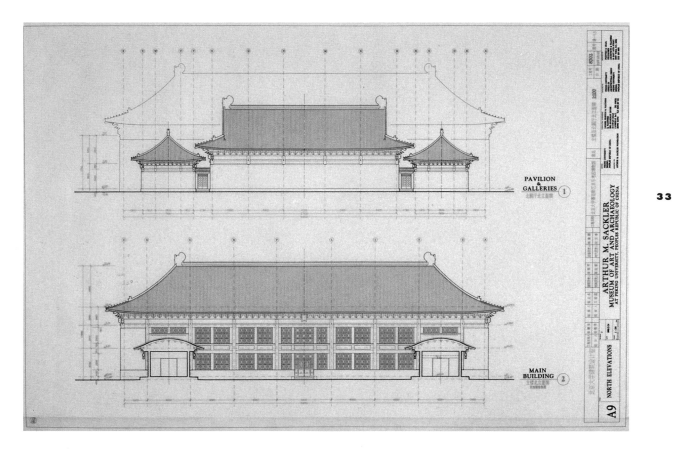

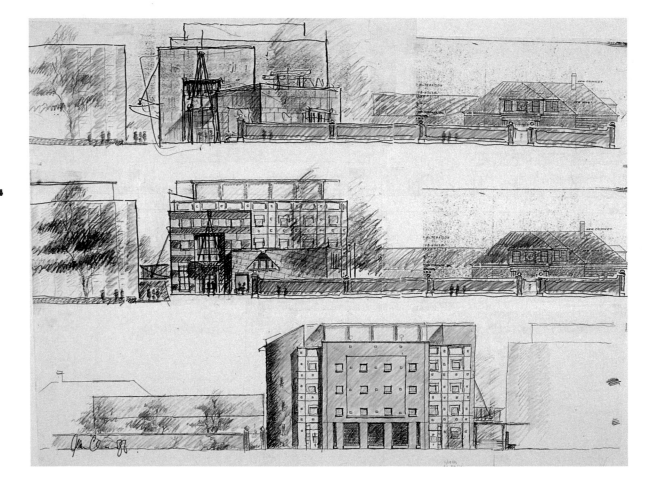

ALAN CHIMACOFF
of The Hillier Group, Princeton, New Jersey (b. 1942)

Materials Science Center, Princeton University,
Princeton, New Jersey, November 15, 1989
Colored pencil on photocopy, mounted on board.
30 × 40 1/16 in.

[THESE DRAWINGS] REPRESENT THE EARLIEST CONCEP-
tual elevations of the Materials Science Center. The
themes for this project are extracted from the discipline of materials science. It should be noted that the
site of the building has been moved since these drawings were executed. Construction is expected to
begin later this year [1991].

[architect's statement]

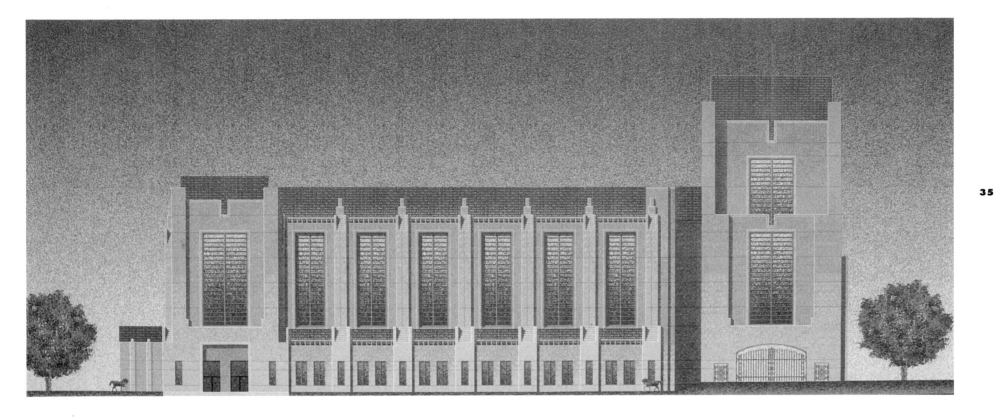

DAVIS, BRODY & ASSOCIATES ARCHITECTS

New York (Lewis Davis, b. 1927, and Samuel Brody, b. 1926)

Competition Entry for a University Library, 1991
Colored ink on paper (computer-aided drawing).
15%⁄16 × 35¹¹⁄16 in.

LUIS CLOTET
Barcelona (b. 1941)

House in Sant Cugat del Vallés, Barcelona, 1982
Black ink and watercolor on paper.
a. 10⅛ × 14¹⁄₁₆ in.
b. 10¹⁄₁₆ × 14¹⁄₁₆ in.

casa en Sant Cugat
Lluis Clotet 1982
51

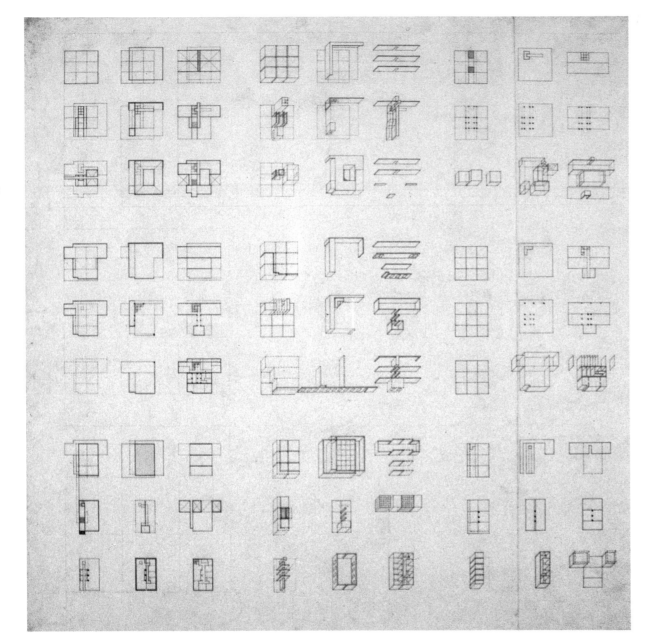

PEGGY DEAMER
of Deamer Phillips, New York (b. 1950)

Analysis of Wittgenstein House, Vienna, 1980
Pencil and colored pencil on Mylar. 30¹⁄₁₆ × 30 in.

THE STONBOROUGH-WITTGENSTEIN HOUSE, DESIGNED by Ludwig Wittgenstein in 1926–28 for his sister's family, was a project undertaken between the writing of his *Tractatus* and *The Philosophical Investigations.* The analysis of this house, unlike others, aligns it with the latter philosophical work and thereby sees the design as a rejection of the possibility of references to external "reality." Instead, like the rules of the "language games" that form the core of the *Investigations'* inquiry—rules at once arbitrary (in relationship to the codes commonly agreed upon by the players)—the "logic" of the house, through acts of spatial displacement, scale alienation and denial of linear narrative, plays games with the viewer's / user's perceptions. The means by which this is done varies from floor to floor.

The only time that one finds oneself centered and located is upon one's expulsion from the house on the roof.

[architect's statement]

NATALIE GRIFFIN DE BLOIS

Austin, Texas (b. 1921)

Harlem from Morningside Park, 1943
Black ink and wash on paper. $11^{15}/_{16} \times 8^{15}/_{16}$ in.

[This drawing dates from the architect's days as a student at Columbia University.]

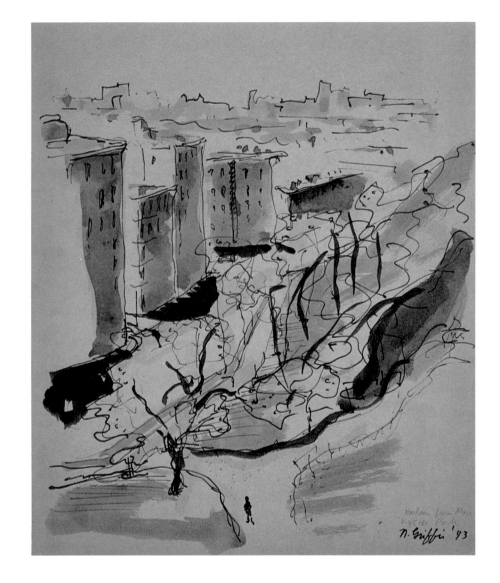

40

ELLERBE BECKET, ARCHITECTS AND ENGINEERS, P.C.
New York and Minneapolis; Peter Pran, Carlos Zapata and Ray Skorupa
BERGERSEN GROMHOLT & OTTAR, OSLO; B.W., OSLO; G&K, OSLO; AND B.C., SWEDEN
Project designers: Tim Arnold, Eduardo Calma, Tim Johnson, Lyn Rice (project architect), Curtis Wagner, Maria Wilthew, Paul Davis, AES, and Dave Koenen, AES

Invited Competition Entry Finalist, Nytt Rikshospital, Oslo, 1991
Colored ink on paper (computer-aided drawing). Each 11 × 17 in.

THIS PROPOSAL REPRESENTS THE HOSPITAL OF THE future, through the most advanced and progressive planning and design. The overall complex gently fits into the landscape and site setting and relates sensitively and creatively to the existing buildings. This solution allows for internal flexibility and external expansion for future needs.

The overall plan has provided for an excellent separate outpatient and inpatient corridor / circulation system.

A gently curved spine / atrium corridor space to the east is the backbone of the proposal.

In general, the second floor contains radiology and emergency; third floor, operating rooms and recovery; fourth floor, university / research functions and administration; and fifth, the main cafeteria / restaurant, with a spectacular view of the Oslofjord.

Daylight is provided for all rooms where staff work more than four hours per day; this provides for a uniquely humane hospital.

[architects' statement]

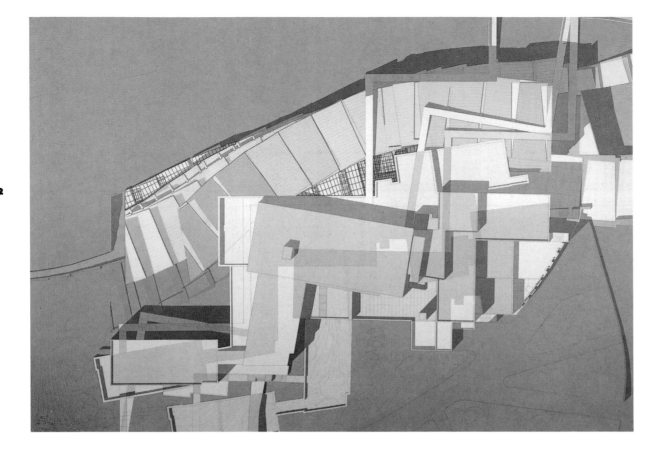

PETER EISENMAN
New York (b. 1932), with John Nichols Printmakers

Roof Plan, College of Design, University of Cincinnati,
Cincinnati, Ohio, 1990–91
Silkscreen on paper. 30 1/16 × 42 3/8 in.

W E N D Y   E V A N S
of Pei Cobb Freed & Partners, Architects, New York (b. 1955)

Conceptual Study of a Roman Palazzo, October 5, 1984
Watercolor on paper. 6¹/₁₆ × 10⅛ in.

THIS DRAWING IS ONE OF A SERIES OF STUDIES I MADE DURING MY STAY AT THE AMERICAN
Academy in Rome in 1984. The image combines a perspective of a palazzo exterior
street facade with that of its courtyard and plan. Both views use the same vanishing
points. Drawing the building in this way allows the architect to design all aspects of
a palazzo simultaneously, thus bringing greater coherence to the facade expressions.

[architect's statement]

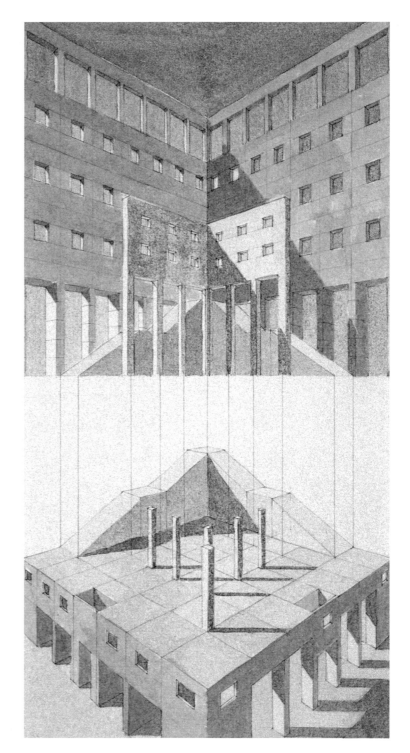

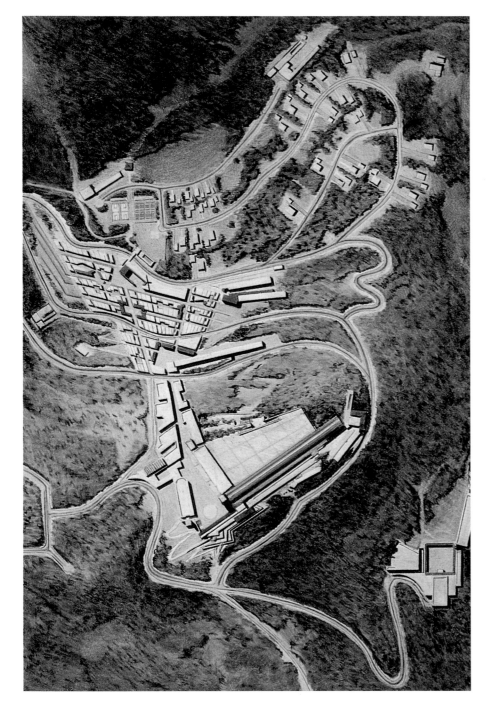

JAMES FAVARO

of Johnson / Favaro, Los Angeles (b. 1956)

Mixed-use Project Adjacent to Yosemite National Park, California, May 1, 1990
Colored pencil on paper. 22¼ × 14½ in.

THIS...PROPOSAL FOR A DEVELOPMENT ON THE BORDER OF YOSEMITE NATIONAL Park...includes two hotels, a commercial center and a small town. The drawing is a site plan of the entire project.

[architect's statement]

ROGER FERRI
for Welton Becket Associates Architects, New York
(b. 1948)

Hudson River Center, unbuilt, New York;
Silverstein Development / MAT Associates, client, 1985
Pencil on tracing vellum, mounted on Mylar.
35¹⁵⁄₁₆ × 44⅞ in.

THIS MIXED-USE DEVELOPMENT [WOULD HAVE BEEN] sited on the Hudson River and connect[ed] directly to the Jacob Javits Convention Center. Four high-rise residential towers and a 1,000-room luxury conference hotel surround a U-shaped marina to create the sense of a hilltop village against the Manhattan skyline.

[architect's statement]

CARLOS FERRATER LAMBARRI

Barcelona (b. 1944)

New Botanical Gardens, Barcelona, 1989
Colored ink and colored pencil on paper. 19⁹⁄₁₆ × 27½ in.

THE GLOBAL PROJECT COMPRISES THE CREATION OF A NEW BOTANICAL GARDEN FOR THE city of Barcelona, specializing in the flora characteristic of areas homoclimatic with the Mediterranean, such as California, Japan, Chile, South Africa and Australia.

The projected garden results from the layout of a triangulated grid which adapts the different formations of vegetation, placing them in "mosaics" (plan) and "transepts" (sections), according to the different ecosystems.

The project tries to formalize the different buildings using the imagery of lightness and transparency which the vegetable world in which they are inserted confers [upon] them.

The buildings, placed strategically at the upper access [to] the highest part of the route through the garden, integrate themselves with the surrounding landscape, remaining as a conspicuous visual reference from the city of Barcelona.

The main building is organized in two volumes placed according to precise orientation requirements. The building destined for research bridges them, creating a "gateway" to the complex. The relationship between the garden and its external surroundings is established by the void left under the bridge. The rest of the different buildings are articulated around them: auditoriums, library, museums and sheds facing north; labs, nurseries and seedbeds facing south.

[architect's statement]

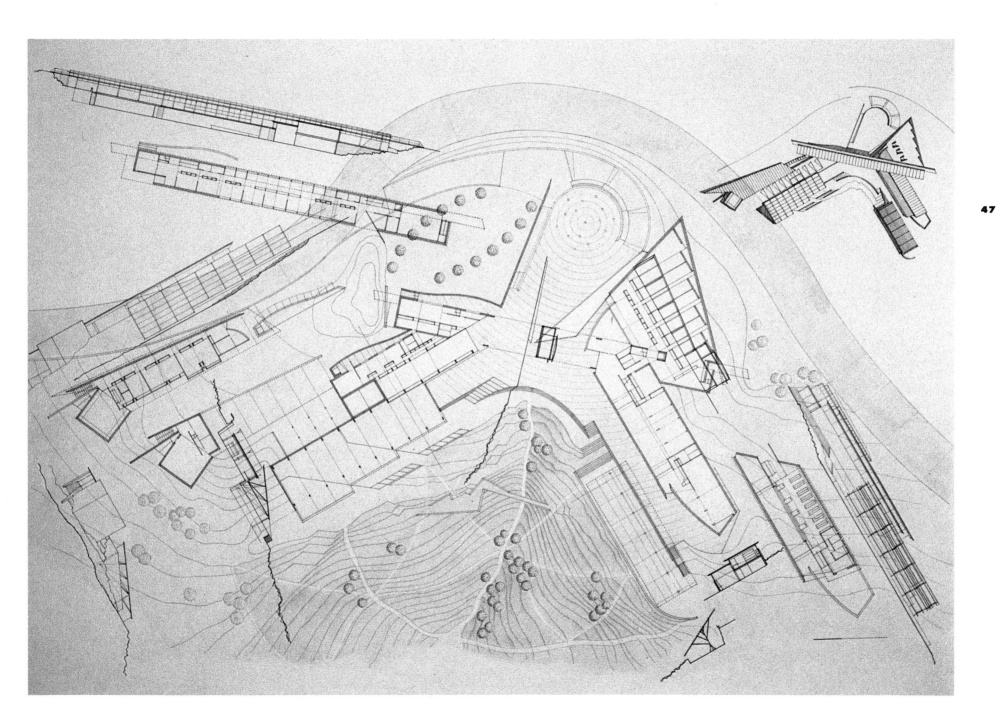

FREDERICK FISHER
Santa Monica, California (b. 1949)

Aobadai Apartments, Tokyo, 1990
Blue pencil and watercolor on paper. 26⅜ × 39⅞ in.

THE AOBADAI APARTMENT COMPLEX IS CONCEIVED as an assemblage of discrete units that index each resi-dent. On the exterior, the mass of the building is clearly articulated into distinct units of shape and material. The separation of apartments by stairs and breezeways provides light and air from all sides to each one.

Like a wood-block puzzle, the disparately shaped parts are identifiable within the single overall shape. The watercolor is an image of the disassembled parts.

[architect's statement]

ULRICH FRANZEN

New York (b. 1921)

Steel-framed Beach House, Long Island, New York, 1975–76
Black, red and blue marker and colored pencil on paper. 9¹/₁₆ × 11¹⁵/₁₆ in.

I HAVE ALWAYS BELIEVED THAT I SHOULD BE ABLE TO make quick freehand sketches of my ideas. My sketches are drawn in a studio away from the office and are generally used as a starting point for further design development in the office. . . .

My drawing hero is Le Corbusier. The sparseness of his line, the single-minded ideas and the swift ink drawing informed by a sharply honed sensibility are fantastic.

Our office has produced, of course, the conventional, large presentation drawings required by client, convention and media. But I have always felt that the *real stuff* is the freehand ink sketch.

[architect's statement]

JAMES FREED
of Pei Cobb Freed & Partners Architects, New York (b. 1930)

Main Public Library, Civic Center, San Francisco, 1989
Black marker on paper. 5⅜ × 8¼ in.

The new Main Library of San Francisco has been designed to complete the Civic Center, one of the few executed, and perhaps the only finished, examples of the City Beautiful Movement of the early 1900s. To achieve this goal the new library is compatible with the massing, materials and formal development of the buildings that now define this great urban space. Its location on a full downtown block makes possible the forging of a vital link between the "contemporary city" and the Civic Center, which is its "public heart"—in short, between the people of San Francisco and the institutions which serve and enrich them.

Like its older counterpart across the street, the new library gestures formally with an L-shaped bar that offers two symmetrical facades complementary to the Civic Center. The library's two other facades make more contemporary response to the commercial district. In response to this part of San Francisco, the library adopts a strategy of urban connection; it is both a destination and a link that permits one to pass into and through the building, weaving the city to the Civic Center and the library to both.

Internally the library is organized around two major spaces: a great open staircase that moves through the building, displaying its activities; and a five-story skylit open space, 60 feet in diameter, that connects the library's various parts. In either case the intention has been to bring natural light inside the 300 × 200–foot building. There are four public elevators facing the organizing open space as well. On its lower level the library houses meeting rooms (with provision for a future auditorium) that can be used by the public when the library proper is not open. Other amenities include literacy programs, services for the deaf and blind and special programs for children. There are, in addition, exhibition spaces, a cafe and a bookstore, a small roof garden and a special reading room—visible from all areas of the building.

The new library has been designed to accommodate collections, services, reading spaces and other related functions in a growth pattern geared to the year 2010. It will have the technological and spatial capacity to be a useful and important institution now and for the future.

[architect's statement]

GREGORY GILMARTIN

for Peter Pennoyer Architects, P.C., New York (b. 1959)

Gazebo at "The Squirrels," Highland Falls, New York, 1989
Pencil on Mylar. 17⅛ × 17¹⁄₁₆ in.

[THIS IS A] DESIGN FOR A NEW GAZEBO TO BE SITED ON the lawn of "The Squirrels," an estate in Highland Falls, New York, overlooking the Hudson.

"The Squirrels," in its present form, is a rambling eighteen-room gabled white clapboard house with additions attributed to Calvert Vaux and Ernest Flagg. The house has remained in the same family since it was a small farm cottage in the 1820s.

The gazebo design is inspired by the Vaux drawings for "The Squirrels" and by other work by Vaux.

[architect's statement]

J O A N   G O O D Y

of Goody, Clancy & Associates, Inc., Architects, Boston (b. 1935)

Biology Building, Massachusetts Institute of Technology, Cambridge, Massachusetts, 1991
a. Black ink on tracing vellum (computer-aided drawing). 15¹⁵/₁₆ × 20 in.
b. Blue marker on tracing paper. 13¹⁵/₁₆ × 18 in.

THE THREE-DIMENSIONAL "LAYERING" SYSTEM THAT we use . . . is a layering in both architectural and computer terms: the building was conceived as a longitudinal core or spine (housing the mechanical and support spaces) with a layer of labs on either side and then outer layers of structural frame, ducts and sun protection. The computer layers don't always coincide with the conceptual layers, but they do in the case of the ducts. The study of the exterior expression of the ducts is important for several reasons besides this: it distinguishes the building by its function (labs requiring great amounts of air to be exhausted), and it provides an opportunity to recall the strong verticals that characterize MIT's original neoclassical buildings with their regular rhythm of columns and pilasters. The structural frame alone is not visually strong enough to do this, and the challenge has been to make a facade that has some of the articulation and rhythm of the old buildings while being expressive of the activities within.

[architect's statement]

PERCIVAL GOODMAN
New York (1904–90)

In the Atrium of the Twelve Pillars, Reconstruction of
the Herodium II after the Description of Josephus, 1989
Pencil on Mylar. 20⅝ × 28½ in.

MICHAEL GRAVES

Princeton, New Jersey (b. 1934)

Additions and Alterations, Whitney Museum
of American Art, New York: Scheme 3,
Madison Avenue Elevation, September, 1988
Pastel on paper. 22¼ × 24¾ in.

New York (b. 1936)

484–490 Broome Street, New York, 1969
Pencil and watercolor on paper. 16⅛ × 12³⁄₁₆ in.

ALTHOUGH THE WATERCOLOR OF 485 BROOME IS A SLIGHT AND UNFINISHED ONE, IT was a pivotal work in my history as an artist interested in architectural subject matter. It was possibly the first work I did focusing on late-nineteenth-century architecture in Soho. It was done in 1969 from my loft directly across the street from this facade on Broome and Wooster, and it was from this watercolor that the accompanying drypoint was done. This formed the first of five drypoints that were then produced of Soho architecture.

Another curious note of circumstance is that my future art dealers and publishers, Brooke and Carolyn Alexander, lived on the fifth floor of this building and happened to see this print, and through that contact became my dealers for the next twenty years.

[artist's statement]

HANRAHAN AND MEYERS

New York (Thomas Hanrahan, b. 1956, and Victoria Meyers, b. 1954)

Interpretive Center, Chattanooga, Tennessee, 1988
Black ink, red pencil and transparent color film on Mylar. 30 × 22¹¹⁄₁₆ in.

HUGH HARDY
of Hardy Holzman Pfeiffer Associates,
New York (b. 1932)

Propylaea, Acropolis, Athens, 1960
Black ink and wash on paper. 8³⁄₁₆ × 11⁵⁄₈ in.

58

CONTEMPORARY ARCHITECTURAL DRAWINGS

J O H N   H E J D U K
with Solo Press, New York (b. 1929)

The Architect's Triangle, 1990
Lithograph on paper. 24⅛ × 17¼ in.

KLAUS HERDEG
New York

Fountain room of Bazaar Amenity, opposite Jarchi Mosque, Isfahan, Iran, 1983
Black ink on Mylar. 48⅛ × 30⅜ in.

THE BAZAAR DATES FROM THE EARLY SEVENTEENTH CENTURY DURING THE REIGN OF
Shah Abbas I.

STEVEN HOLL

New York (b. 1947)

Competition Entry, American Memorial Library
(AGB), Berlin, July 26, 1988
Pencil and watercolor on paper. 12¹/₁₆ × 9 in.

THE ORIGINAL 1951 LIBRARY WAS DESIGNED BY FRITZ
Bornemann, after a competition among German
architects, and built by American funds. The new
extension reverses this by having a competition
limited to Americans but funded by Germans.

Holl's scheme was cited in the first round for the
urban concepts relative to this important city site, at
the terminus of the Friedrichstrasse. The design
extends the philosophical position of the open stack
by organizing the offerings along a "browsing circuit." This circuit spatially frames the old building
and passes over the top of it at one point. Other inno-
vations include a concept for sheared space which
moves diagonally through the main interior of the
extension, a double wall of glass inscribed with a
crisscross of mullions analogous to the mixing of
information categories in the act of browsing, and a
children's library suspended above the existing building which elevates children to the "guardians of this
city."

[office statement]

PAOLA IACUCCI

New York

Walls, Piazza di Aosta, 1989
Pencil, black ink, wash and watercolor on paper. 22 × 30 in.

[THIS DRAWING BELONGS] TO A SMALL SERIES OF drawings that try to investigate the nature of space as matter, and of urban space, with an almost automatic approach. These drawings have helped me to open an idea of space that was totally implosive: to understand relations of discontinuity and movement within the whole of spatial matter.

These drawings are not a project but an ephemeral vision of the possible reality of a space that from this idea can be born. They are like an hallucination, and as such they enclose a moment of experience that is unknown. They are about the secret of making.

[architect's statement]

**SANCTUARY – VISTA GRANDE COMMUNITY CHURCH
UNITED CHURCH OF CHRIST**
CONSTRUCTION COMMENCED APRIL 14, 1986
ELIZABETH WRIGHT INGRAHAM & ASSOCIATES,   ARCHITECT

E L I Z A B E T H   W R I G H T
I N G R A H A M

Colorado Springs, Colorado (b. 1922)

Sanctuary, Vista Grande Community Church,
United Church of Christ, Colorado Springs, 1986
Black ink and pencil on tracing paper. 20 × 32 in.

[THIS IS] A PREMIER INSULATED ARCHITECTURAL CON-
crete sanctuary and fellowship hall. This building
broke ground on a number of new products and new
systems; it was designed wholly within a rectangle
with 180-degree views of the mountains and plains.

[architect's statement]

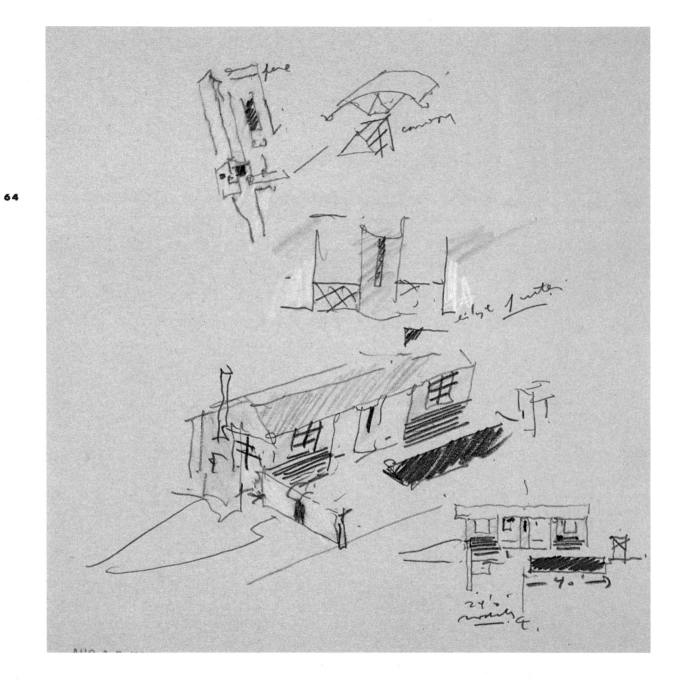

CARLOS JIMENEZ

Houston, Texas (b. 1959)

Fitzpatrick House, Houston, 1987–88
Pencil and colored pencil on paper. 8⁵⁄₁₆ × 8¹⁄₁₆ in.

THE DRAWING . . . IS AN EXPLORATION OF THE ENTRANCES to the house, their design and location in relationship to a swimming pool and court parallel to the house. . . . It contains and illustrates the investigations that are important to me in the design process.

[architect's statement]

J O H N   M .   J O H A N S E N
New York (b. 1916)

Oklahoma Theater Center, Oklahoma City, July 6, 1966
Black marker on paper. 16⅞ × 13⅞ in.

THIS ORIGINAL DRAWING MADE IN FELT PEN IS ONE OF SEVERAL MADE IN 1966 DURING the design process of the Oklahoma Theater Center. It is notable that whereas the construction of the building was completed in 1970 [and] drawings [were] completed in 1968, sketches of the concept were developed in 1966—a long search for an original concept representing, for me, a new architectural vocabulary. This concept introduced a frankly revealed organization of three theaters with various circuits of circulation, "people tubes," distribution of services, in a composition which has little conventional order except what might be called explosive. The underlining order was taken from the operations of electronic devices, made up of a "chassis" or base; "components" and "sub-components," here the major functional elements; and the "harness of circuitry," the circulation connections. Bright-colored sheet metal added much to the original concept.

The Oklahoma Theater Center was the Honor Award by the National AIA, Houston, 1972. The model of this building resides as part of the permanent collection of The Museum of Modern Art.

[architect's statement]

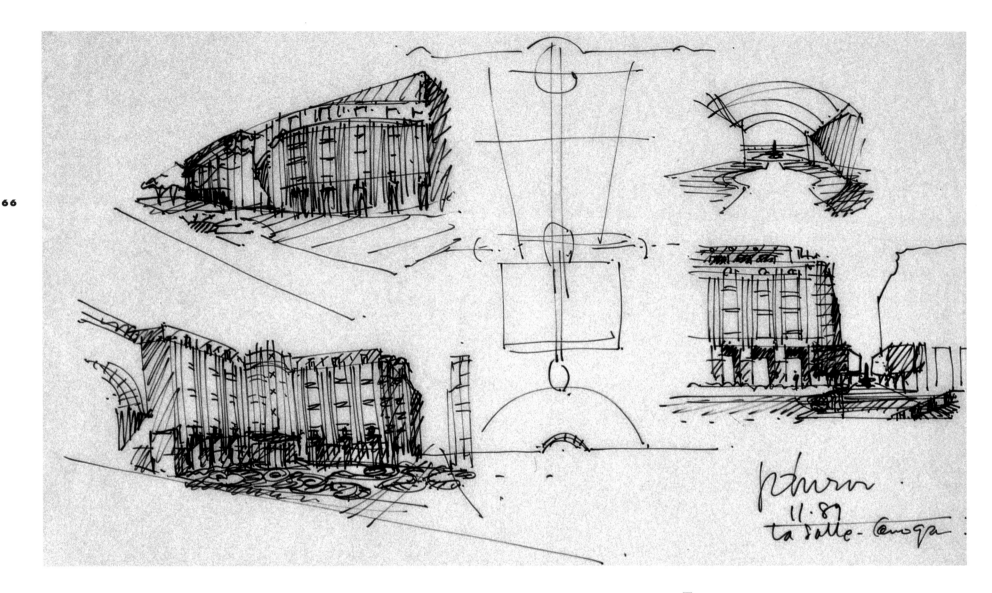

R. SCOTT JOHNSON

of Johnson, Fain and Pereira Associates, Los Angeles
(b. 1951)

6100 Canoga Avenue, Woodland Hills, California;
La Salle Partners, client, November 1989
Black ink on tracing paper. 12 × 15⁵⁄₁₆ in.

This drawing is a design development sketch of the curtain wall of a commercial/office project in Woodland Hills, California, called 6100 Canoga Avenue.... The project consists of four six-story buildings of 142,500 square feet and parking for 2,200 cars. Phase I will begin in October of 1990 and include two six-story buildings and a parking structure.

[architect's statement]

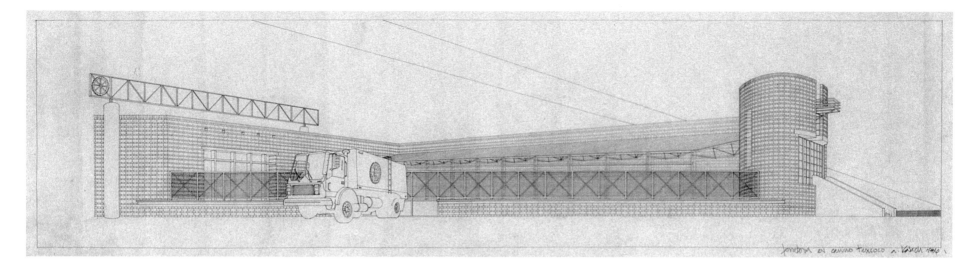

ALBERTO KALACH

Mexico City (b. 1960)

Warehouse, between Mexico City and Texcoco, Mexico,
1985
Black ink on paper. 21⅛ × 50¼ in.

KEENEN RILEY ARCHITECTURE

New York (John Keenen, b. 1957, and Terence Riley, b. 1954)

Mill House Casino, Lambertville, New Jersey, 1989
Black ink and pencil on Mylar. 18 × 22¹¹/₁₆ in.

THE OWNERS OF A WEEKEND COUNTRY HOME, LOCATED ABOUT AN HOUR OUTSIDE OF New York City, wanted a place away from the main house where members of the family or guests could go to play pool [or] Ping-Pong, listen to music, dance or read a book. They also wanted an outdoor room, screened in, where they could go to sit on summer nights. Within this program we saw the elements of a building type largely forgotten in the twentieth century, the casino.

The site is near Lambertville, New Jersey, a small town located on the Delaware River which was settled before the American Revolution. Not far from the main house and off the drive leading into the property are the walls [of] an eighteenth-century millhouse, which will enclose the main space of the casino. Made of 2-foot-thick masonry walls, the ruin is partially burrowed into a steep slope beside the mill stream.

Our intent was to leave the existing stone walls intact. Rather than making new openings into the structure, we wanted to preserve the walls and work with the few doors and windows present.

To bring light into the casino we created a clerestory which runs almost continuously around the building. The clerestory is divided by milled metal posts which help support both the concrete slab and metal railings for the terrace above. The concrete slab becomes the roof of the casino as well as the upper outdoor terrace. On this terrace is the screened room, the roof of which is constructed of metal sheathing over a curved marine plywood subsurface. From the outdoor room and the terrace one has a view of the surrounding property: a stream, a pond, an existing bridge and dam, a swimming pool, the distant hills.

Much of this project refers to the dialectic established between the "heavy" and the "light"—heavy referring to the stone as material, to masonry as a method of construction, density, opacity and immobility; "light" referring to the frame construction, lightweight materials such as metal and glass, and the elements of transparency and spatial complexity.

An attempt has been made to integrate the use of universally produced materials with elements that are more specifically inflected. As a model, we looked to Carlo Scarpa's bridge at Palazzo Querini Stampalia, where the hand-carved rail, produced by Venetian gondola craftsmen, is supported by industrially produced, welded steel sections.

The juxtaposition of the universal and the specific is further articulated by the presence of the millhouse walls. As historical artifacts they lend a singular quality to the project.

[architects' statement]

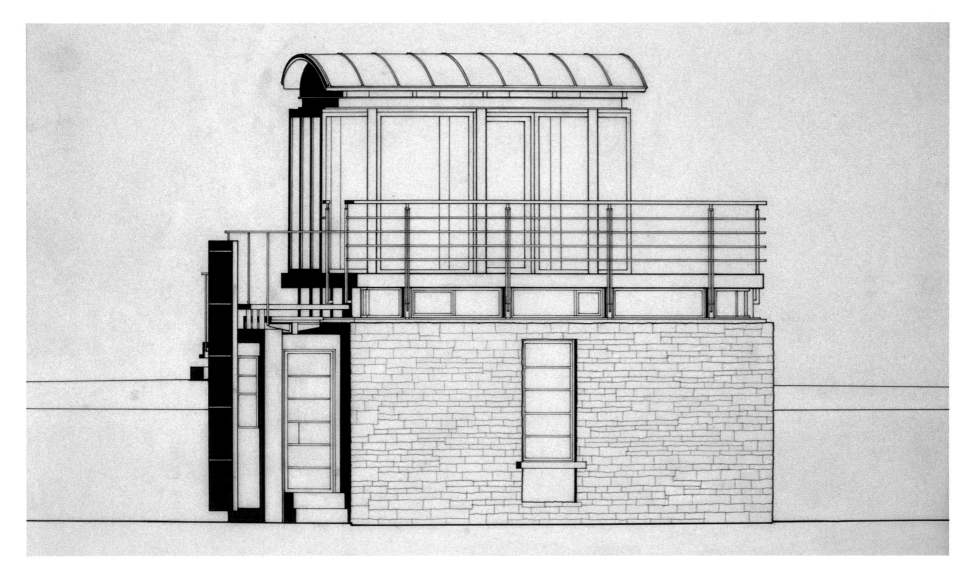

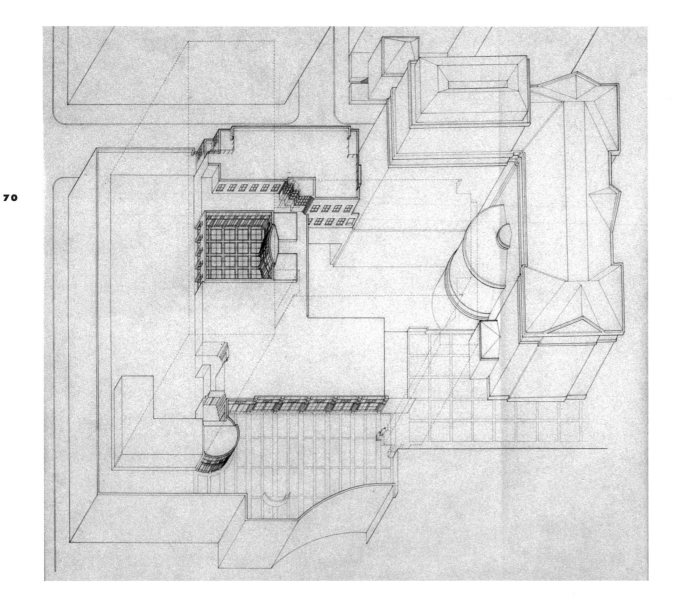

THE BUILDING HOUSES THE DEPARTMENT OF COMputer Sciences, a new department formed within the School of Engineering. The facilities of the department include administrative offices, faculty and graduate student offices, a department lounge, a conference room, computer laboratories, a terminal room and a machine room. Included in the project are a new entrance and a new student lounge for the School of Engineering. The project includes 38,000 square feet, of which 18,000 square feet is renovated space primarily for the computer labs and for mechanical equipment.

The site is at the northeast corner of the McKim, Mead and White Columbia campus plan of 1894. The building is constructed on the four-story podium of the Engineering Terrace building of 1960, south of the Mudd School of Engineering of 1958, both by Voorhees Walker Smith and Haines; north of the Schermerhorn Building of 1897 and the Schermerhorn Extension of 1926, both by McKim, Mead and White; and under the Fairchild Life Sciences building of 1974 by Mitchell / Giurgola.

The building organizes the disparate elements of the context into a coherent whole, and the building is in turn completed by them. The materials and general proportions of the building are drawn from the adjoining buildings: limestone, granite and brick. The primary, elaborated elevations on the east, west, and in the courtyard, are of limestone, with polished granite pilasters that mark the rhythm of the structure, and of bluestone panels that simulate windows or openings to establish the appropriate relationship between solid and void. The secondary, plain walls at courtyard setback and at service court are of brick. The aluminum windows are used throughout.

[architects' statement, from *Architecture and Urbanism,* September, 1984, no. 9, p. 40]

R. M. KLIMENT AND FRANCES HALSBAND ARCHITECTS

New York (Robert Kliment, b. 1933, and Frances Halsband, b. 1943)

Computer Science Building, Columbia University, New York, 1983
Black ink on Mylar. 31⅞ × 42 in.

PIERRE KOENIG
Los Angeles (b. 1925)

Case Study House #22, Los Angeles, 1959–60
Black ink on board. 20 × 30 1/16 in.

KOLATAN / MACDONALD STUDIO

New York (Sulan Kolatan, b. 1958, and
William MacDonald, b. 1957)

Shapiro / Fields Apartment, New York, 1989
Acrylic on Mylar. 24¹³⁄₁₆ × 40⁹⁄₁₆ in.

THE APARTMENT IS COMPOSED OF A MATRIX OF ROOMS arranged around a cruciform distribution of service and circulation elements. There is no view, although the apartment is situated between Broadway and Riverside Drive. This paradoxical relationship led to an idea of creating a "physical path" and a "visual path."

The "physical path" is described by a matrix of rooms, . . . with their independent functional assignments and their usual access routes linked by halls. The "visual path" transcends the position of walls and explores a notion of simultaneity as related to space by creating particular fissures in the walls that align and produce views through the entire apartment; the use of mirrors projects space that exists outside your normal cove of vision to one that exists simultaneously with your natural view; and different sectional ideas of vision, horizontal slots out at eye level alternately placed at standing and sitting heights.

Through an episodic exploration of both the physical and visual realms, the apartment is meant to be engaged and understood in terms of its tactile and conceptual ideas.

[architects' statement, in *GA Houses,* March 1990, vol. 28, p. 74]

KOLATAN / MACDONALD STUDIO

New York (Sulan Kolatan, b. 1958, and
William MacDonald, b. 1957)

Gebekse Hotel, Mamaris, Turkey, 1990
Black ink, white acrylic paint and transparent color film
on electrostatic film. 39⅛ × 35⅞ in.

[THE ARCHITECTS'] IMMEASURABLE SITE FOR THE
Gebekse Hotel and Villas in Mamaris, Turkey, on the
Aegean Sea is caught between the sectional relationship of two horizons, creating a planar, spatial fron-
tality afforded by a vertical condition of tilted land
and the horizontal condition of water.

The occupation and inhabitation of this folded landscape is revealed through a series of "seams" introduced by a variety of operations: incision, insertion,
removal, replacement, extrusion and measurement to
reveal the "land-scape."

The descriptive process of these "seams" is based on
their inherent programmatic value, which, divided
into three constituent parts, became: (1) [the] transit
community, the hotel; (2) the permanent community,
the villas; and (3) the public facilities.

In this project, Kolatan and MacDonald addressed the
issue of cosmopolitan nomadism and people's search
for leisure in "concrete utopia."

[from *Newsline,* December 1989/January 1990, p. 8]

JEREMY KOTAS
of Kotas / Pantaleoni, San Francisco (b. 1943)

Black Spot, 1990
Black ink and colored marker on paper. 11⅛ × 8¹/₁₆ in.

ONE OF A SERIES IN PROGRESS ON "BLACK SPOTS," THIS DRAWING WAS CREATED [IN 1990] using ink on rag paper. The series also could be described as travel sketches.

[architect's statement]

ALEXANDER KOUZMANOFF

New York (b. 1915)

State University College, Old Westbury, Long Island, New York, 1980
Black ink and colored pencil on Mylar. 15⅝ × 23⅝ in.

THE CAMPUS CENTRAL CORE AS DEVELOPED IN THE MASTER PLAN IS A SEPARATE component part of the total college. The generating concept of this building embodies the aims of unity and centrality, which are essential to the satellite growth of this new suburban state university college located thirty miles from a major metropolitan center. Serving as a nucleus for all existing and future campus facilities, this building (constructed in two approximately equal phases) absorbs all major systems of vehicular and pedestrian circulation. The berm-screened parking area is linked to it by two bridges. There is grade access from various pedestrian points of arrival. Core West, the completed phase of this project, includes the central forum; exhibition gallery; cafeteria; bookstore; recital hall; seminar and conference rooms; student activities; administration offices; music, dance and visual arts facilities; and a resources production center. The central forum, the outstanding feature of the building, represents a fusion of several individual lobby, information, lounge and exhibition areas into a single, cohesive, multipurpose space that will provide a greater measure of identity and focus than the sum of the individual programmed parts.

Steel was selected as the material that responded best to the client's needs for flexibility, expansion and open, wide-span spaces. Lightweight, insulated, white metal panels constitute the primary exterior wall material of the building, reflecting the intention to contrast these white opaque volumes with the rolling meadow of golden grass. The entry was seen as a more urban experience, where two steel bridges, capped with a continuous Plexiglas vault, were used to connect the main building and the bermed parking area, spanning the campus loop road below.

[from *Domus,* October 1979, no. 599, pp. 18, 20]

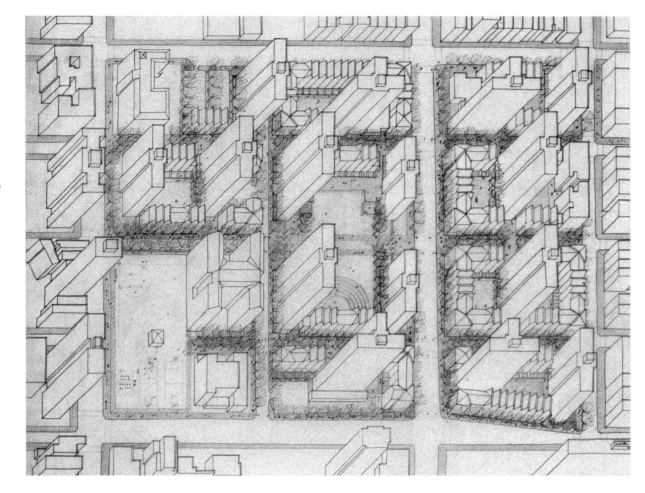

MICHAEL KWARTLER
New York (b. 1944), with Richard Schaffer

Infill Housing at Frederick Douglass Houses,
New York, 1988
Pencil and colored pencil on Mylar. 32⅜ × 36³⁄₁₆ in.

THE DRAWING ILLUSTRATES THE POTENTIAL FOR INFILL affordable housing on the existing Public Housing Authority estate: Frederick Douglass Houses on Manhattan's Upper West Side. It was done in 1988 as part of the West Side Futures project—a preservation and development plan for Community Board 7.

[architect's statement]

A N D R E A   L E E R S

of Leers Weinzapfel Associates, Boston (b. 1942);
John Kuipers, delineator

Tobin Bridge Administration Building, Boston, 1979
Black ink on Mylar. 30 × 30 in.

Technical challenge characterizes this reconstruction of the offices for administration of the
bridge over Boston's Mystic River. The original
building, supported by the bridge structure, lies
directly below a two-level roadway, one hundred feet
above the ground and container port.

A new flush steel panel and window system replaces
the corrugated metal skin, which had been badly cor-
roded by salt washing down over the building from
the roadways above. On the interior, zones of public
and private activity are signaled by shifts in the
width, height, alignment and color of the corridor, at
structural bay lines. Glass block partitions identify
special uses, such as lounge, reception and board
room, and at the same time transmit light into what
was a dark interior.

The building, which is open to administer toll collection twenty-four hours every day, remained in opera-
tion throughout construction. Work on the exterior
was accomplished from scaffolding supported by the
bridge, and materials were hoisted from the ground
below or lowered down from the roadway.

[from *Architecture and Urbanism,* October 1983, no. 157, p. 66]

T O B Y   L E V Y
San Francisco (b. 1951)

Restaurant, Kent Valley, Washington, J. J. and Co., client, 1990
Black ink, colored pencil, and watercolor on paper. 9 × 12⅛ in.

THE PROJECT IS A FREE-STANDING 6,500-SQUARE-FOOT RESTAURANT LOCATED IN THE Kent Valley outside of Seattle, Washington. Kent is a rapidly growing industrial area, with technological industries quickly overtaking the farming aspects of the valley.

The design reflects the many dualities of the project and site. The form combines a simple farm shed perimeter structure around a high-tech center. Individual elements of the program are expressed in their own form: a circle for the bar area and a rectangle for the entry. The center's undulating roof recalls the shape of Mount Rainier in the distance, while suggesting the form of a dragon, a sign of good luck. The perimeter spaces beneath the shed will be dark and earthy, while the center space is designed to be light and airy. The contrast of the spaces and their geometry represent the yin and yang of the program.

The design also took into account the ancient belief of Feng Shui. It seeks to capture the good (cha) spirits that come from the south and to deflect the bad energy from the north. Feng Shui also directs the color of the building, suggesting Red to the south representing fire, Yellow to the east depicting earth, Blue / Green to the west reflecting the sky, and Black to the north alluding to water. The ancient lore suggests many different types of relationships and contrasts, which seem to dovetail easily with the program and environmental directives of the site.

[architect's statement]

79

CONTEMPORARY ARCHITECTURAL DRAWINGS

ROBERT McCARTER
New York (b. 1955)

Berg House, Bridgehampton, Long Island, New York, 1987
Black ink on Mylar. 18 × 27 1/16 in.

IN THIS DESIGN, A PLACE OF GATHERING IS PROPOSED FOR A PERIPATETIC FAMILY. THE house is to be used on weekends and during vacations, and is intended to give this scattered family a place to re-collect themselves. In this sense it is to be their only true dwelling.

The site is within a development laid out over old agricultural fields, looking out to the ocean in the distance. Here the horizon line is the order against which all is measured. The landscape is flat, opening out in all directions, with the line between sea and sky marking the limitless space.

The house begins with the concept of anchorage, a marking-out of place within this endless space. From its center the house grows—spaces are *projected* outward from the hearth, which anchors the volumes. Within the central cubic mass are the fireplace, the kitchen, and, floating between them, the stair up to the master bedroom and library. The dining room and the children's bedrooms are single-story volumes projected out parallel to the distant line of the beach, and the living room is a double-height volume projected out directly toward the water. The pool brings the presence of water into the space of dwelling, and the terrace above the children's bedrooms gives views of the ocean.

The exfoliating roofs and canopies, growing out of the central cubic mass, create shade both inside and outside, marking out a place of inhabitation in this limitless horizontal space. Windows are designed not as holes cut in monolithic walls but as slots of light separating the elements of construction—roofs, columns, walls. Views and passage are allowed between the various interior volumes and between inside and outside by this slicing open of the plan. The place within is made by weaving the linear forms of the tectonic elements of construction to produce space that is open and yet precisely defined.

[architect's statement]

MACHADO AND SILVETTI, INC., ARCHITECTURE AND URBAN DESIGN

Boston (Rodolfo Machado, b. 1942, and Jorge Silvetti, b. 1942)

General Perspective: Panorama of Palermo from Tower, Project for La Porta Meridionale, Palermo, Sicily, 1987
Black ink on Mylar. 28 × 29 in.

PALERMO AND SICILY IN GENERAL ARE OFTEN PERCEIVED OF AS PLACES WHERE THE urbanistic and architectural dreams of Europe are realized; Palermo is a city that attracts and absorbs what is generated elsewhere. These metaphors explain the stylistic, formal and iconographic origins of the most remarkable interventions throughout the city's history. For us, however, they fail to account for the most fascinating aspect of the city's urbanistic and architectonic achievements: its ability to incorporate ideologically diverse products from many Mediterranean cultures. No other place in the Mediterranean matches Palermo's resilience and plasticity to receive, accommodate, transform and implement the disparate influxes of Western culture. All of this serves as the source of Palermo's wisdom and as a paradigm for a certain urbanism that is characterized not by one overriding idea but by an approach where each intervention appears as a striking imposition of a *strong form* on Palermo's urban fabric. These strong forms, now devoid of their original ideological content, are infused with the power of contaminating the organism onto which they are grafted with the luminous emanations of their internal clarity. Although some of the strong forms are conventional architectural monuments, most of them occur as infrastructural interventions such as roads, parks and public spaces.

Today, we are concerned with a critical reinterpretation of architecture, the use and potential invention of late twentieth-century infrastructural and architectural typologies, and the question of *emerging typologies*. We are also interested in the technical *materiality* of buildings, the means and ways of building that are available, contemporary, efficient and durable. This concern for tectonics—the obstinate corporeality of things—is a necessary complement to an attitude of invention. Technical veracity and proficient detailing should be present in the design to demonstrate that what has been dreamt can be made tangible and true. Unprecedented conditions are shown to be possible and better than available precedent by means of a convincing technical materiality which we call *unprecedented realism*.

Furthermore, we are involved in the development of a *personal iconography,* one achieved without reliance on stylistic motives or by the limiting self-abuse of a "language." We are concerned with an individual authorship that runs deeper than language, is more resistant to consumption and risks more in its desire to propose a world and a difference. Finally, we address the issue of *critical design* today—the relentless practice of criticism through design—as part of our desire to work with operations currently common in other artistic practices.

[From *Rodolfo Machado and Jorge Silvetti Buildings for Cities.* Harvard University Graduate School of Design. New York: Rizzoli, 1989, p. 66.]

"OAKLAND SERIES" HOUSE NUMBER ONE.   DONALD MACDONALD '90.

84

DONALD MACDONALD

San Francisco (b. 1935)

Study for a House, Oakland, California, 1990
Black ink and colored pencil on tracing vellum.
$23^{15}/_{16} \times 36^{1}/_{8}$ in.

[THIS DRAWING REPRESENTS] THE FIRST OF A SERIES OF projects in which I am searching for a design vernacular for the environment of Oakland, California. I do not design many houses, but each house that I do design, I use to develop new ideas in my practice.

[architect's statement]

JOSE ANTONIO MARTINEZ LA PEÑA
and
ELIAS TORRES TUR

Barcelona

Facade of the Department Store "El Corte Ingles," Barcelona, 1989
Green wax crayon with black ink on tracing paper. 23¼ × 68⅜ in.

T H O M   M A Y N E
of Morphosis, Santa Monica, California (b. 1944),
with Christopher Wahl and John Nichols Printmakers

Color Proof 1/1, Golf Club at Chiba Prefecture, Japan,
1990
Serigraph on paper. $29\frac{15}{16} \times 29\frac{15}{16}$ in.

THIS PRINT DOCUMENTS THE RELATIONSHIP OF A SITE
strategy to a corresponding architecture. There is an
emphasis on the spatial increment which is fundamental
to the complex's focus on measurement and movement.

[architect's statement]

JOHN MILLER

of Colquhoun, Miller and Partners, London (b. 1930)

La Riba Housing, Alcoy, Spain; Generalitat de Valencia, client, 1989
Pencil and colored pencil on paper. 17¼ × 25⅞ in.

THE GENERALITAT [OF VALENCIA] HAVE APPOINTED SIX European architects to design separate areas of the town as part of an overall reconstruction and improvement programme. Colquhoun, Miller and Partners have been given the central La Riba area.

[The site is] vacant land to [the] east of [the] town center with [a] steep river gorge bounding [its] edge.

[The proposal calls for the] completion of [the] existing town circulation pattern by the development of 135 apartments in buildings of four and five stories with integral basement car-parking for 242 cars. A small shopping arcade with offices above connects the pedestrian circulation with the main public square, and a new road connects two existing streets.

[architect's statement]

87

R I C H A R D   M E I E R
New York (b. 1934), with William Talley and John Nichols Printmakers

Canal +, Paris, 1989
Silkscreen on paper. 29¹³/₁₆ × 47¹³/₁₆ in.

THIS DESIGN FOR A NEW ADMINISTRATIVE HEADQUARTERS AND PRODUCTION FACILITIES for the Canal + television company is located on the left bank of the Seine just west of the Pont Mirabeau. The building is divided into two principal masses: a western wing devoted to administration that faces onto the Seine and a wide eastern wing largely allocated to audiovisual production.

The general organization is a product of the overall context and a number of fairly severe site restrictions. Thus, the thin tapering plan of the administration wing facing the river is a direct result of the boundaries situated to the northeast and the northwest of the L-shaped site. These boundaries define two adjacent sides of a roughly square park that already occupies the best part of the available block.

Conceptually, Canal + depends on a series of delicately tessellated membranes. Of primary importance is the mixture of clear, translucent and opaque white glass that makes up the curtain wall on the western river facade, in conjunction with the projecting, lightweight aluminum *brise soleil* that continues along its entire length. A similarly louvered tessellation appears on the southern facade of the audiovisual wing facing out over the park, with a comparable mixture of clear, translucent and opaque glass. All of this vertical layering is complemented by a series of horizontal light filters, first in the perforated aluminum canopy that crowns the audiovisual block and then in the gridded, top-lit monitor slots that penetrate into the audiovisual block.

All offices in the western wing face the river, and the building is backed by a metal-paneled spine facing the public park behind. Three large, four-story television studios determine the basic shape and mass of the eastern wing, which has been partially sunken so as not to infringe the zoning envelope. Between the two wings is a three-story, skylit glass entry hall that houses the main reception area. This hall provides direct access to all of the studio floors.

It is hoped that the aerodynamic thrust of the office wing-wall opening to the river and the broad contrasting mass of the studios will bring to this somewhat moribund "wasted" quarter of the city a totally new life and sense of civic destiny.

[architect's statement]

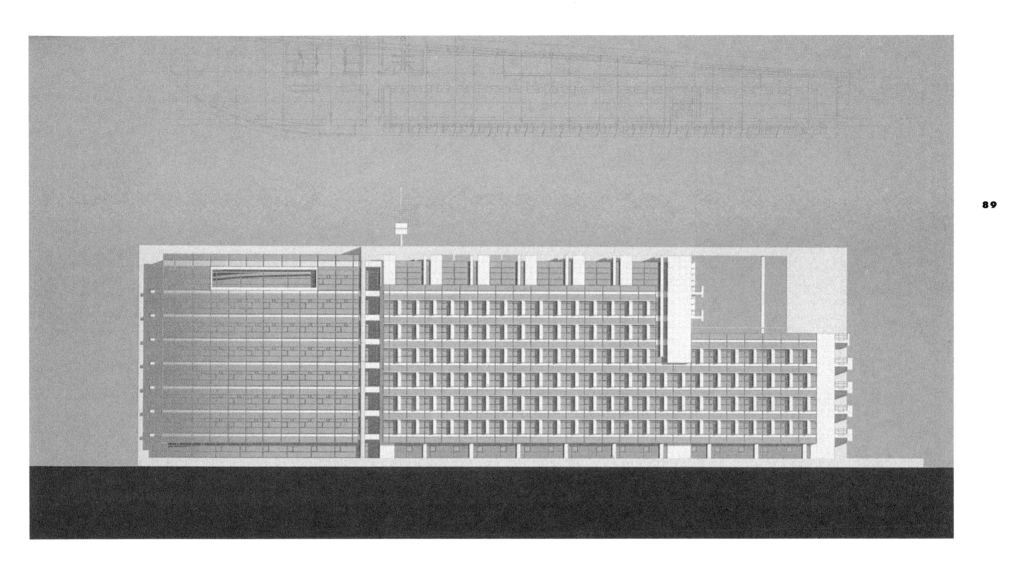

RAFAEL MONEO
Madrid (b. 1937)

Atocha Station, Madrid, c. 1985
Black ink on paper. 8¼ × 11¹¹⁄₁₆ in.

ARTHUR COTTON MOORE

Washington, D.C. (b. 1935)

Retrofitted Window, 1990
Watercolor on paper. 26³⁄₁₆ × 24 in.

I'M AN ARCHITECT AND I PAINT. MY INTENTION HERE IS TO BLUR, FOR THE MOMENT, the distinction between painting and architecture, in order to proffer an aesthetic notion grounded in observations and ideas about art and architecture.

As a very early architectural preservationist in the 1960s, I tried to demonstrate the viability of adapting nineteenth-century industrial structures for modern uses. One of the subliminal lessons for me of that body of architectural work was the easy comfort the nineteenth century had in combining frankly decorative detail with functional structural elements (such as raw riveted steel angles and painted metal floral arrangements)—a visual conversation generally foreign to our eyes today.

The practice of preservation of older buildings has taught that, to humanize and scale a large structure, development of ornamentation is needed which has a declination in scale, telescoped from the large mass to a fine, small, almost tactile perception. Industrial Baroque attempts to enunciate a vocabulary which reinvigorates elements of Modernism by supplying the missing detail in compositions which recall the Baroque period.

Industrial materials are generally perceived as a challenge, perhaps even a threat, to nature—I hope the softening effect of the Baroque-inspired curvilinear form suggests a rapprochement with nature, a recognition that industry is ultimately a part of nature.

These paintings consist of extrapolations from several of my current buildings, manipulations of existing and no longer existing historical structures, and fantasies.

[Arthur Cotton Moore, *Industrial Baroque Paintings and Furniture*. Exhibition catalog, Barbara Fendrick Gallery, New York, 1990.]

91

CHARLES MOORE

Austin, Texas (b. 1925)

Village de Ville, 1985
Etching rendered in watercolor on paper. 13 × 11 in.

A FANTASY DRAWING WHICH DEPICTS AN AIR VILLAGE EMERGING FROM A MOUNTAIN peak with towers and flying banners.

[architect's statement]

BRIAN MURPHY

Pacific Palisades, California (b. 1948)

James Doolittle Theater, Hollywood, California, 1985
Pencil on tracing paper. 21¹⁵⁄₁₆ × 35¹³⁄₁₆ in.

JUAN NAVARRO BALDEWEG
Madrid (b. 1939)

Project for the Renewal of an Industrial Site, Turin, 1986
Black ink, wash and watercolor on paper. 21¼ × 18⅟₁₆ in.

THE FORM AND SCALE OF THE RIVER DORA WITHIN THE CITY OF TURIN GENERATES THE disposition and size of the new buildings planned, as well as the general configuration adopted for the park and the open spaces. The natural landforms and the shapes molded by the river banks have been given a protagonist role in this project: going down to the river is considered an urban gesture. At this point in the city, two geometries dominate: the curvilinear river course and the urban grid that crosses it with difficulty. The solution adopted points toward a balance between these two geometries. The proposed new buildings and the elements that are retained are framed by an interplay of tensions between their autonomous raison d'être and the continuity of the natural forms with the urban grid.

[architect's statement, translated from the Spanish by Angela Giral]

ENRIQUE NORTEN

Mexico City (b. 1954)

Conversion of an Old Wharf into a Cultural and Recreational Center, Manzanilto, Colina,
Mexico, 1987
Black ink on paper. 36³/₁₆ × 23½ in.

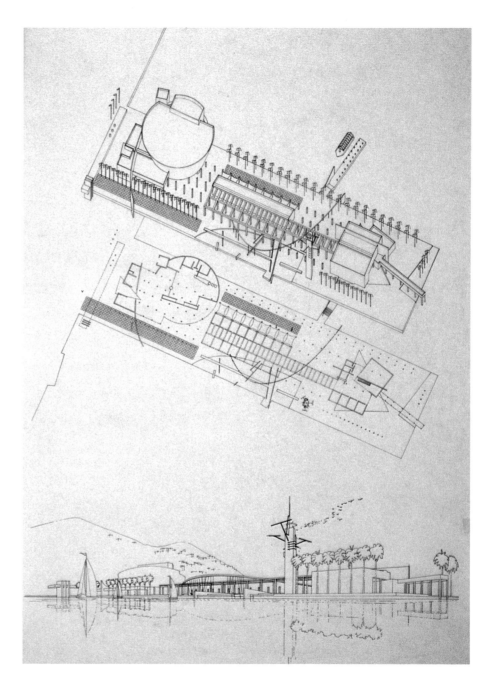

I. M. PEI,   600 Madison Avenue, New York, New York 10022, PL 1-3122

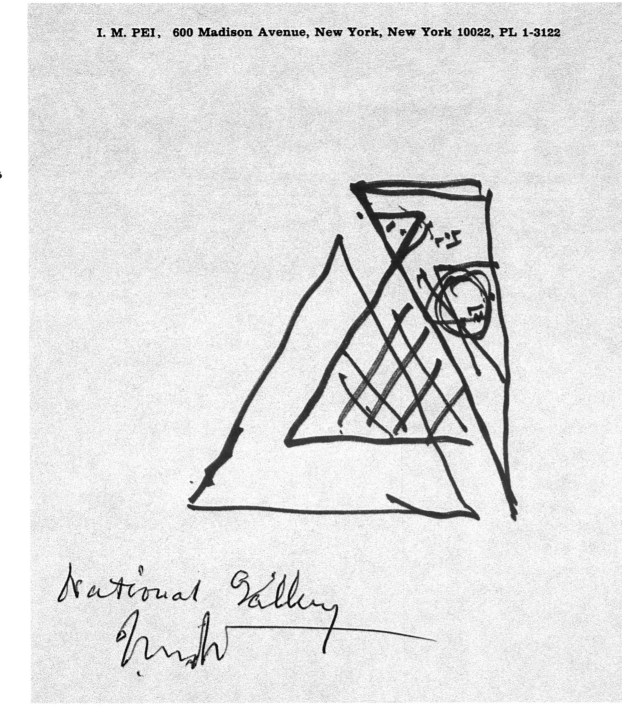

I . M . P E I
of Pei Cobb Freed & Partners, New York (b. 1917)

East Wing, National Gallery of Art, Washington, D.C., c. 1968
Red marker on paper. $8\frac{1}{16} \times 5\frac{1}{2}$ in.

CESAR PELLI

New Haven, Connecticut (b. 1926)

Miglin-Beitler Tower, Chicago, 1990
Pencil on Mylar. 34⁹⁄₁₆ × 26¹³⁄₁₆ in.

THE FIRM HAS BEEN STRUCTURED TO WORK IN TWO MODES: FIRST AS A TRADITIONAL full service firm and second as a specialized design firm capable of working in complex associations and collaborations. This second mode has allowed the firm to be the design architect for very large-scale projects in distant places in the United States and abroad. Successful association with other architects has made it possible for the firm to control design for these projects while still remaining loosely structured as a high-energy atelier, an atmosphere more typical of a much smaller firm.

The crosshatched stabilo rendering style used in this rendering is now the standard style used in our office. Mr. Pelli has described how he learned the technique in Eero Saarinen's office in the 1950s, and that it was previously passed down by Eliel Saarinen.

[office correspondence]

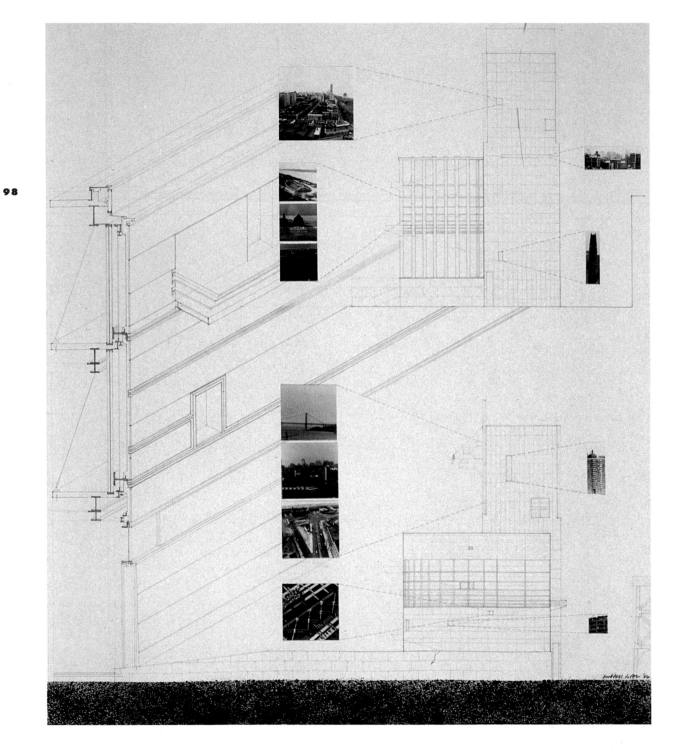

ANNE PERL DE PAL

New York (b. 1960)

Manhattan Boundaries: The Limit of Cities, 1986
Pencil on paper with mounted photographs.
38¼ × 32⅝ in.

THERE ARE TWO COMPONENTS TO THE PROJECT: THE base of the structure, which mediates between the ground edge and the underground 125th Street fault line; and the tower, which mediates between the sky and the base. The curtain walls of the base are different on each side and are fabricated out of ore and bedrock from the site. Specific details from other structures are framed by window and door thresholds. The openings in the tower frame specific limits of Manhattan: the water edge, the street edges, the skyline edge, etc.

[architect's statement]

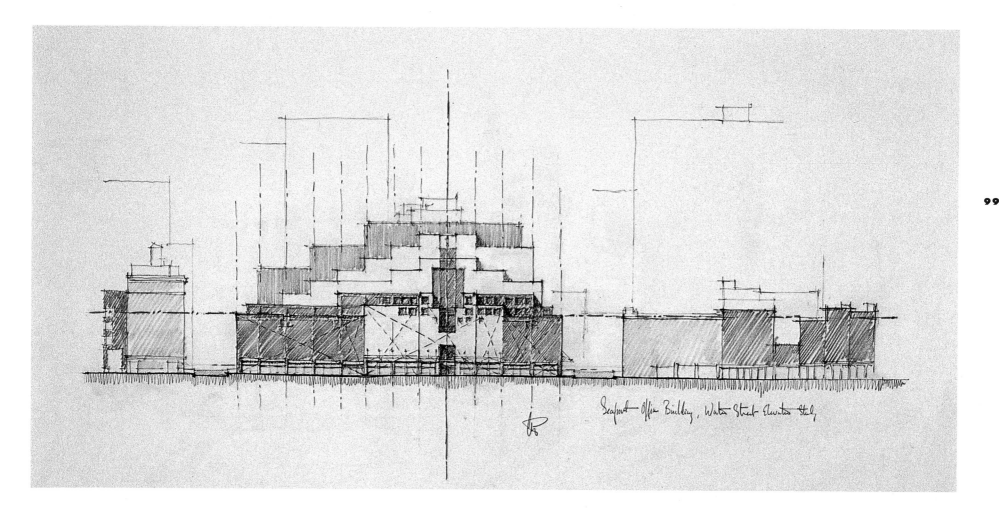

Seaport Office Building, Water Street Elevation Study

CHARLES A. PLATT

of Platt and Byard Architects, New York (b. 1932)

Water Street Elevation Study, Seaport Office Building, New York, 1991
Black ink, pencil and colored pencil on paper. 22⅛ × 29¹³/₁₆ in.

THIS IS A PROPOSAL FOR A TWELVE-STORY OFFICE BUILDING AT 250 WATER STREET IN lower Manhattan, designed to conform to existing zoning—except for the elimination of the arcade—and be appropriate to the South Street Seaport Historic District of which it is a part. The building contains one full floor of retail commercial space at street level and eleven floors of offices for a total of approximately 406,000 gross square feet of built area.

The four- and five-story base of the new building extends the dominant "figure" of the district—a highly varied but consistent cover of brick and granite commercial buildings twenty to forty feet wide and two to five stories high—out to Pearl Street, completing the district's western edge between Beekman Street and Peck Slip. Above the base succeeding floors are set back away from Beekman Street and the entry to the Seaport at Fulton Street toward Peck Slip and Pearl Street. The expression of the base relates closely to the district. The expression of the upper stories relates to the district more abstractly, defining first an "attic" in the setbacks just above the base, then a middle ground of setbacks just above the base, then a middle ground of setbacks clad in cast stone and glass and finally a "core" of setbacks clad variously in clear, reflective and spandrel glass. The varied shapes and colors of the building are integrated into an entirely new form intended to be a worthy and contributing part of the Seaport District.

[architect's statement]

R I C H A R D   P L U N Z
New York (b. 1943)

Portal of Great Theater, Ephesus, Turkey, June 7, 1990
Black ink on paper. 5³⁄₁₆ × 8⁵⁄₁₆ in.

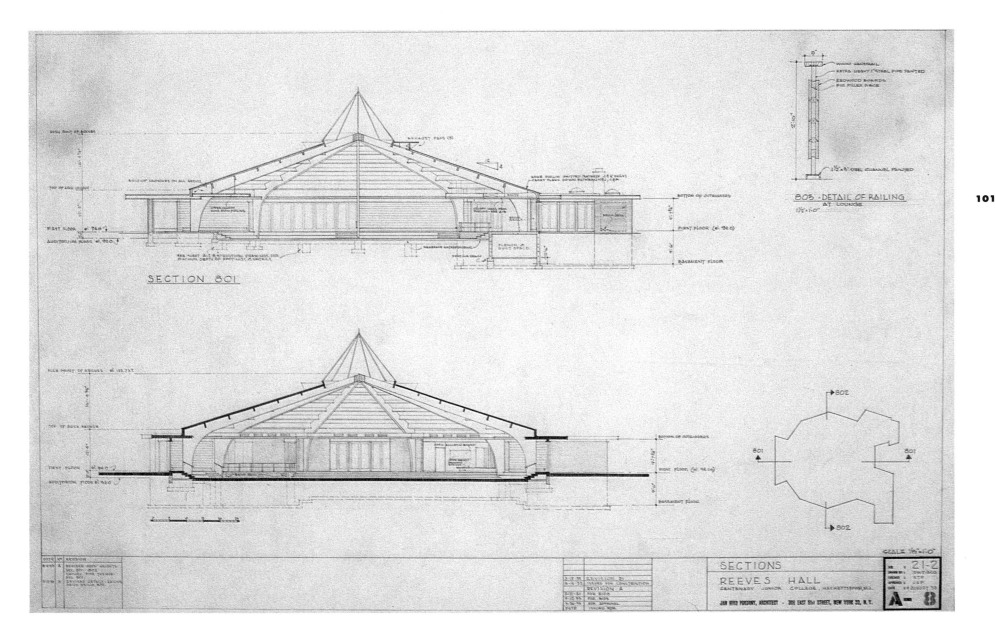

J A N   H I R D   P O K O R N Y

New York (b. 1914)

Reeves Hall, Centenary Junior College, Hackettstown, New Jersey, 1953–54
Pencil on tracing vellum. 24 × 36¼ in.

SO MANY NEW CAMPUS GROUPS ARE USING CIRCULAR OR POLYGONAL BUILDINGS FOR
accent and climax that this kind of feature is almost a 1955 trademark. At Centenary

this focal building shape is unusually appropriate: its tentlike profile, its gay roof, its
sparkling facets and many entrances mark it as a good-time place. Inside, the ten-
sided plan and open structure repeat the light mood, encourage the sweeping, circular movement of the dance.

[from "An Inviting Small Library, a Sociable Student Center," in *Architectural Forum,* vol. 102, no. 3,
March 1955, p. 140]

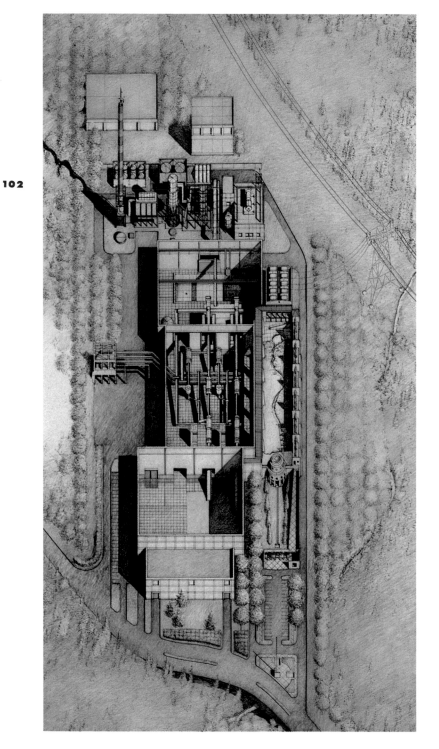

JAMES STEWART POLSHEK AND PARTNERS, ARCHITECTS

New York (James Stewart Polshek, b. 1930; Clem Paulson, delineator)

North County Resource Recovery Facility, San Marcos, California, 1982
Black ink, pencil and colored pencil on Mylar. 35½ × 20⅜ in.

THIS $250-MILLION PIONEER RECYCLING FACILITY, WHICH INCLUDES A MIXED-USE adjunct building and garden, is located at the foot of a landfill. An important model both for the quality of its environmental controls and its efficiency in recycling materials and energy, the facility is also exemplary in its siting and the quality of its architecture. The scheme depends upon the use of landscape both to screen the low-profile metal-clad recycling plant, which covers nearly seven acres, and to serve as a counterpoint to the plant's industrial imagery. The primary program element is the visitors center, which contains an exhibition space, small auditorium, viewing gallery, and garden; its principal objectives are to educate the visitor about the concerns of current waste management systems and to introduce the recycling facility. Conceived as a cluster of articulated, freestanding units oriented perpendicularly to the processing plant, the new visitors building is approached under a trellised walkway. The visitor then enters an exhibition of current waste management systems; proceeds toward an auditorium in an open-air gallery for a film; ascends the stairs to a viewing gallery, which is a bridge of wood trusses and masonry piers; and finally descends to a garden of lush plants and flowers that screens the recycling plant.

[architects' statement]

GERALDINE PONTIUS
for I. M. Pei & Partners, New York (b. 1947)

Charles Shipman Payson Building, Portland Museum
of Art, Portland, Maine, 1979
Black ink, acrylic, pencil and colored pencil on sepia
print (mounted on board). 18⅛ × 29⅜ in.

THE RECIPIENT OF A 1985 AIA HONOR AWARD, THE
Charles Shipman Payson Building is the new wing of
an existing museum complex composed of three
landmark buildings. Located at the intersection of
three streets, the wing provides a street wall for Congress Square that is in scale with this significant public space and respects important vistas and the heights
of neighboring buildings. The curtain wall facade
was constructed with handmade water-struck brick
from Maine with local granite accents for string-
courses, lintels, trim and arcade paving.

This pencil study illustrates an earlier scheme with a
metal-panel facade. The drawing delineates a main
entry portal and three smaller bays with a two-story
arcade running the length of the building. Drawn
from local and regional architectural precedents, the
building's gridlike facade literally recalls the system
of squares in the plan. In the final design, however, the
rectangular forms were transformed into circular and
semicircular bays and openings.

This drawing was one of three by Ms. Pontius published in the September 1982 *AIA Journal* (now
Architecture) as part of a feature honoring the winners
of the magazine's first architectural drawings contest.

[office statement]

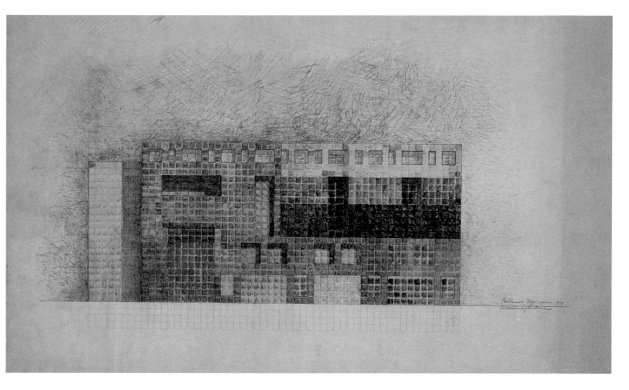

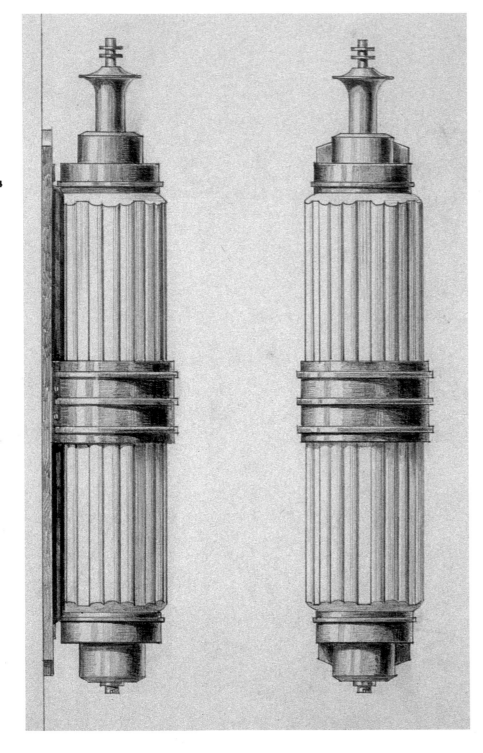

RAMBUSCH, INC.

New York

Light Fixture, n.d.
Pencil on paper. 14⁷⁄₁₆ × 11½ in.

RAMBUSCH HAS BEEN DESIGNING AND FABRICATING OBJECTS MADE OF METAL SINCE the first decade of this century. A creative dynamism reminiscent of the European guilds and ateliers of centuries past pervades their workshops. Unique in the United States, with designers on one floor and craftsmen-artisans on the others, their skills interweave to produce individually designed and custom-made decorative arts for public spaces.

It all began in 1888 when Frode Christian Valdimar Rambusch, master painter and decorator, flipped a coin in his native Denmark to determine his destination: the United States of America or Czarist Russia. In March 1889, he landed in the United States. After two unsuccessful attempts to establish his own business, he entered into a partnership with William C. Hencken in 1898; Hencken was a recent Princeton graduate whose family wanted him to have some business experience. Today, the third generation of Rambusches directs the studio and workshops in Greenwich Village.

Initially, there were commissions for designing and executing painted decoration in public buildings such as banks, theaters, churches, cathedrals and even an opera house in Cincinnati for patron Mark Hanna. Subsequently, workshops for the design and fabrication of lighting fixtures, church furnishings, and, finally, in 1930, stained glass were added, providing clients with the possibility of a completely integrated interior from conceptual phases through design, fabrication and installation.

[from Catha Grace Rambusch, "Rambusch Decorating Company, Ninety Years of Art Metal," in *Journal of Decorative and Propaganda Arts,* Summer 1988, p. 6]

ALDO ROSSI

Milan (b. 1931)

Construzione Marine, 1988
Black ink and pastel on paper. 11 × 8½ in.

[THIS DRAWING IS A] COLLAGE, IN PLAN AND ELEVATION, OF POPULAR IMAGERY USED
by Aldo Rossi surrounding the landscape of the marina.

[office statement]

PAUL RUDOLPH
New York (b. 1918)

Stafford Harbor Housing, near Washington, D.C., 1970
Black ink on tracing vellum. 28½ × 42⅝ in.

DER SCUTT

New York (b. 1934)

Trump Tower, New York, June 1980
Pencil, black ink and colored pencil on tracing paper.
19⅛ × 20 in.

THIS FREEHAND SKETCH ON WHITE TRACING PAPER, using Pentel and Prismacolor, was one of a series of design development studies for the Trump Tower atrium. It was sketched in June 1980, which was when the atrium concept was being finalized. These freehand sketches were literally done in one to two hours and explored color, form and spatial organization. The atrium skylight was still being developed at this time, and this drawing depicts a cubistic version which was later converted to a sloping shape with a space frame.

[architect's statement]

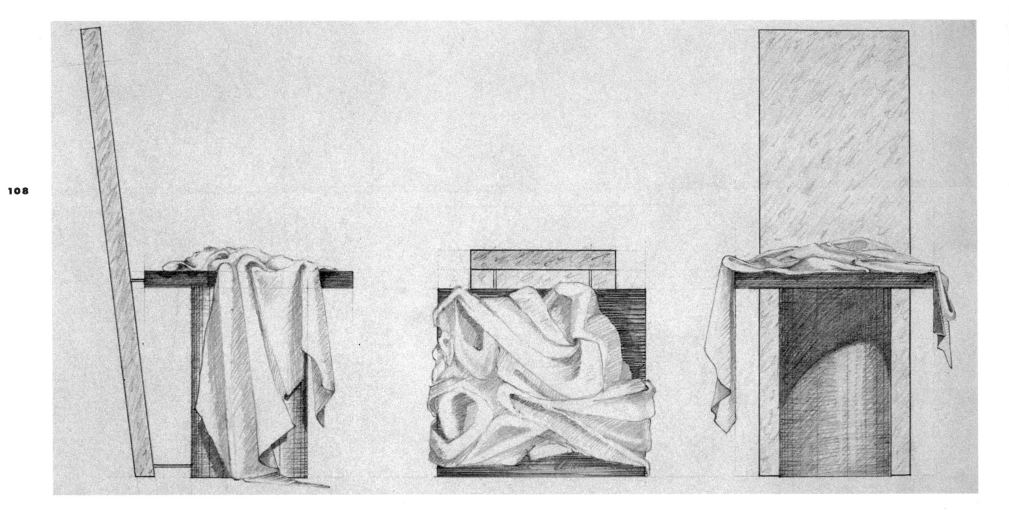

P A T   S A P I N S L E Y

New York (b. 1953)

Itanold Chair, 1985
Pencil on paper, 13⅝ × 15 in.

THE ITANOLD CHAIR IS COMPOSED OF TWO SIMPLE rectilinear planes and a cylinder. These platonic, hard-edged solids are juxtaposed with a softly draped pillow. This juxtaposition sets up a dichotomy of hard architecture and soft accouterments. Both this dichotomy and the use of the simplest platonic solids characterize much of the work of Sapinsley Architecture.

[architect's statement]

PAT SAPINSLEY

New York (b. 1953)

Levy Summer House, Matunuck, Rhode Island,
July 1985
Pencil on vellum. 23⅝ × 30¼ in.

THE CLIENT IS A SINGLE MAN WHO HAS LIVED IN NEW York City all his life. His Manhattan residence overlooks a spectacular and surreal rooftop landscape, the elements of which have come to symbolize "home" to him. The water towers, chimneys and skylight pavilions have become objects of affection and familiarity.

The summer house is an assemblage of pavilions derived from those roofscape elements yet manipulated in order to create an appropriate response to the house's beachfront context. When seen from the beach, the watertank elements (bedrooms), bath and breezeway, elevated as they are, appear to echo the nearby piers and other elevated beach houses.

[architect's statement]

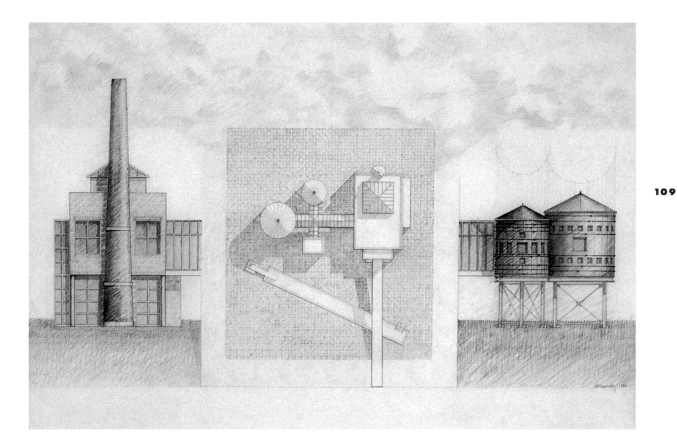

F R E D E R I C   S C H W A R T Z
of Anderson / Schwartz Architects, New York (b. 1951)

Offices for *Rolling Stone* Magazine, New York, February 1, 1990
Collage: Balsa wood, marbleized paper and photocopy on photocopy of a FAX
of a computer-aided drawing. 11 × 16⁹⁄₁₆ in.

DURING THE PAST TWENTY-THREE YEARS, *ROLLING STONE* HAS BECOME AN INSTITUTION in America. From Vietnam to the Berlin Wall, from the Grateful Dead to Public Enemy, from Janis Joplin to Janet Jackson, from Timothy Leary to Lech Walesa, from Mick Jagger to Mick Jagger, *Rolling Stone* has printed "all the news that fits."

The design of the *Rolling Stone / US* magazine offices provided a special and very personal challenge to us in its opportunities to develop an office space for the twenty-first century. The design asserts *Rolling Stone*'s image and distinctive contribution to contemporary culture.

The straightforward and systematic concepts of the design accommodate the ever-changing office adjacency requirements as the needs evolve. The design provides an environment that will aid in the processing and transmittal of information in a thought-provoking and involving manner. The use of natural materials, a variety of textures as well as interior parklike spaces and the views to the outside provide a comfortable experience for all who work in and visit the office.

The design contrasts general downtown loftlike work space with special areas along Sixth Avenue. The design is rich in materials and spaces that are juxtaposed. Industrial jewellike workstations dance on a wooden floor under the grid of concrete beams and columns. Scattered throughout are flourishes like "the wall of the Rolling Stone" at the entry and decorative round columns sprinkled about that are made of tiles, like those found in Gaudi's Park Guell in Barcelona.

The plan combines long-shot vistas running east / west in contrast to short north / south episodic views between the dancing workstations. Between the groupings of private offices located along the perimeter are "free zone" common spaces for informal meetings and work sessions. The program includes two "sight and sound" pavilions along Sixth Avenue behind the curving screen wall of "all the news that fits."

Like the city, where block after block of buildings are interrupted by parks and monuments, . . . the design for the *Rolling Stone* offices [combines] elements that are repetitive and elements that are special. Like a song with its repeating chorus, varied rhythms and big solo, so too is our design. The inner offices are at one beat, the outer offices another beat, the workstations at a constant rhythm and the great curve is the "bridge," the solo along Sixth Avenue that connects the two great halls.

[architect's statement]

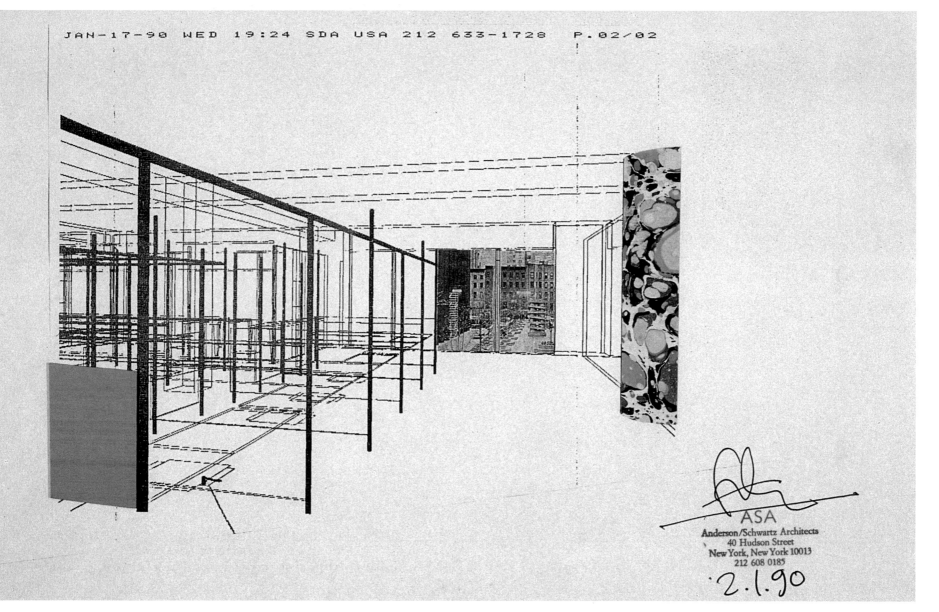

ASA
Anderson/Schwartz Architects
40 Hudson Street
New York, New York 10013
212 608 0185

'2.1.90

EDUARD F. SEKLER
Cambridge, Massachusetts (b. 1920)

The Baptistry at Grado, Italy, July 30, 1969
Black ink on paper. 12⁹⁄₁₆ × 9⁷⁄₁₆ in.

JAMES SHAY

San Francisco (b. 1948)

VanKirk Residence, San Francisco, 1990
Mixed media on paper. 16⅞ × 11⅞ in.

[THIS DRAWING] IS AN ELEVATION STUDY FOR THE VANKIRK RESIDENCE IN SAN
Francisco. It represents the downhill facade of a narrow townhouse on a steeply sloping lot. We are planning to build the house in the color indicated. Construction is
anticipated to begin in the summer of 1991.

[architect's statement]

113

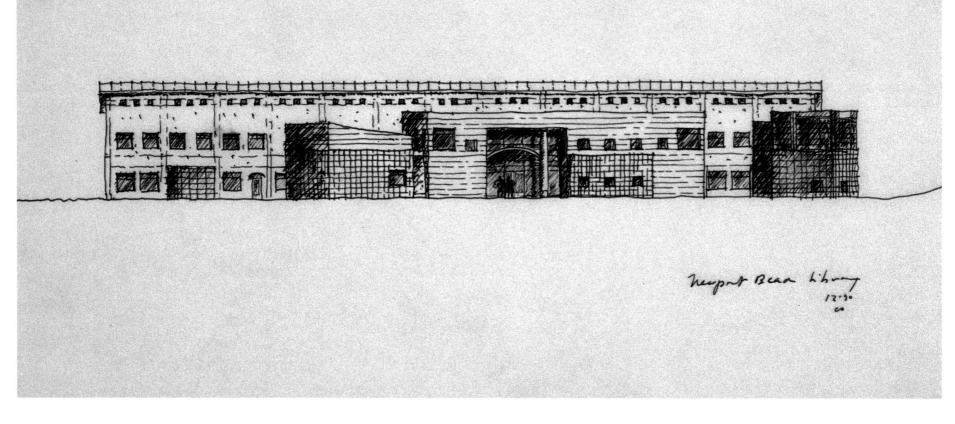

CATHY J. SIMON

of Simon Martin-Vegue Winkelstein Moris Architecture Interior Design, San Francisco
(b. 1943)

Newport Beach Library, Newport Beach, California, 1990
Black ink on paper. 13¹⁵/₁₆ × 16⁷/₈ in.

[This drawing is for] a new 50,000-square-foot Central Library for the City of Newport Beach. It is to be constructed on a complex sloping site as part of a new cultural center that includes a public park to the north and the Newport Harbor Art Museum to the south. The site slopes south toward the Pacific Ocean and affords magnificent views of Catalina Island and the coast. Construction is expected to begin in 1991.

The design of the library consists of a great shed to the north that houses the adult collection, the popular library and the children's library, as well as "back of house" spaces. To the south is a grouping of smaller spaces. On the first floor is the honorific entry to the library, a public meeting room, a children's garden and a special storytelling space; on the second floor is an adult reading room.

The drawing depicts the south elevation. It is a study of the building's facade and the massing of the particularized elements against the long wall of the shed.

[architect's statement]

THOMAS GORDON SMITH

Notre Dame, Indiana (b. 1948)

Diastyle Tetrastyle Portico, Monroe House, Lafayette,
California, 1986
Pencil and watercolor on paper. 15⅝ × 19⅝ in.

THE DORIC PORTICO OF THE MONROE HOUSE LIVING
room wing is presented in perspective / elevation. It is
disengaged from its context in a design for a small
house composed of three pavilions. Metopes and pedi-
mental figures represent personifications of rule and
invention. The drawing represents the specific detail
of the portico but also represents the simple Doric
type of sacred building from which this familiar
domestic element derives.

[architect's statement]

115

A L I S O N   S K Y
of Site, New York (b. 1946)

Addition to Franz Mayer and Co. Inc. Building, Munich, Germany, 1990–91
Pencil and watercolor on paper. 13¹⁵⁄₁₆ × 16⅞ in.

FRANZ MEYER AND CO. INC., FOUNDED IN MUNICH, GERMANY, IN 1845 AND ESTAB-
lished in Fairfield, New Jersey, in 1987, is a renowned studio of stained glass and artistic mosaics.

The Munich studios, constructed in the 1920s, are housed in a landmark masonry
building designed by the architect Theodor Fischer. The existing building is not consistent with the designs of Fischer. It appears to have been intended to continue beyond
the point at which it was cut off and ended in a blank masonry and stucco wall.

The concept, as developed, evolves out of my interest in historical layering and exploration of how new identities can grow out of existing contexts, without destroy-
ing that history. In this project, the historic facade continues to build or "grow,"
metamorphosing into the stained glass "spirit" of the building, within which the
windows and trim float.

The blank exterior wall becomes an interior "studio" wall, revealing doors with
stained glass and mosaic panels; rooms with work tables, work coats, tools and
materials; and mosaic and stained glass works in the process of completion.

By combining opaque and translucent colored glass with illumination, the effect
will be constantly changing. At certain times the "growing" glass wall will glow,
and at other times the "studio" wall will be washed in tones of color.

The concept links the facade to the architectural identity of the building, expressing
the fact that the building was intended to continue and is incomplete as it now
exists. It additionally reflects the fact that this is a creative building, housing studios
and artists working with colored glass and mosaic.

[artist's statement]

ROBERT A. M. STERN ARCHITECTS

New York (Robert A. M. Stern, b. 1939; Andrew Zega, delineator)

Residence at East Hampton, Long Island, New York, 1980–83
Watercolor on paper. 25⅛ × 39¾ in.

THIS RESIDENCE IS A CONTEMPORARY ESSAY IN THE Shingle Style, which flourished in the coastal resorts of northeastern America in the 1880s and 1890s. In the heart of East Hampton's traditional summer colony, the house takes its cues from the imposing Shingle Style "cottages" characteristic of the neighborhood, which were in turn interpretations by nineteenth-century architects of the houses built in the seventeenth century by East Hampton's first English settlers. One of the primary obligations of any work of architecture is to create a sense of place, to respect and enhance a building's physical and cultural context. Another responsibility is to work within a tradition in a scholarly manner—to be succored but not smothered by the values of architectural culture.

In plan, detail and massing this house recaptures the Shingle Style's hybridization of classical and vernacular elements—a synthesis that at once ennobles the rituals of everyday life with memories of cultural traditions inherited from abroad and creates an architectural statement not so much of its time as of its place. The house declares but does not flaunt its modernity; traditional forms are subtly modified, but their representational character is retained and the massing of the house intensified by the geometrical clarity of its predecessors. The iconic elements of the facades—the entrance porch, the eyebrow dormers and the turret overlooking the garden—are applied to the relatively straightforward massing of the house, their slightly inflated scale accentuating the dialogue between the mundane and the meaningful, between a specific place and the memory of grander places long since left behind.

In many ways this house typifies the design process in our office. From my initial conceptual sketches the designs were developed (in drawn and rough model form) by a project team headed by Terry Brown and Roger Seifter. Once the scheme gelled, ink presentation drawings and a more refined cardboard model (the latter now in a private collection) were prepared. The elevational watercolor by Andrew Zega represents the final step in an ongoing graphic process that, as a rule, we have found necessary to our work.

[architect's statement]

ROY STRICKLAND
of Strickland and Carson Associates, New York
(b. 1952)

Apartment Houses, Frederick Douglass Boulevard,
New York, 1989
Black ink on paper. Each 3⅞ × 5¹⁵⁄₁₆ in.

THESE DRAWINGS ARE CONCEPTUAL SKETCHES FOR A
redevelopment project planned in 1990 for Frederick
Douglass Boulevard, 110th Street to 125th Street,
New York City. The low-rise building is a "perimeter"
or courtyard-housing block that would be repeated at
several large, empty sites along the boulevard, especially in the vicinity of 121st Street. The tall building
is located at the triangular intersection of the boulevard, at St. Nicholas Avenue and 120th Street, where
a combined apartment house and community service
facility is proposed. The community service facility
conforms to the site's geometry, while the housing
rises as a tower to mark the intersection as one of a
series of special conditions along Frederick Douglass
Boulevard. Both sketches display the designer's interest in the urban wall and its potential to define space
and/or occupy space.

For this project, drawing was the predominant mode
of design exploration because its flexibility enabled
concepts for the 30-square-block site to be developed
quickly. Small sketches such as the one shown culmi-
nated in hardline plans, elevations and ground-level
and aerial perspectives at a variety of scales.

[architect's statement]

HUGH STUBBINS

Cambridge, Massachusetts (b. 1912)

Minato Mirai 21, Block 25, Yokohama, Japan; Mitsubishi Estate Co., Ltd., May 1990
Pencil and watercolor on paper. 24 × 18¹⁄₁₆ in.

MINATO MIRAI 21 (MM-21) IS PART OF A NEW CITY ON THE WATERFRONT OF
Yokohama, overlooking Tokyo Bay.

The first block is being developed by Mitsubishi Estate Co., Ltd. and is now under
construction.

The complex includes two large high-rise buildings, one including a 600-room
hotel. The remainder of the project is a large shopping and restaurant center.

The project has a total of about 4.5 million square feet and is scheduled for completion in 1993.

The structural elements are steel, and the exterior is clad in a light-colored granite
with a blue-green glass for windows.

[architect's statement]

J O H N S T U B B S
New York (b. 1950)

Restoration of the Forum at Cosa, Orbetello (Ansedonia), Italy, December 1973
Black ink, pencil and colored pencil on tracing vellum. 26 × 43⁹⁄₁₆ in.

ARCHAEOLOGICAL SITE CONSERVATION AND INTERPRETATION IS CURRENTLY A VERY important concern in Italy as well as in many other countries. The conservation of in situ archaeological remains can present perhaps the most complex of all conservation challenges since intervention usually involves protecting historic building fabric and artifacts which were never intended to be exposed to either the elements or tourist wear. Design for accurate interpretation by the average site visitor can also be difficult since it usually involves presenting archaeological remains which are in a ruinous state.

The archaeological site of Cosa is located approximately ninety kilometers north of Rome, near Orbetello, on a promontory projecting into the Tyrrhenian Sea. For over twenty-five years, the site has been excavated under the auspices of the American Academy in Rome, mainly under the direction of Dr. Frank E. Brown.

Cosa was founded in 273 B.C. as a military colony to serve as the northernmost Roman defensive against the inhabitants of Etruria. The walled city, situated above a harbor installation, served as an active seaport for over five centuries. Streets of the city were laid out in a basic grid pattern on a northwest-southeast axis, and a temple dedicated to Jupiter occupied the highest elevation of the site. At its peak stage of development the town, including its immediate hinterlands, had an estimated population of 30,000 and contained essentially the same public amenities as Rome, i.e., temples, a forum, a commitium, a basilica, a bath and a number of governmental structures called atrium publica.

The effort represented in this project has been directed toward suggesting a comprehensive approach for effectively preserving and presenting the most significant public space at the site. The principal objective was to provide an acceptable proposal for conserving irreplaceable archaeological materials while also utilizing recent scholarly findings to communicate an accurate general interpretation of the forum space and its buildings. Proposed treatment of extant architectural fabric involved reconstruction (minimal), structural consolidation, protective shelters, an attempt at innovative interpretive aids, landscape design and reburial—an intervention which remains the most effective way of preserving in situ archaeological material. Special design requirements included using durable and easily maintained construction materials, fencing off the area to protect a livestock herd and preserving a number of randomly placed olive trees.

Preparation for this project involved two summers of field experience at Cosa as a site surveyor and illustrator, and touring a number of conserved sites in western Europe and North Africa.

[architect's statement]

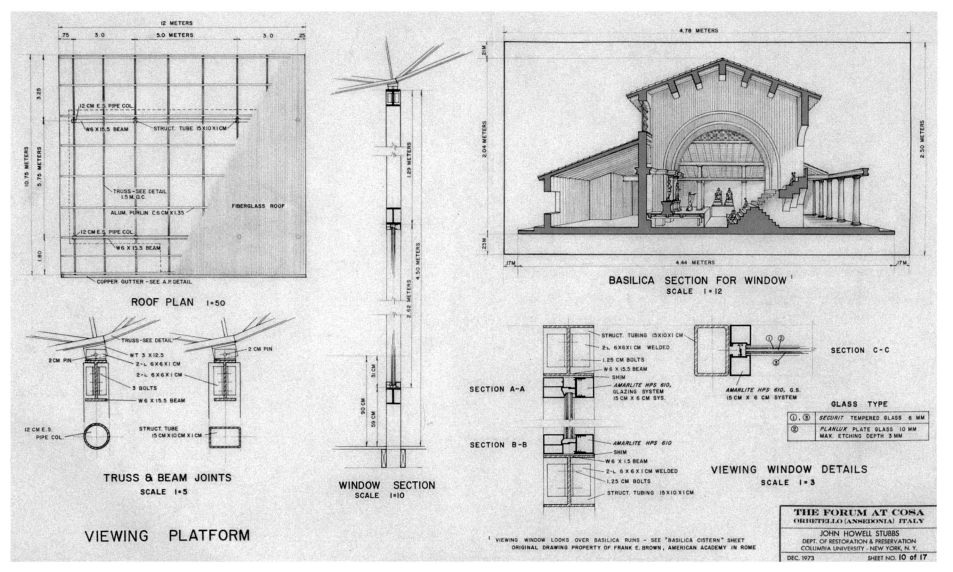

ROOF PLAN 1=50

12 METERS

.75 3.0 5.0 METERS 3.0 25

12 CM E.S. PIPE COL.
W6 X 15.5 BEAM
STRUCT. TUBE 15X10X1 CM
TRUSS-SEE DETAIL 1.5 M.O.C.
ALUM. PURLIN C6 CM X 1.35
FIBERGLASS ROOF
12 CM E.S. PIPE COL.
W 6 X 15.5 BEAM
COPPER GUTTER - SEE A.P. DETAIL

TRUSS & BEAM JOINTS
SCALE 1=5

TRUSS-SEE DETAIL
2 CM PIN
2 CM PIN
WT 3 X 12.5
2-L 6X6X1 CM
2-L 6X6X1 CM
3 BOLTS
W 6 X 15.5 BEAM
12 CM E.S. PIPE COL.
STRUCT. TUBE 15 CM X 10 CM X 1 CM

VIEWING PLATFORM

WINDOW SECTION
SCALE 1=10

30 CM
90 CM
59 CM

1.29 METERS
4.50 METERS
2.62 METERS

BASILICA SECTION FOR WINDOW'
SCALE 1=12

4.78 METERS
4.44 METERS
2.50 METERS
2.04 METERS
21 M
25 M
17 M
17 M

SECTION A-A

STRUCT. TUBING 15X10X1 CM
2-L 6X6X1 CM WELDED
1.25 CM BOLTS
W 6 X 15.5 BEAM
SHIM
AMARLITE HPS 610, GLAZING SYSTEM 15 CM X 6 CM SYS.

SECTION C-C

AMARLITE HPS 610, G.S.
15 CM X 6 CM SYSTEM

SECTION B-B

AMARLITE HPS 610
SHIM
W 6 X 1.5 BEAM
2-L 6 X 6 X 1 CM WELDED
1.25 CM BOLTS
STRUCT. TUBING 15 X 10 X 1 CM

GLASS TYPE

①,③ SECURIT TEMPERED GLASS 6 MM
② PLANLUX PLATE GLASS 10 MM MAX. ETCHING DEPTH 3 MM

VIEWING WINDOW DETAILS
SCALE 1=3

' VIEWING WINDOW LOOKS OVER BASILICA RUINS - SEE "BASILICA CISTERN" SHEET
ORIGINAL DRAWING PROPERTY OF FRANK E. BROWN, AMERICAN ACADEMY IN ROME

THE FORUM AT COSA
ORBETELLO (ANSEDONIA) ITALY

JOHN HOWELL STUBBS
DEPT. OF RESTORATION & PRESERVATION
COLUMBIA UNIVERSITY · NEW YORK, N. Y.

DEC. 1973   SHEET NO. 10 of 17

JAMES TICE
Ardsley, New York

Competition Entry, First Prize, Shinkenchiku Housing, Japan; sponsored by *Japan Architect,* 1978
Black ink on paper. 20⅛ × 26¹⁵/₁₆ in.

THE ARCHITECTURAL GROUP CONSISTS OF A CONTINUOUS WALL OF ROW HOUSING alternating with the open space of the street, the sunken courtyard and the terraced gardens opposite. Urbanistically, only one side of the street is designed as building. The resulting ensemble of building and "park" reinterprets late-eighteenth- and early-nineteenth-century housing exemplified in the work of John Wood and John Nash.

The two different housing types on either side of the street have been designed in accordance with their urban role while still providing living amenities for the individual.

The row house unit distinguishes between front and rear. The arcaded street side is public: it presents a polite, predictable facade to the park, its added height determined by the scale of the open space opposite. In contrast, the rear gardens are private and informal and allow for a greater degree of choice and whimsy. This unit type adopts the conventional slotted row house as a model; however, its rear portion is transformed into a version of Swiss stepped housing in order to provide sunny terraces with a view. In these units the generous accommodations range up to four bedrooms and a studio. Living zones are conventionally organized with living and dining on the entry level, services and parking below with sleeping / private space above.

The entry to the atrium house opposite is disguised as a garden gate. Its sunken courtyard provides a focus for the various spaces surrounding it. This unit owes more to very old courtyard examples, Renaissance garden grottos and the English green house than to the twentieth-century *Siedlung*. Yet its modest size allows for interesting living alternatives. For instance, it is possible to interpret the unit as three separate studios, each retaining a separate entry off the court. Or these may become the separate domain of individual family members.

The project respects the street and therefore could be introduced, either in whole or in part, as a fragment into an existing urban context. Of course it suggests applications in new residential areas as well, for its passages and linkages provide continuity with complementary parts of the city.

[architect's statement]

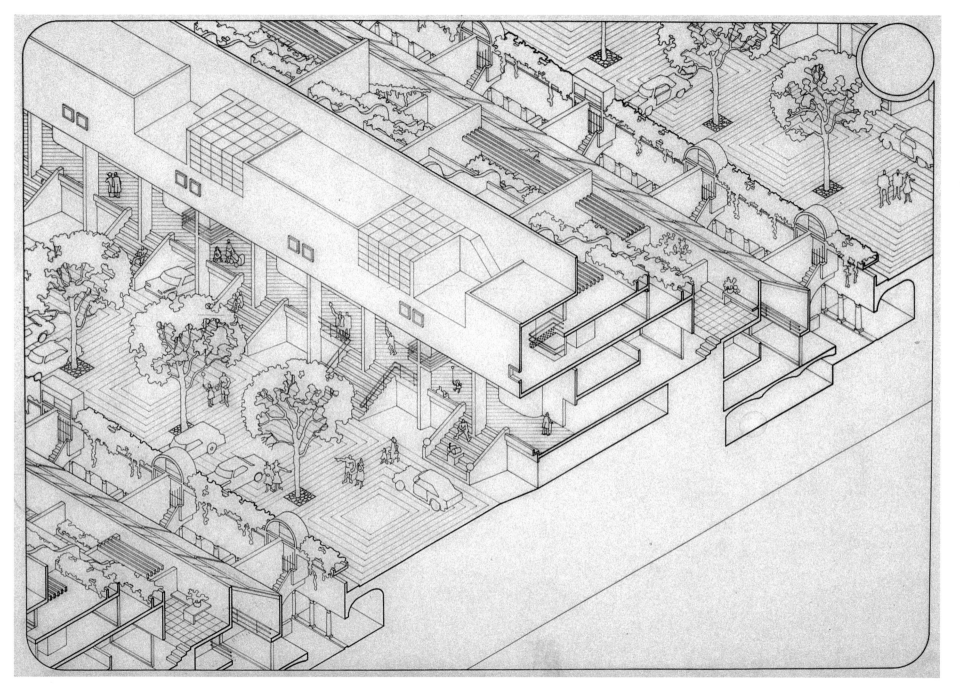

CONTEMPORARY ARCHITECTURAL DRAWINGS

S U S A N A   T O R R E
New York (b. 1944)

A Public Park on Ellis Island, New York, 1981
Pencil and yellow pencil on tracing paper. 39 × 29 in.

THE PROJECT PROPOSES THE TRANSFORMATION OF ELLIS ISLAND, A PLACE OF HOPE AND despair, into a place of remembrance and celebration. If built, this park would be the first to celebrate in its design and proposed uses the plurality of influences that have shaped a civilization.

Half of the island is retained as museum, the main Immigration Station left empty, filled with silence where names of every nationality were once shouted. Upon exiting the building through the low railroad addition, the visitors find themselves at the edge of a reflecting pool that follows the outline of Fort Gibson's wall, built in 1812. Beyond is a high wall with a walkway atop supported by shallow masonry arches on one side. This wall follows the outline of Ellis Island during the building of the Immigration Station and the years of peak immigration influx.

The visitors may walk beyond this wall by following the curved walkways, a fragment of the intended but never-built garden. In so doing, they will pass under the flag—a reenactment of the immigrants' rite of passage and their confrontation with the values of a civilization as yet unknown to them. Beyond the wall is a grassy area with a wooden boardwalk intended to recall the loading docks where many immigrants waited to be transported to the mainland. The walkway above the wall, accessible from stairs and ramps, functions as a vantage point to view Manhattan and the Statue of Liberty, restoring to the singular prowlike shape its meaning as carrier of an earlier memory of the site: Fort Gibson's garrison wall and gun battery.

The central, green space will be used for picnics, parades, concerts, games and festivals. This space marks the intersection of two major influences on American attitudes toward landscape. Along the southwest-northeast axis it is experienced as the ceremonial foreground to a formal garden beyond, while along the northwest-southeast axis it functions like town and college greens, recalling Jefferson's plan for the University of Virginia with a prominent building at its head. Narrow pools beside the long edges of the green suggest the once-separate islands.

The garden opposite the former hospital has an oval pool with a 24-foot-high waterfall around its edge. The monumental stairs at the center lead to checkered terraces of paving and grass to either side, forming a stadium in which to view the events occurring in the central green, and to an upper terrace, also accessible by a ramp. Here is a labyrinth garden, the archetypal form associated with the act and process of dwelling.

The edge of the island facing the Statue of Liberty functions like a ship's deck lined with various small ethnic restaurants and shops. Along this street the visitors may pause and enjoy an imaginary voyage while relaxing and eating on the deck's upper level. The street is only interrupted at its center, behind the great waterfall. Water pumped from the sea to form the waterfall is recycled through large circular openings in the seawall.

Either at their arrival or at their departure from the island the visitors may stop at the restored Art Deco ferry house to view an audiovisual presentation about Ellis Island's history or buy postcards and souvenirs. They may also enjoy a walk through the forest facing New Jersey, a reminder of the American wilderness cherished by Europeans and Americans alike at the turn of the century. Finally, they may participate in an event taking place at the bermed building that is at the head of the central green. This building is the transformed ruin of the former recreation structure where immigrants enjoyed some sociability and entertainment. The 45-degree berm covering the building's sides is planted with 3-foot-high "Christmas tree" pines. Stairs lead to an upper balcony around the building's perimeter and mark the entrance. As one enters through an opening in the hearth, the skylight above fills the buried building with light.

On special occasions like the Fourth of July or the anniversary of the Statue of Liberty's dedication, powerful water cannons at either end of the island shoot a spray into the air, causing a rainbow to form.

[architect's statement]

125

CONTEMPORARY ARCHITECTURAL DRAWINGS

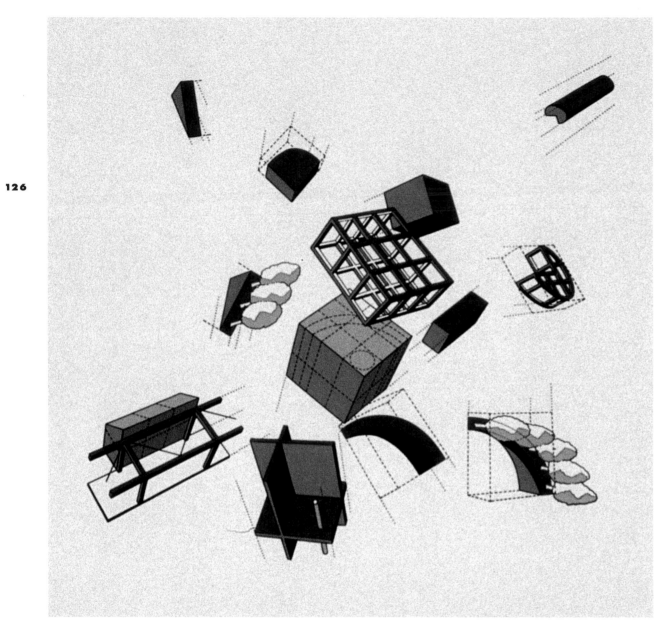

BERNARD TSCHUMI
New York (b. 1944)

Blue Folie L7 and Gallery, La Villette, Paris, 1986
Black and red ink and wash on paper. 19⅝ × 27⁹⁄₁₆ in.

E U G E N E   T S U I
Emeryville, California (b. 1954)

Aquaterra, February 1991
Black ink, colored pencil and metallic paint on blackline print. 25¹/₁₆ × 36 in.

AQUATERRA IS A TOURIST/PUBLIC VISITATION HOUSE SHOWING THE CAPABILITIES OF composite plastic materials for use in the building industry. The house introduces construction uses of these plastics as strong, durable, maintenance-free materials for residential development. Subsequent designs will be far more economical. The aerodynamic, air-cooled design gracefully accommodates any site in an earthquake-prone region.

Specially designed spring-loaded rubber gasket "cones" create an earthquake-proof foundation. The house is laterally reinforced by its "X-wing" bridge structure with two walkway bridges which act as stabilizing elements tying the structure to its hill-side terrain.

Aquaterra features two pools: a small roof-deck pool acts as a skylight for the living area below. Water falling from the roof-deck pool plunges into a 100-foot diameter circular see-through swimming pool with 60-foot recycling waterfall. Both pools are designed to create solar barriers to control heat gain.

The power for this water-cooled house is generated by two 60-foot vertical windmill generators called "egg-beaters." These eggbeaters convert 40 to 45 percent of the incoming wind energy to electricity. Attached to the wind power is a continuous bank of photovoltaic panels on the upper surface of the structure to assist with the rest of the power needed for the house.

The house contains six bedrooms (two convert to independent apartments), five bathrooms, a three-car garage and two large open-air patios with pools. A water-cooled smoke filtration system and an air cleaning system of irrigated plants produces a zero pollution home.

Aquaterra's playful, reflecting waters create the ambiance of a beautiful aquatic environment.

[architect's statement]

"AQUATERRA"

PERSPECTIVE VIEW   SAN RAFAEL, CALIFORNIA, USA

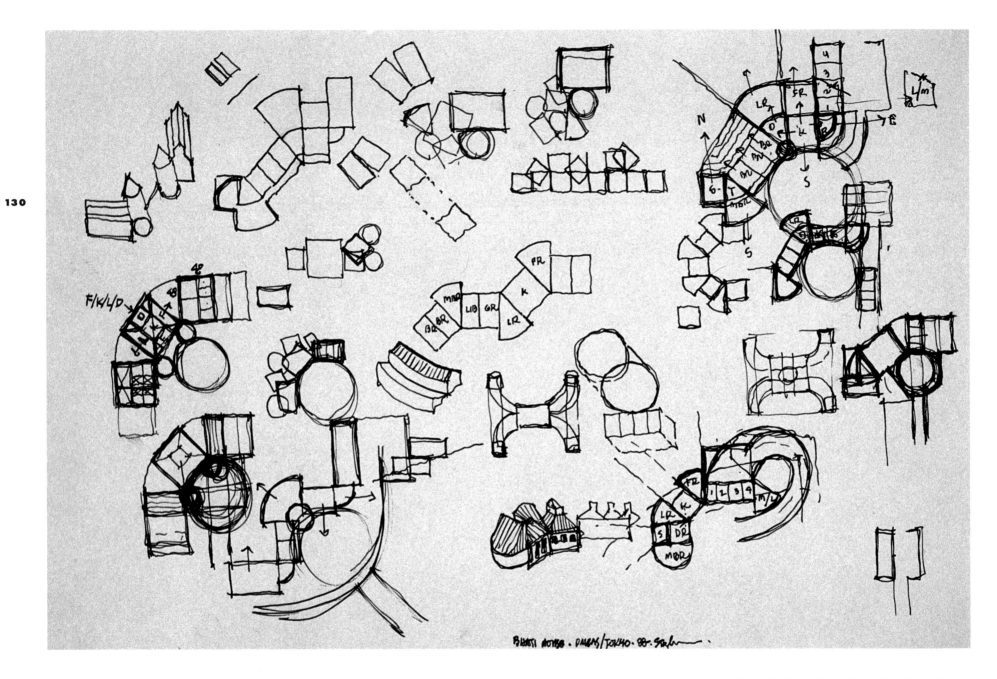

STANLEY TIGERMAN

of Tigerman McCurry Architects, Chicago (b. 1930)

Unbuilt House Project, Cincinnati, Ohio 1988–89
Black ink on paper. 7^{11}/$_{16}$ × 11^{11}/$_{16}$ in.

WILLIAM TURNBULL

San Francisco (b. 1935)

Zimmerman House, Great Falls, Virginia, Fall, 1972
Black marker on paper. 10^{15}/$_{16}$ × 8^{7}/$_{16}$ in.

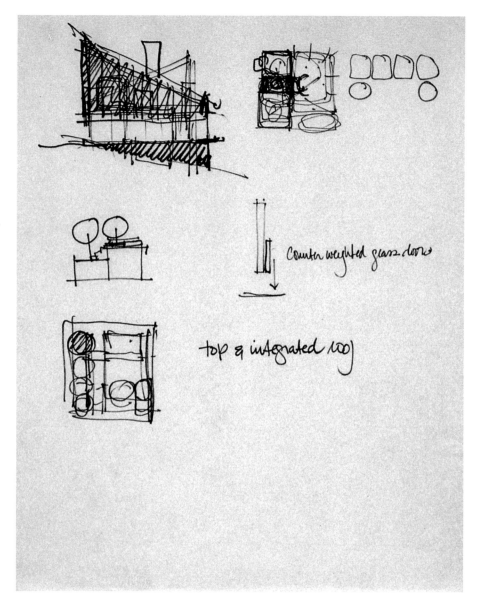

THE OWNERS DESIRED A RESIDENCE WITH TWO DISTINCT QUALITIES: A BRIGHT, LIGHT-filled house, and a house with lots of porches. Out of this paradox grew the solution of a house that is a porch.

Within an outer "porch house"—a timber structure of built-up wood members, sheathed in redwood lattice and covered with a translucent plastic roof—sits a house designed for specific functions. This inner house is of conventional wood frame construction. Interior walls are gypsum board, exterior siding is resawn plywood. White inside and out, the inner house is a freestanding object within the naturally weathering "porch house."

A giant skylight, the translucent roof, fills the inside of the "porch house" with natural light while a light tower from the inner house projects through the roof to flood the interior with bright light. Under the skylight the roof surfaces of the inner house are finished with a synthetic decking material and become multileveled porches. Intended for summer living and sleeping, the lattice-enclosed porches form an air space to cool the house during the hot Virginia summers. Openings cut into the lattice are located to frame views out and are super-scaled to emphasize the porch quality of the house.

Backed by old oaks and maples, the house is sited on the first rise of ground overlooking the long hay fields which are the flood plain of the Potomac River. A long linear lake runs along the base of the hill. Scaled to the site, the form of the house is simple, almost barnlike on the landscape.

[architect's statement]

KAREN VAN LENGEN

New York (b. 1951); Michael Gorski, delineator

Competition Entry, The American Memorial Library (AGB), Berlin, September 1988
Black ink and pigment on Mylar with applied paper, backed with paper. 18 × 48½ in.

Problem

The division of West Berlin after World War II resulted in the loss of the city's urban center. Consequently, the emergence of smaller nodes within the Western sector has established a new urban hierarchy. The Landwehrkanal, the major east-west artery of West Berlin, functions as a spine which organizes a series of spaces serving as gateways to the various neighborhoods of the city. The Amerika Gedenkbibliothek (AGB), at the Blucherplatz, is located at the intersection of the canal and the historically charged Friedrichstrasse. Presently, this plaza is fragmented and incoherent. Our proposal for the library addition addresses the urbanistic considerations as well as the functional requirements of the library program.

Site

Our solution creates a large plaza or "carpet" situated directly in front of the existing AGB. In the tradition of the European piazza, it gathers and organizes the various commercial, ecclesiastical and institutional facilities of the neighborhood.

Library Functions

Each upper level is divided into four zones. The southern end contains the circulation desk and book transport system. Its large windows face an expansive view of South Kreuzberg. The eastern and northern zones contain combined reading and stack areas, which overlook the garden and plaza respectively. The west side of the atrium is densely packed with carrels and stacks where views are least desirable and visitors may enjoy a sense of privacy among the books.

Structural System

The four upper levels of the open-access departments which surround the atrium are conceived of as a single rigid structural frame, which is hung from the concrete atrium structure, which in turn carries the load to the ground. The ground floor and mezzanine level (Berlin Collection) are supported by their own structural system which acts independently from the upper levels.

Conclusion

Our design for the AGB addition transforms the existing site and building into a vital center for cultural life. The site solution brings order to the competitive requirements of the neighborhood, while the addition itself provides new focus for the library complex. As the new wing thrusts itself to the north, it suggests the possibility of increased development along the Friedrichstrasse and the hope for a unified city.

[architect's statement]

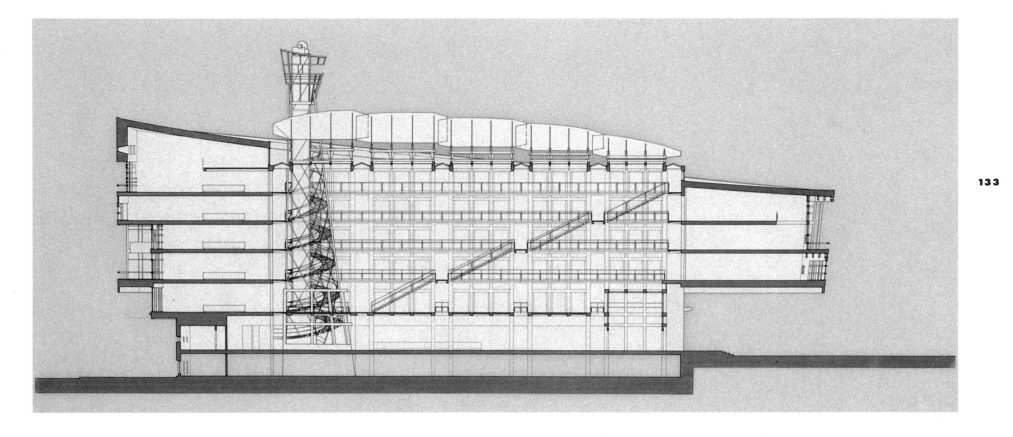

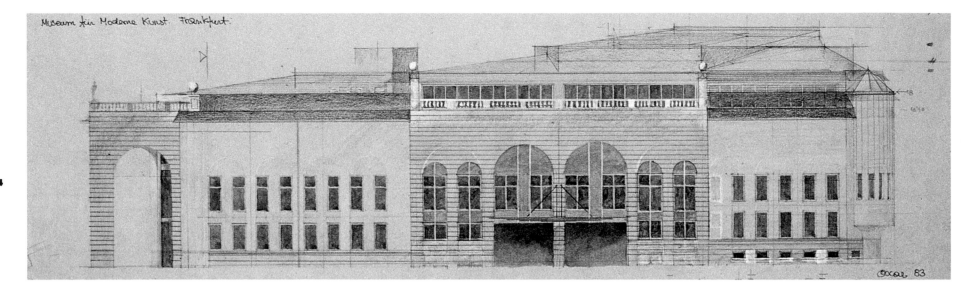

Museum für Moderne Kunst. Frankfurt.

OSCAR TUSQUETS BLANCA

Barcelona (b. 1941)

Modern Art Museum, Frankfurt, Germany, April 1983
Colored pencil and watercolor on blueline print. $5^{11}/_{16} \times 18^{3}/_{4}$ in.

VENTURI, RAUCH AND SCOTT BROWN

Philadelphia

Sainsbury Wing, National Gallery, London,
March 8, 1989
Black, red and green ink on tracing vellum (computer-
aided working drawing). 36 × 53⁹⁄₁₆ in.

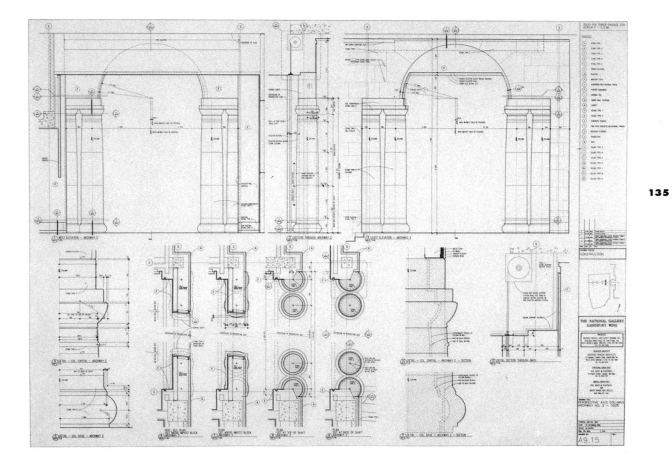

135

LAURETTA VINCIARELLI

New York

Water Enclosure, June 1988
Brown ink and watercolor on paper. 29¹⁵⁄₁₆ × 22¼ in.

VOORSANGER & ASSOCIATES, ARCHITECTS

New York (Bartholomew Voorsanger, b. 1937)

Addition to Pierpont Morgan Library, New York, 1990
Black ink, metallic paint and foil on Mylar. 40$\frac{15}{16}$ × 30$\frac{15}{16}$ in.

137

HARRY WEESE

Chicago (b. 1915)

Milwaukee Performing Arts Center, Milwaukee, Wisconsin, c. 1966
Pencil on tracing paper. 27⅜ × 34¾ in.

DURING HIS MANY TRIPS ABROAD, MR. WEESE often visited Paris, his favorite city, and the Paris Opera House. From that interior he drew inspiration for his concept design for Milwaukee, reflected in the accompanying drawing.

This project, completed in 1969, was the first performing arts facility done by Harry Weese & Associates. George Izenour was the theatre/acoustic consultant.

The Milwaukee Performing Arts Center was given a National Honor Award by the American Institute of Architects in 1970.

[office statement]

COLIN ST. JOHN WILSON

London (b. 1922)

Entrance Hall, British Library, London, 1985
Pencil and watercolor on paper. 20⅞ × 14⅞ in.

[This] is a study that I made for the entrance hall of the British Library, and its subtitle is "It looks like an Academy of Secret Police—H. R. H. The Prince of Wales."

This may puzzle you unless you know of the running battle some of us are having with our self-appointed Royal Pundit. It is also part of the history of this drawing that it made top-price for a drawing at the auction for the Pevsner Memorial Trust in April [1989].

[architect's statement]

J A M E S   W I N E S
of Site, New York (b. 1932)

Bedford House, 1982
Brown ink wash on paper. 14⅛ × 23 in.

Most artists attempt to extend or examine people's values. No true artist just paints a painting; it is always about something. The subject matter of our work is architecture, and I don't think that should be offensive to people, but it often is. There is a line that has been drawn around architecture in terms of what is acceptable and what is not. This has gone on for a long time, and it is really destructive. . . .

The architectural language you use—Modernism, Historicism—doesn't matter, as long as you use it in a vital way. In every cliche there are endless possibilities because it is so loaded. To imitate the Villa Savoye is one thing, but to take its imagery, which is constantly being recycled, and invert or twist its meaning is potentially quite wonderful. Using history as a resource can be bad or very good based on your ability to manipulate its language. The history of art is full of examples of cliches turned into something new. The essence of the matter is: Why is architecture this bland little road that we all have to travel along?

[from an interview with James Wines, in *Progressive Architecture*, August 1990, vol. 71, no. 8, p. 117]

WORKSHOP, INC., ARCHITECTURE AND PLANNING

Tokyo

4 Torri, Takamatsu, Skikoku Islands, Japan, 1990
Black ink, gray screen print and red ink airbrush on paper (computer-aided drawing).
14¼ × 31⅝ in.

THIS DRAWING IS A COMPOSITION OF NINE DIFFERENT ANGLE VIEWS OF THE BUILDING named "4 Torri" in the center of Takamatsu, Shikoku Island, Japan.

4 Torri consists of a restaurant, bar, shops and art gallery, and it has access stairways that rise directly up to the sixth floor. All of the drawing except the red air-brushed figures was created through computer-aided devices.

[architects' statement]

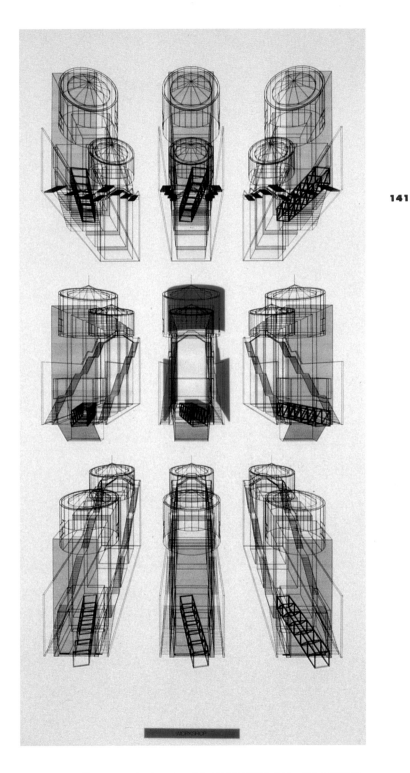

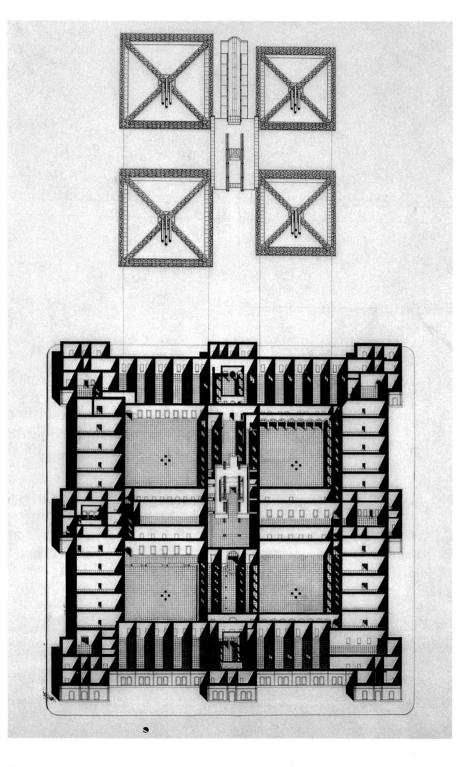

ABRAHAM ZABLUDOVSKY
Mexico City (b. 1924)

Public Library of Mexico, Mexico City, 1987
Black ink on paper. 35¹³⁄₁₆ × 25⁷⁄₁₆ in.

THIS WORK WAS A RESTORATION . . . OF A BUILDING CONSTRUCTED IN THE EIGHTEENTH century as a tobacco factory, which now is part of the vast cultural heritage of Mexico City.

The whole building was adapted for its new function by using the old patios of the factory as large reading rooms, which were covered with a roof resting on four metal poles located in the center of the patios. . . . This roof never touches the old building.

[architect's statement]